Mike Geig

D1397066

Sams **Teach Yourself**

# Unity® Game Development

in **24 Hours**

**SAMS**   800 East 96th Street, Indianapolis, Indiana, 46240 USA

**Sams Teach Yourself Unity® Game Development in 24 Hours**

Unity is a trademark of Unity technologies.

Kinect is a trademark of Microsoft®.

PlayStation and PlayStation Move are trademarks of Sony®.

Wii is a trademark of Nintendo®.

ISBN-13: 978-0-672-33696-6
ISBN-10: 0-672-33696-6

Library of Congress Control Number: 2013950040

Printed in the United States of America

First Printing November 2013

**Trademarks**

**Warning and Disclaimer**

**Bulk Sales**

Sams Publishing offers excellent discounts on this book when ordered in quantity for bulk purchases or special sales. For more information, please contact

U.S. Corporate and Government Sales
1-800-382-3419
corpsales@pearsontechgroup.com

For sales outside of the U.S., please contact

International Sales
international@pearsoned.com

**Editor-in-Chief**
Mark Taub

**Executive Editor**
Laura Lewin

**Senior Development Editor**
Chris Zahn

**Managing Editor**
Kristy Hart

**Project Editor**
Andy Beaster

**Copy Editor**
Keith Cline

**Indexer**
Brad Herriman

**Proofreader**
Sheri Cain

**Technical Editors**
Tim Harrington
Valerie Shipbaugh
Jeff Somers

**Publishing Coordinator**
Olivia Basegio

**Interior Designer**
Gary Adair

**Cover Designer**
Mark Shirar

**Compositor**
Gloria Schurick

# Contents at a Glance

# Table of Contents

# Preface

The Unity game engine is an incredibly powerful and popular choice for professional and amateur game developers alike. This book has been written to get readers up to speed and working in Unity as fast as possible (about 24 hours to be exact) while covering fundamental principles of game development. Unlike other books that only cover specific topics or spend the entire time teaching a single game, this book covers a large array of topics while still managing to contain four games! Talk about a bargain. By the time you are done reading this book, you won't have just theoretical knowledge of the Unity game engine. You will have a portfolio of games to go with it.

## Who Should Read This Book

This book is for anyone looking to learn how to use the Unity game engine. Whether you are a student or a development expert, there is something to learn in these pages. It is not assumed that you have any prior game development knowledge or experience, so don't worry if this is your first foray into the art of making games. Take your time and have fun. You will be learning in no time.

## How This Book Is Organized and What It Covers

Following the Sam's Teach Yourself approach, this book is organized into 24 chapters that should take approximately 1 hour each to work through. The chapters include the following:

▶ Hour 1, "Introduction to Unity": This hour gets you up and running with the various components of the Unity game engine.

▶ Hour 2, "Game Objects": Hour 2 teaches you how to use the fundamental building blocks of the Unity game engine: the game object. You also learn about coordinate systems and transformations.

▶ Hour 3, "Models, Materials, and Textures": In this hour, you learn to work with Unity's graphical asset pipeline as you apply shaders and textures to materials. You also learn how to apply those materials to a variety of 3D objects.

▶ Hour 4, "Terrain": In Hour 4, you learn to sculpt game worlds using Unity's terrain system. Don't be afraid to get your hands dirty as you dig around and create unique and stunning landscapes.

▶ Hour 5, "Environments": In this hour, you learn to apply environmental effects to your sculpted terrain. Time to plant some trees!

▶ Hour 6, "Lights and Cameras": Hour 6 covers lights and cameras in great detail.

▶ Hour 7, "Game 1: *Amazing Racer*": Time for your first game. In Hour 7, you create Amazing Racer, which requires you to take all the knowledge you have gained so far and apply it.

▶ Hour 8, "Scripting Part 1": In Hour 8, you begin your foray into scripting with Unity. If you've never programmed before, don't worry. We go slowly as you learn the basics.

▶ Hour 9, "Scripting Part 2": In this hour, you expand on what you learned in Hour 8. This time, you focus on more advanced topics.

▶ Hour 10, "Collision": Hour 10 walks you through the various collision interactions that are common in modern video games. You learn about physical as well as trigger collisions. You also learn to create physical materials to add some variety to your objects.

▶ Hour 11, "Game 2: *Chaos Ball*": Time for another game! In this hour, you create Chaos Ball. This title certainly lives up to its name as you implement various collisions, physical materials, and goals. Prepare to mix strategy with twitch reaction.

▶ Hour 12, "Prefabs": Prefabs are a great way to create repeatable game objects. In Hour 12, you learn to create and modify prefabs. You also learn to build them in scripts.

▶ Hour 13, "Graphical User Interfaces": In Hour 13, you learn to implement graphical user interfaces (GUIs) in Unity. You learn the various components and how to position them on a 2D interface.

▶ Hour 14, "Character Controllers": In this hour, you learn how to create your own character controllers. You finish up the chapter by building your own custom controller.

▶ Hour 15, "Game 3: *Captain Blaster*": Game number 3! In this hour, you make Captain Blaster, a retro-style spaceship shooting game.

▶ Hour 16, "Particle Systems": Time to learn about particle effects. In this chapter, you experiment with Unity's legacy particle system and its new Shuriken particle system. You learn how to create cool effects and apply them to your projects.

▶ Hour 17, "Animations": In Hour 17, you get to learn about animations and Unity's legacy animation system. You experiment with bringing models to life using assets from the Asset Store.

▶ Hour 18, "Animators": Hour 18 is all about Unity's new Mecanim animation system. You learn to remap model riggings and apply universal animations to them.

▶ Hour 19, "Game 4: *Gauntlet Runner*": Lucky game number 4 is called Gauntlet Runner. This game explores a new way to scroll backgrounds and how to implement animator controllers to build complex blended animations.

▶ Hour 20, "Audio": Hour 20 has you adding important ambient effects via audio. You learn about 2D and 3D audio and their different properties.

▶ Hour 21, "Mobile Development": In this hour, you learn how to build games for mobile devices. You also learn to utilize a mobile device's built-in accelerometer and multi-touch display.

▶ Hour 22, "Game Revisions": It's time to go back and revisit the four games you have made. This time you modify them to work on a mobile device. You get to see which control schemes translate well to mobile and which don't.

▶ Hour 23, "Polish and Deploy": Time to learn how to add multiple scenes and persist data between scenes. You also learn about the deployment settings and playing your games.

▶ Hour 24, "Wrap Up": Here, you look back and summarize the journey you went on to learn Unity. This hour provides useful information about what you have done and where to go next.

# Unity Engine Versions

This book was made with the Unity engine version 4.1 and 4.2. The two different versions are nearly identical for your purposes, but do note that some visual elements might have shifted place. For example, in some of the screen images you may note a Terrain menu item in the menu bar at the top of the Unity editor. In version 4.2, that has been moved. Do not worry. All explanations involving the creation and management of terrain have been updated to illustrate the new process. I am just writing this here so that you are not confused if a couple of things look slightly different.

Thank you for reading my preface! I hope you enjoy this book and learn much from it. Good luck on your journey with the Unity game engine!

# About the Author

**Mike Geig** is both an experienced teacher and game developer, with a foot firmly in both camps. He is currently teaches game design and development at Stark State College and the Cleveland Institute of Art. Mike also works as a screencaster for Unity Technologies and is a member of Unity's Learn department. His Pearson video, *Game Development Essentials with Unity 4 LiveLessons*, is a key title on Unity. Mike was once set on fire and has over a million "likes" on Facebook.

# Dedication

*To Dad: Everything worth learning, I learned from you.*

# Acknowledgments

A big "thank you" goes out to everyone who helped me write this book.

First and foremost, thank you Kara for keeping me on track. I don't know what we'll be talking about when this book comes out, but whatever it is, you are probably right. Love ya, babe.

Link and Luke: We should take it easy on mommy for a little while. I think she's about to crack.

Thanks to my parents. As I am now a parent myself, I recognize how hard it was for you not to strangle or stab me. Thanks for not strangling or stabbing me.

Thanks to Angelina Jolie. Due to your role in the spectacular movie Hackers (1995), I decided to learn how to use a computer. You underestimate the impact you had on 10-year-olds at the time. You're elite!

To the inventor of beef jerky: History may have forgotten your name, but definitely not your product. I love that stuff. Thanks!

Thank you to my technical editors: Valerie, Jim, and Tim. Your corrections and insights played a vital role in making this a better product.

Thank you, Laura, for convincing me to write this book. Also thank you for buying me lunch at GDC. I feel that lunch, the best of all three meals, specifically enabled me to finish this.

Finally, a "thank you" is in order for Unity Technologies. If you never made the Unity game engine, this book would be very weird and confusing.

# We Want to Hear from You!

As the reader of this book, you are our most important critic and commentator. We value your opinion and want to know what we're doing right, what we could do better, what areas you'd like to see us publish in, and any other words of wisdom you're willing to pass our way.

We welcome your comments. You can email or write to let us know what you did or didn't like about this book—as well as what we can do to make our books better.

Please note that we cannot help you with technical problems related to the topic of this book.

When you write, please be sure to include this book's title and author as well as your name and email address. We will carefully review your comments and share them with the author and editors who worked on the book.

Email:   consumer@samspublishing.com

Mail:    Sams Publishing
         ATTN: Reader Feedback
         800 East 96th Street
         Indianapolis, IN 46240 USA

# Reader Services

Visit our website and register this book at informit.com/register for convenient access to any updates, downloads, or errata that might be available for this book.

# HOUR 1
# Introduction to Unity

**What You'll Learn in This Hour:**

▶ How to install Unity

▶ How to create a new project or open an existing project

▶ How to use the Unity editor

▶ How to navigate inside the Unity Scene view

This hour focuses on getting you ready to rock and roll in the Unity environment. We start by looking at the different Unity licenses, choosing one, and then installing it. Once that is installed, you learn how to create new projects as well as open existing ones. You open the powerful Unity editor, and we examine its various components. Finally, you learn to navigate a scene using mouse controls and keyboard commands. This chapter is meant to be hands-on, so download Unity while reading and follow along.

## Installing Unity

To begin using Unity, you first need to download and install it. Software installation is a pretty simple and straightforward process these days, and Unity is no exception. Before we can install anything, though, we need to look at the two available Unity licenses: Unity Free and Unity Pro. Unity Free is more than sufficient to complete all the examples and projects in this book. In fact, Unity Free contains everything you need to make games commercially. If you feel like working with more power (and spending money), Unity Pro provides a suite of extended tools that gives you a true "high-priced" game engine experience. If you are curious about Unity Pro but don't want to commit to purchasing it, Unity Free comes with a 30-day trial of the Pro license. Feel free to play around with the Pro features and determine whether it is right for you. While on the Unity website, you might notice the Android and iOS plug-in licenses as well. As of the most recent release of Unity, the basic mobile plug-ins are free and come with Unity.

## Downloading and Installing Unity

For the purposes of this chapter, we will assume you are sticking with the Unity Free license. If you went with the Pro version, the process will be very similar, only deviating when it comes time to choose the license. When you are ready to begin downloading and installing Unity, follow these steps:

1. Download the Unity installer from the Unity3D download page at http://unity3d.com/unity/download/.

2. Run the installer and follow the prompts as you would with any other piece of software.

3. When prompted, be sure to leave the **Example Project**, **Unity Development Web Player**, and **MonoDevelop** check boxes checked (see Figure 1.1).

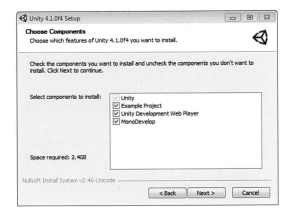

**FIGURE 1.1**
Prompt to choose the installed components.

4. Choose an install location for Unity (see Figure 1.2). It is recommended that you leave the default unless you know what you are doing.

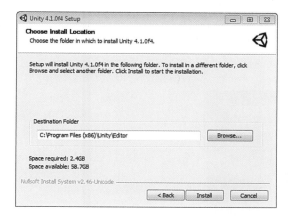

**FIGURE 1.2**
The prompt to choose the install location.

**5.** At this point, the installation will finish.

**6.** When you run Unity for the first time, you will be asked to activate your license (see Figure 1.3). At this point, you can select whether you want to use Unity Free or start a 30-day trial of Unity Pro. If you purchased Unity Pro, you can enter your serial number to unlock it. We will operate under the assumption that you chose Unity Free for now.

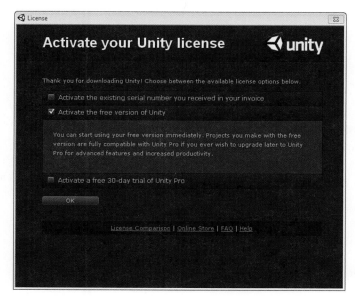

**FIGURE 1.3**
The Unity license selection screen.

**7.** You will be prompted to log in to a Unity account (see Figure 1.4). If you have one, enter it here. If you don't have one, choose the **Create Account** option and fill out the required form.

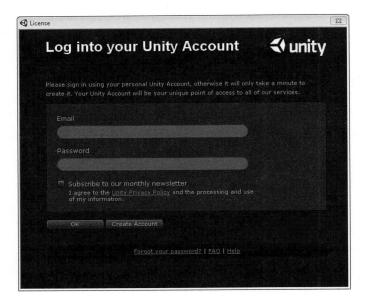

**FIGURE 1.4**
The prompt to log in to a Unity account.

**8.** That's it! Unity installation is now complete.

NOTE

## Supported Operating Systems and Hardware

To use Unity, you must be using a Windows PC or a Macintosh computer. Although it is possible to build your projects to run on a Linux machine, the Unity editor itself will not. Your computer must also meet the minimum requirements outlined here (taken from the Unity website at the time of writing):

▶ Windows: XP SP2 or later. Mac OS X: Intel CPU and Snow Leopard 10.6 or later. Note that Unity was not tested on server versions of Windows and OS X.

▶ Graphics card with DirectX 9 (Shader Model 2.0) capabilities. Any card made since 2004 should work.

▶ Using occlusion culling requires a GPU with occlusion query support (some Intel GPUs do not support that).

Note that these are *minimum* requirements.

CAUTION

**Internet Links**

All Internet links are current as of the time of this writing. Web locations do change sometimes, though. If the material you are looking for is no longer provided at the links I give you, a good Internet search should turn up what you are looking for.

# Getting to Know the Unity Editor

Now that you have Unity installed, you can begin exploring the Unity editor. The Unity editor is the visual component that enables you to build your games in a "what you see is what you get" fashion. Because most interaction we have is actually with the editor, we often just refer to it as Unity. The next portion of this chapter examines all the different elements of the Unity editor and how they fit together to make games.

## The Project Dialog

The first window you see when opening Unity for the first time is the Project dialog (see Figure 1.5). This window is what we use to open recent projects, browse for projects that have already been created, or start new projects.

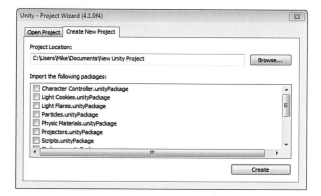

**FIGURE 1.5**
The Project dialog.

If you have created a project in Unity already, whenever you open Unity, it will go directly into that project. To get back to the Project dialog, you go (from inside Unity) to **File > New Project** to get to the Create New Project dialog, or you go to **File > Open Project** to get to the Open Project dialog.

TIP

## Opening the Project Dialog

When you run Unity, the last project you were working on opens automatically. If you want to open the Project dialog instead of the last project, you can do so by holding the **Alt** key (**Control** on a Mac) while clicking the **Unity** icon. If you would like Unity to behave this way all of the time, you can set it to do so by going to **Edit > Preferences** and checking the box **Always Show Project Wizard**.

▼ TRY IT YOURSELF

## Creating Our First Project

Let's go ahead and create a project now. You want to pay special attention to where you save the project so that you can find it easily later if necessary. Figure 1.6 shows you what the dialog window should look like before creating the project:

1. Open the Create New Project dialog.

2. Select a location for your project. If you are unsure where to put your project, you can leave the default location. If you decide to choose a custom location, select an empty folder to put your project in. The empty folder will dictate the name of the project.

3. Name your project **Chapter1_Trial**. The project name is the last bit of text in the Project Location text box.

4. Leave unchecked all the packages under Import the Following Packages. We will discuss packages later.

5. Click **Create**.

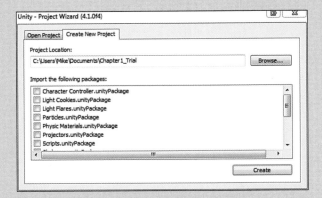

**FIGURE 1.6**
The settings used for our first project.

## CAUTION

### Projects and Packages

At first, you might be tempted to select a bunch of packages in the Create New Project dialog. I want to caution you against frivolously adding packages to your project, however, because unneeded items can add size and lag. Unused packages just take up space and provide no real benefit. With that in mind, it is better to wait until you actually need a package to import it. Even then, only import the parts of the package that you intend to use.

# The Unity Interface

So far, we have installed Unity and looked at the Project dialog. Now it is time to dig in and start playing around. When you open a new Unity project for the first time, you will see a collection of gray windows (called *views*), and everything will be rather empty (see Figure 1.7). Never fear, we will quickly get this place hopping. In the following sections, we look at each of the unique views one by one. First, though, I want to talk about the layout as a whole.

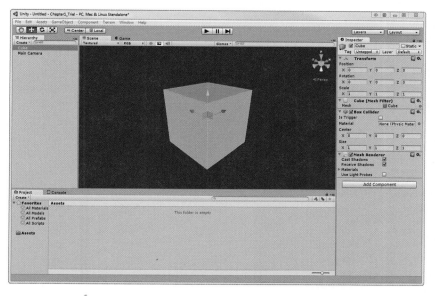

**FIGURE 1.7**
The Unity interface.

For starters, Unity allows the user to determine exactly how they want to work. This means that any of the views can be moved, docked, duplicated, or changed. For instance, if you click the word *Hierarchy* (on the left) to select the Hierarchy view and drag it over to the Inspector (on the right), you can tab the two views together. You can also place your cursor on any line between views and resize the windows. In fact, why don't you take a moment to play around and move things so that they are to your liking. If you end up with a layout that you don't much care for, never fear. You can quickly and easily switch back to the built-in default view by going to **Window > Layouts > Default Layout**. While we are on the topic of built-in layouts, go ahead and try out a few of the other layouts (I'm a fan of the Wide layout). If you create a custom layout you like, you can always save it by going to **Window > Layouts > Save Layout**. Now if you accidentally change your layout, you can always get it back.

NOTE

### Finding the Right Layout

No two people are alike, and likewise, no two ideal layouts are alike. A good layout will help you work on your projects and make things much easier for you. Be sure to take the time to fiddle around with the layout to find the one that works best for you. You will be working a lot with Unity. It pays to set your environment up in a way that is comfortable.

If you would like to duplicate a view, it is a fairly straightforward process as well. You can simply right-click any view tab (the *tab* is the part sticking up with the views name on it), hover the mouse cursor over **Add Tab**, and a list of views will pop up for you to choose from (see Figure 1.8). You may wonder why you would want to duplicate a view. It is possible that in your view-moving frenzy, you accidentally closed the view. Re-adding the tab will give it back to you. Also, consider the capability to create multiple Scene views. Each Scene view could align with a specific element or axis within your project. If you want to see this in action, check out the four Split built-in layout by going to **Window > Layouts > 4 Split**. (If you created a layout that you like, be sure to save it first.)

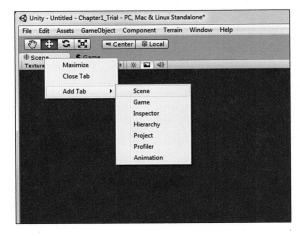

**FIGURE 1.8**
Adding a new tab.

Now, without further ado, let's look at the specific views themselves.

# The Project View

Everything that has been created for a project (files, scripts, textures, models, and so on) can be found in the Project view (see Figure 1.9). This is our window into all the assets and organization of our entire project. When you create a new project, you will notice a single folder item called Assets. If you go to the folder on your hard drive where you save the project, you will also find an Assets folder. This is because Unity mirrors the Project view with the folders on the hard drive. If you create a file or folder in Unity, the corresponding one appears in the explorer (and vice versa). You can move items in the Project view simply by dragging and dropping. This enables you to place items inside folders or reorganize your project on-the-fly.

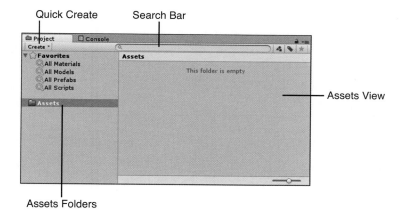

**FIGURE 1.9**
The Project view.

NOTE

## Assets

An *asset* is any item that exists as a file in your assets folder. All textures, meshes, sound files, scripts, and so on are considered assets. In contrast, if you create a game object, but it doesn't create a corresponding file, it is not an asset.

CAUTION

## Moving Assets

Unity maintains links between the various assets associated with projects. As a result, moving or deleting items outside of Unity could cause potential problems. As a general rule, it is a good idea to do all of your asset management inside Unity.

Whenever you click a folder in the Project view, the contents of the folder will be displayed under the Assets section on the right. As you can see in Figure 1.9, the Assets folder is currently empty, and therefore nothing is appearing on the right. If you would like to create assets, you can do so easily by clicking the Create drop-down menu. This menu enables you to add all manner of assets and folders to your project.

TIP

### Project Organization

Organization is extremely important for project management. As your projects get bigger, the number of assets will start to grow until finding anything can be a chore. You can help prevent a lot of frustration by employing some simple organization rules:

▶ Every asset type (scenes, scripts, textures, and so on) should get its own folder.

▶ Every asset should be in a folder.

▶ If you are going to use a folder inside another folder, make sure that the structure makes sense. Folders should become more specific and not be vague or generalized.

Following these few, simple rules will really make a difference.

One of my favorite additions to the Project view in Unity 4 would be the addition of favorites and the integration of the Unity Asset Store. The Favorites buttons enable you to quickly select all assets of a certain type. This makes it possible for you to get an "at a glance" view of your assets quickly. When you click one of the Favorites buttons (**All Models**, for instance) or perform a search with the built-in search bar, you will see that you can narrow down the results between Assets and Asset Store. If you click **Asset Store**, you will be able to browse the assets that fit your search criteria from the Unity Asset Store (see Figure 1.10). You can further narrow your results down by free and paid assets. To me, this is a fantastic addition because it enables you to go and grab assets that you need for your project without ever leaving the Unity interface.

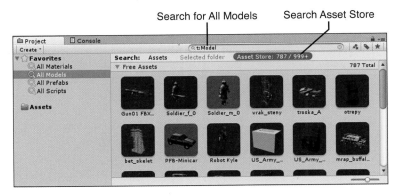

**FIGURE 1.10**
Searching the Unity Asset Store.

# The Hierarchy View

In many ways, the Hierarchy view (see Figure 1.11) is a lot like the Project view. The difference is that the Hierarchy view shows all the items in the current scene instead of the entire project. When you first create a project with Unity, you get the default scene, which is empty except for a single item: the Main Camera. As you add items to your scene, they will appear in the Hierarchy view. Just like with the Project view, you can use the Create menu to quickly add items to your scene, search using the built-in search bar, and click and drag items to organize and "nest" them.

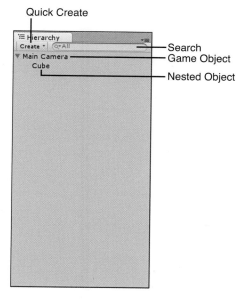

Quick Create

Search
Game Object
Nested Object

**FIGURE 1.11**
The Hierarchy view.

---

TIP

## Nesting

*Nesting* is the term for establishing a relationship between two or more items. In the Hierarchy view, clicking and dragging an item onto another item will nest the dragged item under the other. This is commonly known as a parent/child relationship. In this case, the object on top is the parent, and any objects below it are children. You will know when an object is nested because it will become indented. As you will see later, nesting objects in the Hierarchy view can affect how they behave.

---

TIP
_____

## Scenes

A _scene_ is the term Unity uses to describe what you might already know as a level. As you develop a Unity project, each collection of objects and behaviors should be its own scene. Therefore, if you were building a game with a snow level and a jungle level, those would be separate scenes.

_____

TIP
_____

## Scene Organization

The first thing you should do when working with a new Unity project is create a Scenes folder under Assets in the Project view. This way, all your scenes (or levels) will be stored in the same place. Be sure to give your scenes a descriptive name. Scene1 may sound like a great name now, but when you have 30 scenes, it can get confusing.

_____

# The Inspector View

The Inspector view enables you to see all of the properties of a currently selected item. Simply click any asset or object from the Project or Hierarchy view, and the Inspector view automatically propagates with information.

In Figure 1.12, we can see the Inspector view after the Main Camera object was selected from the Hierarchy view.

Let's break down some of this functionality:

▶ If you click the check box next to the object's name, it will become disabled and not appear in the project.

▶ Drop-down lists (such as the Layer or Tag lists; more on those later) are used to select from a set of predefined options.

▶ Text boxes, drop-downs, and sliders can have their values changed, and the changes will be automatically and immediately reflected in the scene—even if the game is running!

▶ Each game object acts like a container for different components (such as Transform, Camera, and GUILayer in Figure 1.12). You can disable these components by unchecking them or remove them by right-clicking and selecting **Remove Component**.

▶ Components can be added by clicking the **Add Component** button.

Name

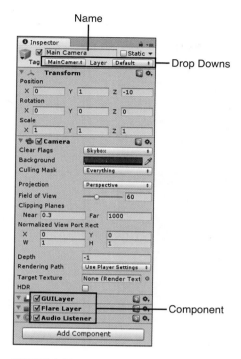

Drop Downs

Component

**FIGURE 1.12**
The Inspector view.

---

CAUTION

## Changing Properties While Running a Scene

The capability to change the properties of an object and seeing those changes reflected immediately in a running scene is very powerful. It enables you to tweak things like movement speed, jumping height, collision power, and so on all on-the-fly without stopping and starting the game. Be wary, though. Any changes you make to the properties of an object while the scene is running will be changed back when the scene finishes. If you make a change and like the result, be sure to remember what it was so that you can set it again when the scene is stopped.

---

# The Scene View

The Scene view is the most important view you work with because it enables you to see your game visually as it is being built (see Figure 1.13). Using the mouse controls and a few hotkeys, you can move around inside your scene and place objects where you want them. This gives you an immense level of control.

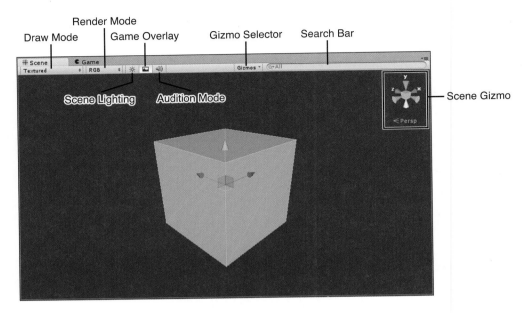

**FIGURE 1.13**
The Scene view.

In a little bit, we will talk about moving around within a scene, but first, let's focus on the controls that are a part of the Scene view:

▶ **Draw mode:** This controls how the scene is depicted. By default it is set to Textured, which means objects will be drawn with their textures.

▶ **Render mode:** This controls how the objects in the scene are drawn. By default, the Render mode is RGB, which means that objects will be drawn in their full color.

▶ **Scene lighting:** This control determines whether objects in the Scene view will be lit by default ambient lighting or by lights that actually exist within the scene. The default is to use the built-in ambient lighting, but that gets changed once the first light is added to the scene.

▶ **Game overlay:** This determines whether items like skyboxes and graphical user interface (GUI) components appear in the Scene view. This also controls whether the placement grid is visible.

▶ **Audition mode:** This control sets whether an audio source in the Scene view functions or not.

▶ **Gizmo selector:** This control enables you to choose which "gizmos" appear in the Scene view. A gizmo is an indicator that gives visual debugging or aids in setup.

▶ **Scene gizmo:** This control serves to show you which direction you are currently facing and to align the Scene view with an axis.

---

NOTE

### The Scene Gizmo

The scene gizmo gives you a lot of power over the Scene view. As you can see, the control has an X, Y, and Z indicator that aligns with the three axes. This makes it easy to tell exactly which way you are looking in the scene. We discuss axes and 3D space more in a later chapter. The gizmo also gives you active control over the scene alignment. If you click one of the gizmo's axes, you will notice that the Scene view immediately snaps to that axis and gets set to a direction like top or left. Clicking the box in the center of the gizmo toggles you between Iso and Persp modes. Iso stands for Isometric and is the 3D view with no perspective applied. Inversely, Persp stands for Perspective and is the 3D view with perspective applied. Try it out for yourself and see how it affects the Scene view.

---

NOTE

### Different Versions, Different Buttons

If you are using Unity 4.2 or earlier, your scene view menus will look as listed in Figure 1.13. If you are using Unity 4.3 or later, however, things will look a little different. Don't worry, the options are all still there. They will now just be under an Effects drop-down menu. You may also notice a new 2D button not illustrated in the previous images. This enables Unity's new 2D capabilities. Because this book focuses on 3D games, however, don't worry about those options for now.

---

## The Game View

The last view to go over is the Game view. Essentially, the Game view allows you to "play" the game inside the editor by giving you a full simulation of the current scene. All elements of a game will function in the Game view just as they would if the project were fully built. Figure 1.14 shows you what a Game view looks like. Note that although the Play, Pause, and Step buttons are not technically a part of the Game view, they control the Game view and therefore are included in the image.

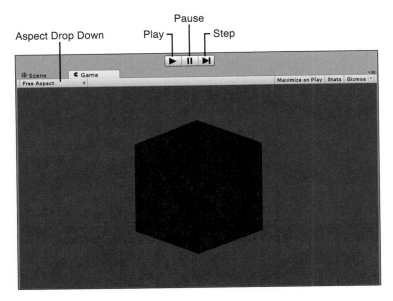

**FIGURE 1.14**
The Game view.

TIP

## Missing Game View

If you find that the Game view is hidden behind the Scene view, or that the Game view tab is missing entirely, don't worry. As soon as you click the **Play** button, a Game view tab will appear in the editor and begin displaying the game.

The Game view comes with some controls that assist us with testing our games:

▶ **Play:** The Play button enables you to play your current scene. All controls, animations, sounds, and effects will be present and working. Once a game is running, it will behave just like the game would if it were being run in a standalone player (such as on your PC or mobile device). To stop the game from running, click the Play button again.

▶ **Pause:** The Pause button pauses the execution of the currently running Game view. The game will maintain its state and continue exactly where it was when paused. Clicking the Pause button again will continue running the game.

▶ **Step:** The Step button works while the Game view is paused and causes the game to execute a single frame of the game. This effectively allows you to "step" through the game slowly and debug any issues you might have. Pressing the Step button while the game is running will cause the game to pause.

▶ **Aspect drop-down:** From this drop-down menu, you can choose the aspect ratio you want the Game view window to display in while running. The default is Free Aspect, but you can change this to match the aspect ratio of the target platform you are developing for.

▶ **Maximize on Play:** This button determines whether the Game view takes up the entirety of the editor when run. By default, this is off, and a running game will only take up the size of the Game view tab.

▶ **Stats:** This button determines whether rendering statistics are displayed on the screen while the game is running. These statistics can be useful for measuring the efficiency of your scene. This button is set to off by default.

▶ **Gizmos:** This is both a button and a drop-down menu. The button determines whether gizmos are displayed while the game is running. The button is set to off by default. The drop-down menu (the small arrow) on this button determines which gizmos appear if gizmos are turned on.

NOTE

**Running, Paused, and Off**

It can be difficult at first to determine what is meant by the terms *running*, *paused*, and *off*. When the game is not executing in the Game view, the game is said to be off. When a game is off, the game controls do not work and the game cannot be played. When the Play button is pressed and the game begins executing, the game is said to be running. Playing, executing, and running all mean the same thing. If the game is running and the Pause button is pressed, the game stops running but still maintains its state. At this point, the game is paused. The difference between a paused game and an off game is that a paused game will resume execution at the point it was paused while an off game will begin executing at the beginning.

# Honorable Mention: The Toolbar

Although not a view, the toolbar is an essential part of the Unity editor. Figure 1.15 shows the toolbar components:

▶ **Transform tools:** These buttons enable you manipulate game objects and are covered in greater detail later. Pay special attention to the button that resembles a hand. This is the Hand tool and is described later in this chapter.

▶ **Transform gizmo toggles:** These toggles manipulate how gizmos appear in the Scene view. Leave these alone for now.

▶ **Game view controls:** These buttons control the Game view.

▶ **Layers drop-down:** This menu determines which object layers appear in the Scene view. By default, everything appears in the Scene view. Leave this alone for now. Layers are covered in a later chapter.

▶ **Layout drop-down:** This menu allows you to quickly change the layout of the editor.

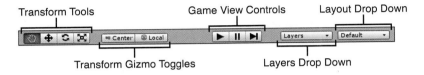

**FIGURE 1.15**
The toolbar.

# Navigating the Unity Scene View

The Scene view gives you a lot of control over the construction of your game. The ability to place and modify items visually is very powerful. None of this is very useful though if you cannot move around inside the scene. This section covers a couple of different ways to change your position and navigate the Scene view.

## The Hand Tool

The Hand tool (hotkey: **Q**) provides you a simple mechanic to move about the Scene view with the mouse (see Figure 1.16). This tool proves especially useful if you are using a mouse with only a single button (because other methods require a two-button mouse). Table 1.1 briefly explains each of the Hand tool controls.

**TABLE 1.1**  The Hand Tool Controls

| Action | Effect |
| --- | --- |
| Click-drag | Drags the camera around the scene |
| Hold **Alt** and click-drag | Orbits the camera around the current pivot point |
| Hold **Ctrl** (**Command** on Mac) and right-click-drag | Zooms the camera |

**FIGURE 1.16**
The Hand tool.

You can find all the Unity hotkeys here:

`http://blogs.unity3d.com/2011/08/24/unity-hotkeys-keyboard-shortcuts-in-unity/`

CAUTION

**Different Cameras**

When working in Unity, you will be dealing with two types of cameras. The first is the standard game object camera. You can see that you already have one in your scene (by default). The second type is more of an imaginary camera. It is not a camera in the traditional sense. Instead, it is what determines what we can see in the Scene view. In this chapter, when the camera is mentioned, it is the second type that is being referred to. You will not actually be manipulating the game object camera.

# Flythrough Mode

Flythrough mode enables you to move about the scene using a tradition first-person control scheme. This mode will feel right at home for anyone who plays first-person 3D games (such as the first-person shooter genre). If you don't play those games, this mode might take a little getting used to. Once you become familiar with it, though, it will be second nature.

Holding down the right mouse button will put you into Flythrough mode. All the actions laid out for you in Table 1.2 require that the right mouse button be held down.

**TABLE 1.2** Flythrough Mode Controls

| Action | Effect |
| --- | --- |
| Move the mouse | Causes the camera to pivot, which gives the feeling of "looking around" within the scene. |
| Press the **WASD** keys | The WASD keys move you about the scene. Each key corresponds with a direction: forward, left, back, and right, respectively. |
| Press the **QE** keys | The QE keys move you up and down, respectively, within the scene. |
| Hold **Shift** while pressing **WASD** or **QE** keys | Has the same effect as before, but it is much faster. Consider Shift to be your "sprint" button. |

TIP

## Zoom

Regardless of what method you are using for navigation, scrolling the mouse wheel will always zoom the view within a scene. By default, the scene zooms in and out of the center of the Scene view. If you hold **Alt** while scrolling, however, you zoom in and out of wherever the mouse is currently pointing. Go ahead and give it a try!

TIP

## Snap Controls

You have many ways to attain precious control over the scene navigation. Sometimes, you just want to quickly get around the scene though. For times like these, it is good to use what I call *snap controls*. If you want to quickly navigate to, and zoom in on, a game object in your scene, you can do so by highlighting the object in the Hierarchy view and pressing **F**. You will notice that the scene "snaps" to that game object. Another snap control is one you have seen already. The scene gizmo allows you to quickly snap the camera to any axis. This way, you can see an object from any angle without have to manually move the scene camera around. Be sure to learn the snap controls and navigating your scene quickly with become a snap!

# Summary

In this hour, you took our first look at the Unity game engine. You started off by downloading and installing Unity. From there, you learned how to open and create projects. Then you learned about all the different views that make up the Unity editor. You also learned how to navigate around the Scene view.

# Q&A

**Q.** **Are assets and game objects the same?**

**A.** Not exactly. Basically the big difference is that assets have a corresponding file or group of files on the hard drive, whereas a game object does not. An asset may or may not contain a game object.

**Q.** **There are a lot of different controls and options. Will I need to memorize them all right away?**

**A.** Not at all. Most controls and options will already be set to a default state that covers most situations. As your knowledge of Unity grows, you can continue to learn more about the different controls that you have available to you. This chapter is just meant to show you what's there and to give you some level of familiarity.

# Workshop

Take some time to work through the questions here to ensure that you have a firm grasp of the material.

## Quiz

1. True or False: You must purchase Unity Pro to make games.

2. Which view enables us to manipulate objects in a scene visually?

3. True or False: You should always move your asset files around within Unity and not use the operating system's file explorer.

4. True or False: When creating a new project, you should include every asset that you think is awesome.

5. What mode do you enter in the Scene view when you hold down the right mouse button?

## Answers

1. False

2. The Scene view

3. True

4. False

5. Flythrough mode

# Exercise

Take a moment and practice the concepts studied in this chapter. It is important to have a strong foundational understanding of the Unity editor because everything you will learn from here on out will utilize it in some way. To complete this exercise, do the following:

1. Create a new scene by going to **File > New Scene** or by pressing **Ctrl+N** (**Command+N** on a Mac).

2. Create a Scene folder under Assets in the Project view.

3. Save your scene by going to **File > Save Scene** or by pressing **Ctrl+S** (**Command+S** on a Mac). Be sure to save the scene in the Scenes folder you created and name it something descriptive.

4. Add a cube to your scene. To do this click the **GameObject** menu at the top, place your mouse over **Create Other**, and select **Cube** from the pop-up menu.

5. Select the newly added cube in the Hierarchy view and experiment with its properties in the Inspector view.

6. Practice navigating around the Scene view using Flythrough mode, the Hand tool, and snap controls. Use the cube as a point of reference to help you navigate.

# HOUR 2
# Game Objects

**What You'll Learn in This Hour:**

▶ How to work with 2D and 3D coordinates
▶ How to work with game objects
▶ How to work with transforms

Game objects are the foundational components of a Unity game project. Every item that exists in a scene is, or is based on, a game object. In this hour, you learn about game objects within Unity. Before you can start working with objects in Unity, however, you must first learn about the 2D and 3D coordinate systems. Then you will begin working with the built-in Unity game objects, and you will wrap up the hour by learning about the various game object transformations. Information gained this hour is foundational to everything else in this book. Be sure to take your time and learn it well.

## Dimensions and Coordinate Systems

For all of their glitz and glamour, video games are mathematical constructs. All the properties, movements, and interactions can be boiled down to numbers. Luckily for you, a lot of the groundwork has already been laid. Mathematicians have been toiling away for centuries to discover, invent, and simplify different processes so that you can more easily build your games with modern software. You may think the objects in a game just exist in space randomly, but really every game space has dimensions, and every object is placed in a coordinate system (or grid).

# Putting the D in 3D

As mentioned previously, every game uses some level of dimensions. The most common dimension systems, the ones you are most likely familiar with, are 2D and 3D (short for two-dimensional and three-dimensional). A 2D system is a flat system. In a 2D system, you deal only with vertical and horizontal elements (or to put it another way: up, down, left, and right). Games like *Tetris*, *Pong*, and *Pac Man* are good examples of 2D games. A 3D system is like a 2D system, but it obviously has one more dimension. In a 3D system, you not only have horizontal and vertical (up, down, left, and right), you also have depth (in and out). Figure 2.1 does a good job of illustrating the difference between a 2D square and a 3D square, otherwise known as a *cube*. Notice how the inclusion of the depth axis in the 3D cube makes it seem to "pop out."

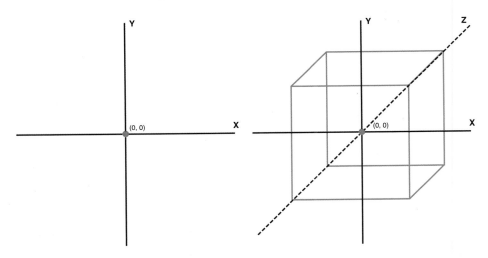

**FIGURE 2.1**
2D square versus 3D cube.

NOTE

## Learning About 2D and 3D

Unity is a 3D engine. Therefore, all the projects made with it will inherently use all three dimensions. You might be wondering why then we bother to cover 2D systems at all. The truth is that even in 3D projects, there are still a lot of 2D elements. Textures, screen elements, and mapping techniques all use a 2D system. It is worth learning about 2D systems because they aren't going away any time soon.

# Using Coordinate Systems

The mathematical equivalent of a dimension system is a coordinate system. A coordinate system uses a series of lines, called *axes* (the plural of axis), and locations, called *points*. These axes correspond directly with the dimensions that they mimic. For instance, a 2D coordinate system has the x axis and y axis, which represent the horizontal and vertical directions, respectively. If an object is moving horizontally, we say it is moving "along the x axis." Likewise, the 3D coordinate system uses the x axis, the y axis, and the z axis for horizontal, vertical, and depth, respectively.

NOTE
_____

**Common Coordinate Syntax**

When referring to an object's position, you will generally list its coordinates. Saying that an object is 2 on the x axis and 4 on the y axis can be a little cumbersome. Luckily, a shorthand way of writing coordinates exists. In a 2D system, you write coordinates like (x, y), and in a 3D system, you write them like (x, y, z). Therefore, this example would instead be written as (2, 4). If that object were also 10 on the z axis, it would be written as (2, 4, 10).
_____

Every coordinate system has a point where all the axes intersect. This point is called the *origin*, and the coordinates for the origin are always (0, 0) in a 2D system and (0, 0, 0) in a 3D system. This origin point is very important because it is the basis by which all other points are derived. The coordinates for any other point are simply the distance of that point from the origin along each axis. A point's coordinates will get larger as it moves away from the origin. For example, as a point moves to the right, its x axis value gets larger. When it moves left, the x axis value gets smaller until it passes through the origin. At that time, the x value of the point begins getting larger again, but it also becomes negative. Consider Figure 2.2. This 2D coordinate system has three points defined. The point (2, 2) is 2 *units* away from the origin in both the x and y directions. The point (–3, 3) is 3 units to the left of the origin and 3 units above the origin. The point (2, –2) is 2 units to the right of the origin and 2 units below the origin.

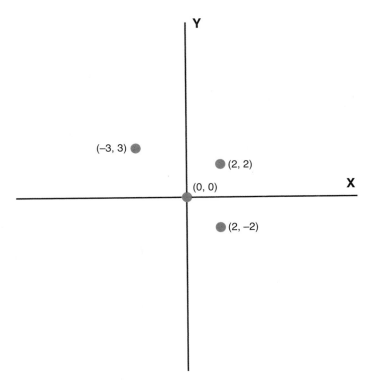

**FIGURE 2.2**
Points in relation to the origin.

# World Versus Local Coordinates

You have now learned about the dimensions of a game world and about the coordinate systems that compose them. What you have been working with so far is considered the *world* coordinate system. At any given time, there is only a single x, y, and z axis in the world coordinate system. Likewise, there is only one origin that all objects share. What you might not know is that there is also something called the *local* coordinate system. This system is unique to each object, and it is completely separate from other objects. This local system has its own axes and origin that other objects don't use. Figure 2.3 illustrates the world versus local coordinate systems by showing the four points that make of a square for each.

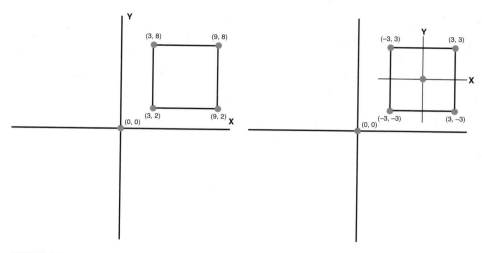

**FIGURE 2.3**
World coordinates versus local coordinates.

You might be wondering what the local coordinate system is for if the world coordinate system is used for the position of objects. Later in this hour, you will look at transforming game objects and at parenting game objects. Both of these require the local coordinate system.

# Game Objects

Every shape, model, light, camera, particle system, and so on in a Unity game all have one thing in common: They are all game objects. The game object is the fundament unit of any scene. Even though they are simple, they are very powerful. At their root, game objects are little more than a transform (as discussed in greater detail later in the hour) and a container. This container exists to hold the various components that make objects more dynamic and meaningful. What you add to your game objects is up to you. There are many components, and they add a huge amount of variety. Throughout the course of this book, you will be learning to use many of these components.

NOTE

## Built-In Objects

Not every game object you use will start as an empty object. Unity has several built-in game objects available to use right out of the box. You can see the large amount of items available by clicking the **GameObject** menu item at the top of the Unity editor and hovering over **Create Other**. A large portion of learning to use Unity is learning to work with built-in and custom game objects.

### Creating Some Game Objects

Let's take some time now to work with game objects. You will be creating a few basic objects and examining their different components:

1. Create a new project or create a new scene in a project you already have.

2. Add an empty game object by clicking the **GameObject** menu item and selecting **Create Empty** (Note: You could also create an empty game object by pressing **Ctrl+Shift+N** for PC users or **Command+Shift+N** for Mac users.)

3. Look in the Inspector view and notice how the game object you just created has no components other than a transform. All game objects have a transform. Clicking the **Add Component** button in the Inspector will show you all the components you could add to the object. Don't select any components at this time.

4. Add a cube to your project by clicking the **GameObject** menu item, hovering the cursor over **Create Other**, and selecting **Cube** from the list.

5. Notice the various components the cube has that the empty game object doesn't. The mesh components make the cube visible, and the collider makes it able to interact with other objects.

6. Finally, add a point light to your project by clicking the **Create** drop-down in the Hierarchy view and selecting **Point Light** from the list.

7. You can see that the point light doesn't share any components with the cube and is instead focused entirely upon emitting light. You might also notice that your other objects went dark when the light was added to the scene. This is normal. Because a light exists in the scene, Unity turns off its ambient lighting.

# Transforms

At this point, you have learned and explored the different coordinate systems and experimented with some game objects. It is time to put the two together. When dealing with 3D objects, you will often hear the term *transform*. Depending on the context, transform is either a noun or a verb. All objects in 3D space have a position, a rotation, and a scale. If you combine them all together, you get an object's transform (noun). Alternatively, *transform* can be a verb if it refers to changing an object's position, rotation, or scale. Unity combines the two meanings of the word with the *transform component*. You will recall that the transform component is the only component that every game object has to have. Even empty game objects have transforms. Using this component, you can both see the current transform of the object as well as change (or transform) the transform of the object. It might sound confusing now, but it is fairly simple. You will get the hang of it in no time. Because the transform is made up of the position, rotation,

changing the transform: translation, rotation, and scaling (respectively). These transformations can be achieved using either the Inspector or the transform tools. Figures 2.4 and 2.5 illustrate which Inspector components and tools correlate with which transforms.

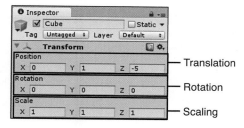

**FIGURE 2.4**
Transform options in the Inspector.

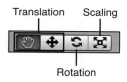

**FIGURE 2.5**
The transform tools.

# Translation

Changing the coordinate position of an object in a 3D system is called *translation*, and it is the simplest transform that you can apply to an object. When you translate an object, it is shifted along an axis. Figure 2.6 demonstrates a square being translated along the x axis.

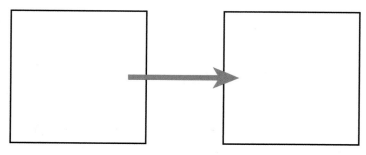

**FIGURE 2.6**
Sample translation.

When you select the Translate tool (hotkey: **W**), you will notice that whatever object you have selected will change slightly in the Scene view. More specifically, you will see three arrows appear pointing away from the center of the object along the three axes. These are translation gizmos, and they help you move your objects around in the scene. Clicking and holding on any of these axis arrows causes them to turn yellow. Then, if you move your mouse, the object will move along that axis. Figure 2.7 shows you what the translation gizmos look like. Note that the gizmos appear only in the Scene view; if you are in the Game view, you will not see them.

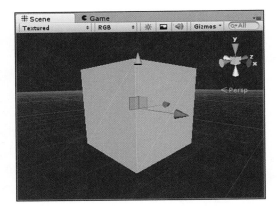

**FIGURE 2.7**
Translation gizmos.

TIP

### The Transform Component and Transform Tools

Unity provides two ways to manage the transform of your objects. Knowing when to use each is important. You will notice that when you change an object's transform in the Scene view with a transform tool, the transform data also changes in the Inspector view. It is often easier to make large changes to an object's transform using the Inspector view because you can just change the values to what they need to be. The transform tools, however, are more useful for quick, small changes. Learning to use both together will greatly improve your workflow.

## Rotation

Rotating an object does not move it in space. Instead, it changes the object's relationship to that space. More simply stated, rotation enables you to redefine which direction the x, y, and z axes for a particular object point. When an object rotates around an axis, it is said to be rotating *about* that axis. Figure 2.8 shows a square being rotated about the z axis.

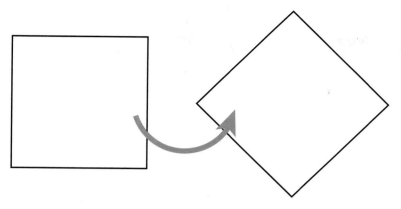

**FIGURE 2.8**
Rotation about the Z axis.

TIP

## Determining the Axis of Rotation

If you are unsure which axis you need to rotate an object about to get a desired effect, you can use a simple mental method. One axis at a time, pretend that the object is stuck in place by a pin that is parallel with that axis. The object can only spin around the pin stuck in it. Now, determine which pin allows the object to spin the way you want. That is the axis you need to rotate the about around.

Just as with the Translate tool, selecting the Rotate tool (hotkey: **E**) causes rotation gizmos to appear around your object. These gizmos are circles representing the object's rotation path about the axes. Clicking and dragging on any of these circles turns them yellow and rotates the object about that axis. Figure 2.9 shows you what the rotation gizmos look like.

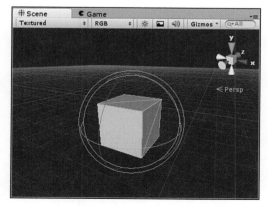

**FIGURE 2.9**
The Rotate tool gizmos.

# Scaling

Scaling causes an object to grow or shrink within a 3D space. This transform is really straightforward and simple in its use. Scaling an object on any axis causes its size to change on that axis. Figure 2.10 demonstrates a square being scaled down on the x and y axis. Figure 2.11 shows you what the scaling gizmos look like when you select the Scaling tool (hotkey: **R**).

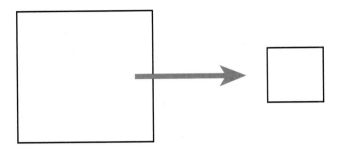

**FIGURE 2.10**
Scaling on the x and y axis.

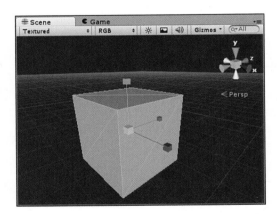

**FIGURE 2.11**
The scaling gizmos.

# Hazards of Transformations

As mentioned before, transformations use the local coordinate system. Therefore, the changes that are made can potentially impact future transformations. Consider Figure 2.12. Notice how the same two transformations, when applied in reverse order, have very different effects.

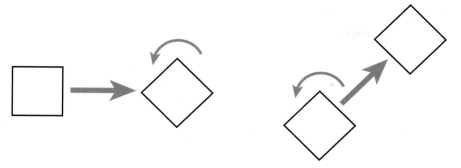

**FIGURE 2.12**
Effects of transformation order.

As you can see, not paying attention to transformation order can have unexpected consequences. Luckily, the transformations have consistent effects that can be planned on:

▶ **Translation:** Translation is a fairly inert transformation. That means that any changes applied after it generally won't be affected.

▶ **Rotation:** Rotation changes the orientation of the local coordinate system axes. Any translations applied after a rotation would cause the object to move along the new axes. If you were to rotate an object 180 degrees about the z axis, for example, and then move in the positive y direction, the object would appear to be moving down instead of up.

▶ **Scaling:** Scaling effectively changes the size of the local coordinate *grid*. Basically, when you scale an object to be larger, you are really scaling the local coordinate system to be larger. This causes the object to seem to grown. This change is multiplicative. For example, if an object is a scaled to 1 (its natural, default size) and then translated 5 units along the x axis, the object appears to move 5 units to the right. If the same object were to be scaled to 2, however, then translating 5 units on the x axis would result in the object appearing to move 10 units to the right. This is because the local coordinate system is now double the size and 5 times 2 equals 10. Inversely, if the object were scaled to .5 and then moved, it would appear to only move 2.5 units (.5 * 5 = 2.5).

Once you understand these rules, determining how an object will change with a set of transformations becomes easy.

## Transforms and Nested Objects

In Hour 1, "Introduction to Unity," you learned how to nest game objects in the Hierarchy view (drag one object onto another one) and that doing so changes the way transformations work slightly. Recall that when you have an object nested inside another one, the top-level object is the parent, and the other object is the child. Transformations applied to the parent object work as normal. The object can be moved, scaled, and rotated. What's special is how the child object behaves. Once nested, a child object's transform is relative to that of the parent object, not the world. Therefore, a child object position is not based on its distance from the origin, but the distance from the parent object. If the parent object is rotated, the child object would move with it. If you looked at the child's rotation, however, it would not register that it had rotated at all. The same goes for scaling. If you scale the parent object, the child also changes in size. The scale of the child object would remain unchanged. You might be confused by why this is. Remember, when a transformation is applied, it is not applied to the object, but to the object's coordinate system. An object isn't rotated, its coordinate system is. The effect is that the object turns. When a child object's coordinate system is based on the local coordinate system of the parent, any changes to the parent system will directly change the child (without the child knowing about it).

# Summary

In this hour, you learned all about game objects in Unity. You started off by learning all about the differences between 2D and 3D. From there, you looked at the coordinate system and how it breaks the "world" concepts down mathematically. You then began working with game objects, including some of the built-in ones. You ended by learning all about transforms and the three transformations. You got to try out the transforms, learn about some of the hazards, and how they affect nested objects.

# Q&A

**Q. Is it important to learn both the 2D and 3D concepts?**

**A.** Yes. Even games that are entirely 3D still utilize some of the 2D concepts on a technical level.

**Q. Should I learn to use all the built-in game objects right away?**

**A.** Not necessarily. There are many game objects, and it can be overwhelming to attempt to learn them all right away. Take your time and learn about the objects as they are covered here.

**Q. What is the best way to get familiar with transforms?**

**A.** Practice. Keep working with them; eventually, they will become quite natural.

# Workshop

Take some time to work through the questions here to ensure that you have a firm grasp of the material.

## Quiz

1. What does the *D* in 2D and 3D stand for?

2. How many transformations are there?

3. True or False: Unity has no built-in objects and you must create your own.

4. If you want an object to be "laying on its side" 5 units to the right of its current position, would you rotate the object and then translate it or translate the object and then rotate it?

## Answers

1. Dimension.

2. Three.

3. False. Unity provides many built-in objects for you.

4. Translate and then rotate.

# Exercise

Take a moment to experiment with the way transformations work in a parent/child object scenario. You will get a better feel for exactly how the coordinate systems change the way things are oriented.

1. Create a new scene or project.

2. Add a cube to the project and place it at (0, 2, –5). Remember the shorthand notation for coordinates. The cube should have an x value of 0, a y value of 2, and a z value of –5. You can set these values easily in the transform component in the Inspector view.

3. Add a sphere to your scene. Pay attention to the sphere's x, y, and z values.

4. Nest the sphere under the cube by dragging the sphere in the Hierarchy view onto the cube. Notice how the position values changed. The sphere is now located relative to the cube.

5. Place the sphere at (0, 1, 0). Notice how it doesn't go to right above the origin and instead sits right above the cube.

6. Now experiment with the various transformations. Be sure to try them on the cube as well as the sphere and see how different they behave for a parent versus a child object.

# HOUR 3
# Models, Materials, and Textures

---

**What You'll Learn in This Hour:**

▶ The fundamentals of models
▶ How to import custom and premade models
▶ How to work with materials and shaders

In this hour, you learn all about models and how they are used in Unity. You start by looking at the fundamental principles of meshes and 3D objects. From there, you learn how to import your own models or use ones acquired from the Asset Store. You finish this hour by examining Unity's material and shader functionality.

## The Basics of Models

Video games wouldn't be very *video* without the graphical components. In 2D games, the graphics consist of flat images called *sprites*. All you needed to do was change the x and y positions of these sprites and flip several of them in sequence and the viewer's eye was fooled into believing that it saw true motion and animation. In 3D games, however, things aren't so simple. In worlds with a third axis, objects need to have volume to fool the eye. Because games use a large number of objects, the need to process things quickly was very important. Enter the mesh. A mesh, at its most simple, is a series of interconnected triangles. These triangles build off of each other in strips to form basic to very complex objects. These strips provide the 3D definitions of a model and can be processed very quickly. Don't worry, though; Unity handles all of this for you so that you don't have to manage it yourself. Later in this hour, you'll see just how triangles can make up various shapes in the Unity Scene view.

NOTE

### Why Triangles?

You might be asking yourself why 3D objects are made up entirely of triangles. The answer is simple. Computers process graphics as a series of point, otherwise known as *vertices*. The fewer vertices an object has, the faster it can be drawn. Triangles have two properties that make them desirable. The first is that whenever you have a single triangle, you need only one more vertex to make another. To make one triangle, you need three vertices, two triangles take only four, and three triangles require only five. This makes them very efficient. The second is that by using this practice of making strips of triangles, you can model any 3D object. No other shape affords you that level of flexibility and performance.

NOTE

### Model or Mesh?

The terms *model* and *mesh* are similar, and you can often use them interchangeably. There is a difference, however. A mesh contains all the vertex information that defines the 3D shape of an object. When you refer to the shape or form of a model, you are really referring to a mesh. A model, therefore, is an object that contains a mesh. A model has a mesh to define its dimensions, but it can also contain animations, textures, materials, shaders, and other meshes. A good general rule is this: If the item in question contains anything other than vertex information, it is a model; otherwise, it is a mesh.

## Built-In 3D Objects

Unity comes with a few basic built-in meshes (or primitives) for you work with. These tend to be simple shapes that serve simple utilities or can be combined to make more-complex objects. Figure 3.1 shows the available built-in meshes. (You worked with the cube and sphere in the previous hours.)

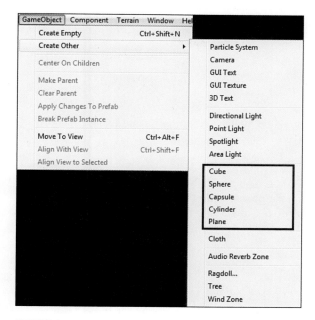

**FIGURE 3.1**
The built-in meshes in Unity.

TIP

## Modeling with Simple Meshes

Do you need a complex object in your game but you can't find the right type of model to use? Nesting objects in Unity enables you to easily make simple models using the built-in meshes. Just place the meshes near each other so that they form the rough look you want. Then nest all the objects under one central object. This way, when you move the parent, all the children move, too. This might not be the prettiest way to make models for your game, but it will do in a pinch!

# Importing Models

Having built-in models is nice, but most of the time, your games will require art assets that are a little more complex. Thankfully, Unity makes it rather easy to bring your own 3D models into your projects. Just placing the file containing the 3D model in your Assets folder is enough to bring it into the project. From there, dragging it into the scene or hierarchy builds a game object around it. Natively, Unity supports .fbx, .dae, .3ds, .dxf, and .obj files. This enables you to work with just about any 3D modeling tool.

## ▼ TRY IT YOURSELF

### Importing Your Own 3D Model

Let's walk through the steps required to bring custom 3D models into a Unity project:

1. Create a new Unity project or scene.

2. In the Project view, create a new folder named **Models** under the Assets folder. (Right-click the Assets folder and select **Create > Folder.**)

3. Locate the Torus.fbx file provided for you in the Hour 3 folder of the book files.

4. With both the operating system's file browser and the Unity editor open and side by side, click and drag the Torus.fbx file from the file browser into the Models folder that you created in step 2. In Unity, click the **Models** folder to see the new Torus file. If done correctly, your Project view will resemble Figure 3.2. Notice the Materials folder that was added for you. You will learn more about this later.

**FIGURE 3.2**
The Project view after the Torus model was added.

5. Click the **Torus** asset in the Models folder and look at the Inspector view. Change the value of the scale factor from 0.01 to 1 and click **Apply.**

6. Drag the Torus asset from the Models folder onto the Scene view. Notice how a Torus game object was added to the scene containing a mesh filter and mesh rendered. These allow the Torus to be drawn to the screen. If you click the **Torus** object, you see how it is made up of many connected triangles.

---

### CAUTION

### Default Scaling of Meshes

Most of the Inspector view options for meshes are advanced and are not covered right now. The property you are interested in is the scale factor. By default, Unity imports meshes scaled down. By changing the value of the scale factor from 0.01 to 1, you are telling Unity to allow the model to enter the scene as the same size as it was created.

---

# Models and the Asset Store

You don't have to be an expert modeler to make games with Unity. The Asset Store provides a simple and effective way to find premade models and import them into your project. Generally speaking, models on the Asset Store are either free or paid and come alone or in a collection of similar models. Some of the models come with their own textures, and some of them are simply the mesh data.

---

## TRY IT YOURSELF ▼

### Downloading Models from the Asset Store

Let's learn how to find and download models from Unity's Asset Store. We will be acquiring a model named Robot Kyle and importing it into our scene:

1. Create a new scene (click **File > New Scene**). In the Project view, type **t:Model** into the search bar (see Figure 3.3).

2. In the search filter section, click the **Asset Store: 999+/999+** button (see Figure 3.3). If these words aren't visible, you may need to resize your editor window or Project view window.

3. Locate **Robot Kyle** and select it.

**FIGURE 3.3**
Steps to locate a model asset.

4. In the Inspector view, click **Import Package**. At this point, you may be prompted to provide your Unity account credentials.

5. When the Importing Package dialog opens, leave everything checked and select **Import**.

6. There will now be a new asset folder called Robot Kyle. Locate the robot model under **Assets > Robot Kyle > Model** and drag it into the Scene view (see Figure 3.4). Note that the model will be fairly small in the Scene view; you might need to move closer to see it.

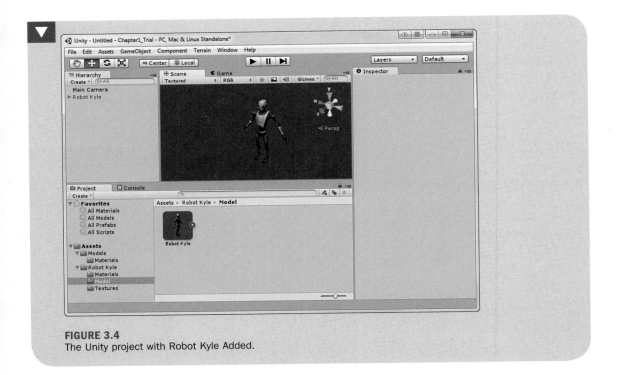

**FIGURE 3.4**
The Unity project with Robot Kyle Added.

# Textures, Shaders, and Materials

Applying graphical assets to 3D models can be daunting if you are not familiar with it. Unity uses a simple and specific workflow that gives you a lot of power when determining exactly how you want things to look. Graphical assets are broken down into textures, shaders, and materials. Each of these is covered individually in its own section, but Figure 3.5 shows you how they fit together. Notice that textures are not applied directly to models. Instead, textures and shaders are applied to materials. Those materials are in turn applied to the models. This way, the look of a model can be swapped or modified quickly and cleanly without a lot of work.

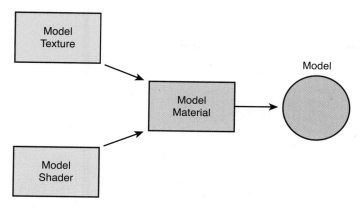

**FIGURE 3.5**
The model asset workflow.

# Textures

Textures are flat images that get applied to 3D objects. They are responsible for models being colorful and interesting instead of blank and boring. It can be strange to think that a 2D image can be applied to a 3D model, but it is a fairly straightforward process once you are familiar with it. Think about a soup can for a moment. If you were to take the label off of the can, you would see that it is a flat piece of paper. That label is like a texture. After the label was printed, it was then wrapped around the 3D can to provide a more pleasing look.

Just like all other assets, adding textures to a Unity project is easy. Start by creating a folder for your textures; a good name would be Textures. Then drag any textures you want in your project into the Textures folder you just created. That's it!

NOTE

## That's an Unwrap!

Imagining how textures wrap around cans is fine, but what about more complex objects? When creating an intricate model, it is common to generate something called an *unwrap*. The unwrap is somewhat akin to a map that shows you exactly how a flat texture will wrap back around a model. If you look in the Robot Kyle > Textures folder from earlier this hour, you notice the Robot_Color texture. It looks strange, but that is the unwrapped texture for the model. The generation of unwraps, models, and textures is an art form to itself and is not covered in this text. A preliminary knowledge of how it works should suffice at this level.

CAUTION

## Weird Textures

Later in this hour, you will apply some textures to models. You might notice that the textures warp a bit or get flipped in the wrong direction. Just know that this is not a mistake or an error. This problem occurs when you take a basic rectangular 2D texture and apply it to a model. The model has no idea which way is correct, so it applies the texture however it can. If you want to avoid this issue, use textures specifically designed for (unwrapped for) the model that you are using.

# Shaders

If the texture of a model determines what is drawn on its surface, the shader is what determines *how* it is drawn. Here's another way to look at this: A material contains properties and textures, and shaders dictate what properties and textures a material can have. This might seem nonsensical right now, but later when we create materials you will begin to understand how they work. Much of the information about shaders is covered later this hour, because you cannot create a shader without a material. In fact, much of the information to be learned about materials is actually about the material's shader.

TIP

## Thought Exercise

If you are having trouble understanding how a shader works, consider this scenario: Imagine you have a piece of wood. The physicality of the wood is its mesh; the color, texture, and visible element are its texture. Now take that piece of wood and pour water on it. The wood still has the same mesh. It still is made of the same substance (wood). It looks different, though. It is slightly darker and shiny. The water in this example is the shader. The shader took something and made it look a little different without actually changing it.

# Materials

As mentioned earlier, materials are not much more than containers for shaders and textures that can be applied to models. Most of the customization of materials depends on which shader is chosen for it, although all shaders have some common functionality.

To create a new material, start by making a Materials folder. Then right-click the folder and select **Create > Material**. Give your material some descriptive name and you are done. Figure 3.6 shows two materials with different shaders selected. Notice how they each have a base texture, main color, tilling and offsets, and a preview of the material (blank now because there is no texture). The Shiny material, however, uses a specular shader and comes with properties for specular color and shininess. All these properties are covered later in this hour.

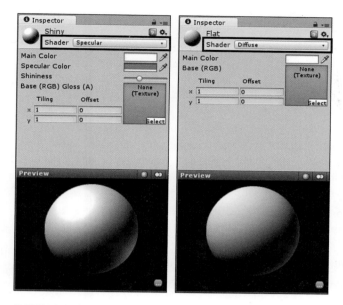

**FIGURE 3.6**
Two materials with different shaders.

# Shaders Revisited

Now that you understand textures, models, and shaders, it is time to look at how it all comes together. Unity has a lot of built-in shaders, but this book is concerned with only a few of the Normal family of shaders. These shaders are the most basic and should be useful for everyone. Table 3.1 lists some of the basic shaders and describes them.

**TABLE 3.1    Basic Normal Family of Shaders**

| Shader | Description |
| --- | --- |
| Diffuse | Diffuse is the default shader for materials and is also the most basic. Light is evenly distributed across the diffuse object's surface. |
| Specular | Specular textures make an object look shiny. If you want to make an object seem to reflect a lot of light, this is the shader to use. |
| Bumped | Bumped shaders are generally used in conjunction with other shaders (as in bumped-diffuse or bumped-specular). These shaders use a normal map to give the flat texture a 3D, or bumpy, look. These are a great way to give your models a lot of physical detail without requiring complex modeling. |

Now that you are familiar with a few of the built-in shaders, it is time to look at some of the common shader properties that you will be working with. Table 3.2 describes the common shader properties.

**TABLE 3.2    Common Shader Properties**

| Property | Description |
|---|---|
| Main Color | The Main Color property defines what color of ambient light shines on the object. This does not change the color of the object itself; it just makes the object appear different. For example, an object with a blue texture and a yellow main color will not turn yellow but green (because blue with yellow light looks green). If you want your model's color to remain unchanged, select white. |
| Specular Color | The Specular Color property determines what color the "shiny" parts of a specular model are. Generally speaking, this will be white unless you intend for it to appear as if another color of light is shining on the object. |
| Shininess | The Shininess property determines how shiny a specular object is. |
| Texture | The Texture block contains the texture you want to apply to your model. |
| Normal Map | The Normal Map block contains the normal map that will be applied to your model. A normal map can be used to apply bumpiness to a model. This is useful when calculating lighting to give the model more detail than it would otherwise have. |
| Tiling | The Tiling property defines how often a texture can repeat on a model. It can repeat in both the x and y axes. |
| Offset | The Offset property defines whether a gap will exist between edges of the object and the texture. |

This might seem like a lot of information to take in, but once you become more familiar with the few basics of textures, shaders, and materials, you'll find this a smooth process.

## Applying Textures, Shaders, and Materials to Models

Let's put all of our knowledge of textures, shaders, and materials together and create a decent-looking brick wall:

1. Start a new project or scene. Note that creating a new project will close and reopen the editor.

2. Create a Textures and a Materials folder.

3. Locate the Brick_Texture.png file in the book files and drag it into the Textures folder created in step 2.

4. Add a cube to the scene. Position it at (0, 1, −5). Give it a scale of (5, 2, 1). See Figure 3.7 for the cube properties.

**FIGURE 3.7**
The properties of the cube.

5. Create a new material (right-click the Materials folder and select **Create > Material**) and name it **BrickWall**.

6. Leave the shader as Diffuse, and in the texture block click **Select**. Select **Brick_Texture** from the pop-up window.

7. Click and drag the brick wall material from the Project view onto the cube in the Scene view.

8. Notice how the texture is stretched across the wall a little too much. With the material selected, change the value of the x tiling to be **3**. Now the wall looks much better.

9. Add a directional light to your scene (click **GameObject > Create Other > Directional Light**). Position it at (0, 10, −10) and give it a rotation of (30, 0, 0). We will discuss lighting more in a later hour. This is just here to make your brick wall "pop."

10. You now have a textured brick wall in your scene. Figure 3.8 contains the final product.

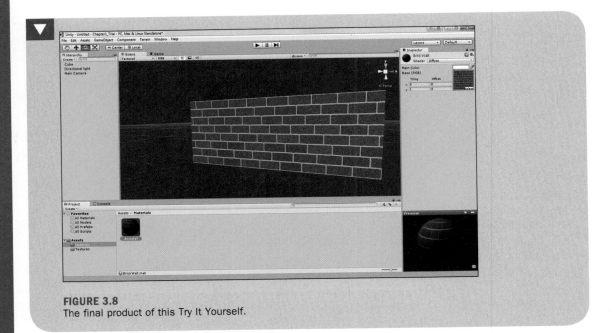

**FIGURE 3.8**
The final product of this Try It Yourself.

# Summary

In this hour, you learned all about models in Unity. You started by learning about how models are built with collections of vertices called meshes. Then, you discovered how to use the built-in models, import your own models, and download models from the Asset Store. You then learned about the model art workflow in Unity. You experimented with textures, shaders, and materials. You finished by creating a textured brick wall.

# Q&A

**Q. Will I still be able to make games if I'm not an artist?**

**A.** Absolutely. Using free online resources and the Unity Asset Store, you can find various art assets to put in your games.

**Q. Will I need to know how to use all the built-in shaders?**

**A.** Not necessarily. Many shaders are very situational. Start with the shaders covered in this chapter and learn more if a game project requires it.

**Q.** **If there are paid art assets in the Unity Asset Store, does that mean I can sell my own art assets?**

**A.** Yes, it does. In fact, it is not limited to only art assets. If you can create high-quality assets, you can certainly sell them in the store.

# Workshop

Take some time to work through the questions here to ensure that you have a firm grasp of the material.

## Quiz

1. True or False: Because of their simple nature, squares make up meshes in models.

2. What file formats does Unity support for 3D models?

3. True or False: Only paid models can be downloaded from the Unity Asset Store.

4. Explain the relationship between textures, shaders, and materials.

## Answers

1. False, meshes are made up of triangles.

2. .fbx, .dae, .3ds, .dxf, and .obj files.

3. False. There are several free models.

4. Materials contain textures and shaders. Shaders dictate the properties that can be set by the material and how the material gets rendered.

# Exercise

Let's experiment with the effects shaders have on the way models look. You will use the same mesh and texture for each model; only the shaders will be different. The project created in this exercise is named Hour3_Exercise and is available in the Hour 3 book files.

1. Create a new scene or project.

2. Add a Materials and a Textures folder to your project. Locate the files Brick_Normal.png and Brick_Texture.png in the Hour 3 book files and drag them into the Textures folder.

3. In the Project view, select **Brick_Texture**. In the Inspector view, change the aniso level from 1 to 3 to increase the texture quality for curves. Click **Apply**.

4. In the Project view, select **Brick_Normal**. In the Inspector view, change the texture type to **Normal Map**. Click **Apply**.

5. Add a directional light to your project (click **GameObject > Create Other > Directional Light**) and give it a position of (0, 10, −10) with a rotation of (30, 40, 0).

6. Add four spheres to your project. Scale them each to (2, 2, 2). Spread them out by giving them positions of (2, 0, −5), (−2, 0, −5), (−2, 2, −5), and (2, 2, −5).

7. Create four new materials in the Materials folder. Name them **DiffuseBrick**, **SpecularBrick**, **BumpedBrick**, and **BumpedSpecularBrick**. Figure 3.9 contains all the properties of the four materials. Go ahead and set their values.

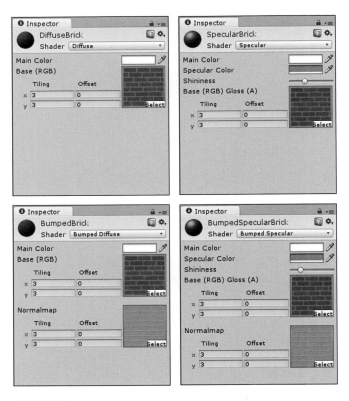

**FIGURE 3.9**
Material properties.

8. Click and drag each of the materials onto one of the four spheres. Notice how the light and the curvature of the spheres interact with the different shaders. Remember that you can move about the Scene view to see the spheres at different angles.

# Terrain

**What You'll Learn in This Hour:**

▶ The fundamentals of terrain
▶ How to sculpt terrain
▶ How to decorate your terrain with textures

In this hour, you learn about terrain generation. You learn what terrain is, how to create it, and how to sculpt it. You also get hands on with texture painting and fine-tuning. In addition, you learn to make large, expansive, and realistic-looking terrain pieces for your games.

## Terrain Generation

All 3D game levels exist in some form of a world. These worlds can be highly abstract or realistic. Often, games with expansive "outdoor" levels are said to have a terrain. The term *terrain* refers to any section of land that simulates a world's external landscape. Tall mountains, far plains, or dank swamps are all examples of possible game terrain.

In Unity, terrain is a flat mesh that can be sculpted into many different shapes. It may help to think of terrain as the sand in a sandbox. You can dig into the sand or raise sections of it up. The only thing basic terrain cannot do is overlap. This means that you cannot make things like caves or overhangs. Those items have to be modeled separately. Also, just like any other object in Unity, terrain has a position, rotation, and scale (although they aren't usually changed).

## Adding Terrain to Your Project

Creating a flat terrain in a scene is an easy task with some basic parameters. To add terrain to a scene, just click the menu items **GameObject > Create Other > Terrain**. You will see that an object called Terrain has been added. If you navigate around in your Scene view, you may also notice that the terrain piece is very large. In fact, the piece is much larger than we could possibly need right now. Therefore, we need to modify some of the properties of this terrain.

To make this terrain more manageable, you need to change the terrain resolution. By modifying the resolution, you can change the length, width, and maximum height of your piece of terrain. The reason the term *resolution* is used will become more apparent later when you learn about heightmaps. To change the resolution of the terrain piece, follow these steps:

1. Select your terrain in the Hierarchy view. In the Inspector view, locate and click the **Terrain Settings** button (see Figure 4.1).

2. Locate the Resolution settings.

3. Currently, the terrain width and length are set to 2000. Set these values both to **50**.

**FIGURE 4.1**
The Resolution settings.

The other options in the Resolution settings modify how textures are drawn and the performance of your terrain. Leave these alone for now. After you change the width and the height, you will see that the terrain is much smaller and manageable. Now it is time to start sculpting.

CAUTION

**Terrain Size**

Currently, you are going to be working with terrain that is 50 units long and wide. This is purely for manageability while learning the various tools. In a real game, the terrain would probably be a bigger size to fit your needs. It is also worth noting that if you already have a heightmap (covered in the next section), you will want the terrain ratio (the ratio of length and width) to match the ratio of the heightmap.

# Heightmap Sculpting

Traditionally, 256 shades of gray are available in 8-bit images. These shades range from 0 (black) to 255 (white). Knowing this, you can take a black-and-white image, often called a *grayscale* image, and use it as something called a *heightmap*. A heightmap is a grayscale image that contains elevation information similar to a topographical map. The darker shades can be thought of as low points, and the lighter shades are high points. Figure 4.2 is an example of a heightmap. It might not look like much, but a simple image like that can produce some dynamic scenery.

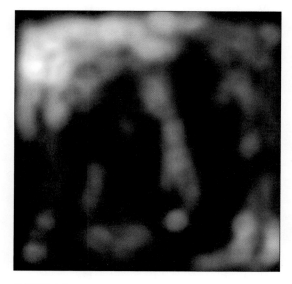

**FIGURE 4.2**
A simple heightmap.

Applying a heightmap to your currently flat terrain is simple. You simply start with a flat terrain and import the heightmap onto it, as follows.

▼ TRY IT YOURSELF

## Applying a Heightmap to Terrain

Let's walk through the steps of importing and applying a heightmap:

1. Locate the terrain.raw file in the Hour 4 files and put it somewhere you can easily find it.

2. With your terrain selected in the Hierarchy view, click the **Terrain Settings** button. (See Figure 4.1 if you don't remember where that is.) In the Heightmap section, click **Import Raw**.

3. The Import Raw Heightmap dialog will open. Locate the terrain.raw file from step 1 and click **Open**.

4. The Import Heightmap dialog will open (see Figure 4.3). Leave all options as they appear and click **Import**. Right about now, your terrain is looking strange. The problem is that when you set the length and width of your terrain to be more manageable, you left the height at 600. This is obviously much too high for your current needs.

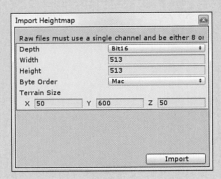

**FIGURE 4.3**
Import Heightmap dialog.

5. Change the terrain resolution by going back to the Resolution section in the Terrain Settings in the Inspector view. This time, change the height value to **60**. The result should be something much more pleasant (see Figure 4.4).

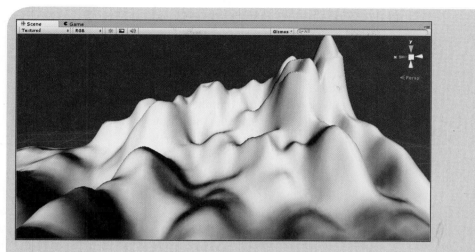

**FIGURE 4.4**
Terrain after you import a heightmap.

TIP

## Calculating Height

So far, the heightmap might seem random, but it is actually quite easy to figure out. Everything is based on a percentage of 255 and the maximum height of the terrain. The max height of the terrain defaults to 600 but is easily changeable. If you apply the formula of (Gray shade) / 255 * (Max height), you can easily calculate any point on the terrain. For instance, black has a value of 0, and so any spot that is black will be 0 units high (0 / 255 * 600). White has a value of 255 and therefore produces spots that are 600 units high (255 / 255 * 600). If you have a medium gray with a value of 125, any spots that color will produce terrain that is about 294 units high (125 / 255 * 600).

NOTE

## Heightmap Formats

In Unity, heightmaps must be grayscale images in the .raw format. There are many ways to generate these types of images; you can use a simple image editor or even Unity itself. If you create a heightmap using an image editor, try to make the map the same length and width ratio as your terrain. Otherwise, some distortion will be apparent. If you sculpt some terrain using Unity's sculpting tools and you want to generate a heightmap for it, you can by going to the Heightmap section in the Terrain Settings in the Inspector view and clicking **Export Raw**.

## Unity Terrain Sculpting Tools

Unity gives you multiple tools for hand sculpting your terrain. You can see these tools in the Inspector view under the component Terrain (Script). These tools all work under the same premise: You use a brush with a given size and opacity to "paint" terrain. In effect, what you are doing behind the scene is painting a heightmap that is translated into changes for the 3D terrain. The painting effects are cumulative, which means that the more you paint an area, the stronger the effect is on that area. Figure 4.5 shows identifies these tools. Using these tools, you can generate pretty much any landscape you can imagine.

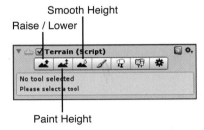

**FIGURE 4.5**
The terrain sculpting tools.

The first tool you will learn to use is the Raise/Lower tool. This tool, just as it sounds, enables you to raise or lower the terrain wherever you paint. To sculpt with this tool, follow these steps:

1. Select a brush. Brushes determine the size and shape of the sculpting effect.

2. Choose a brush size and opacity. The opacity determines how strong the sculpting effect is.

3. Click and drag over the terrain in the Scene view to raise the terrain. Holding Shift when you click and drag will instead lower the terrain.

Figure 4.6 illustrates some good starting options for sculpting given the terrain size 50 x 50 with a height of 60.

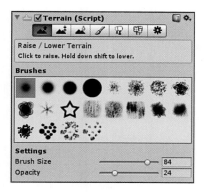

**FIGURE 4.6**
Good starting properties for sculpting.

The next tool is the Paint Height tool. This tool works almost exactly as the Raise/Lower tool except that it paints your terrain to a specified height. If the specified height is higher than the current terrain, painting raises the terrain. If the specified height is lower than the current terrain, however, the terrain is lowered. This proves useful for creating mesas or other flat structures in your landscape. Go ahead and try it out!

TIP

**Flattening Terrain**

If, at any time, you want to reset your terrain back to being flat, you can do so by going to the Paint Height tool and clicking **Flatten**. One added benefit of this is that you can flatten the terrain to a height other than its default 0. If your maximum height is 60 and you flatten your heightmap to 30, you have the ability raise the terrain by 30 units, but you can also lower it by 30 units. This makes it easy to sculpt valleys into your otherwise flat terrain.

The final tool you will use is the Smooth Height tool. This tool doesn't alter the terrain in highly noticeable ways. Instead, it removes a lot of the jagged lines that appear when sculpting terrain. Think of this tool as a polisher. You will really only use it to make minor tweaks after your major sculpting is done.

▼ TRY IT YOURSELF

### Sculpting Terrain

Now that you have learned about the sculpting tools, let's practice using them. In this exercise, you attempt to sculpt a specific piece of terrain:

1. Create a new project or scene and add a terrain. Set the resolution of the terrain to 50 x 50 and give it a height of 60.

2. Flatten the terrain to a height of 20 by clicking the **Paint Height** tool, changing the height to **20**, and clicking **Flatten**.

3. Using the sculpting tools, attempt to create a landscape similar to Figure 4.7.

4. Continue to experiment with the tools to try to add unique features to your terrain.

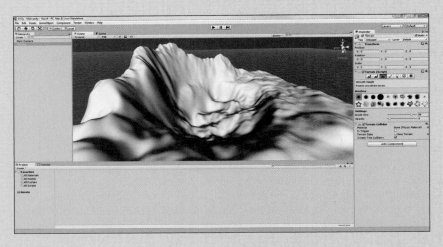

**FIGURE 4.7**
A sample terrain.

TIP

### Practice, Practice, Practice

Developing strong, compelling levels is an art form itself. Much thought has to be given to the placement of hills, valleys, mountains, and lakes. Not only do the elements need to be visually satisfying, they also need to be placed in such a way as to make the level playable. This type of skill doesn't develop overnight. Be sure to practice and refine your level-building skills to make exciting and memorable levels.

# Terrain Textures

You now know how to make the physical dimensions of a 3D world. Even though there may be a lot of features to your landscape, it is still bland and difficult to navigate. It is time to add some character to your level. In this section, you learn how to texture your terrain to give it an engaging look.

## Importing Terrain Assets

Like sculpting terrain, texturing terrain works a lot like painting. You select a brush and a texture and paint it onto your world. Before you can begin painting the world with textures, however, you need some textures to work with. Unity has some terrain assets available to you, but you need to import them first. To load these assets, click **Assets > Import Package > Terrain Assets**. The Importing Package dialog will appear (see Figure 4.8). This dialog is where you specify exactly which assets you want to import. Deselecting unneeded items is a good idea if you want to keep your project size down. For now, just leave all options checked and click **Import**. You should now have a new folder under Assets in the Project view called Standard Assets. This folder contains all the terrain assets you will be using in the rest of this hour.

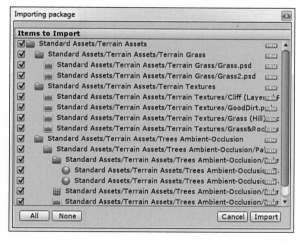

**FIGURE 4.8**
The Importing Package dialog.

## Texturing Terrain

The terrain texturing procedure is simple in Unity and works a lot like the sculpting. The first thing you need to do is load a texture. Figure 4.9 illustrates the texturing tool in the Inspector. Pay attention to the three numeric properties: brush size, opacity, and target strength. You should be familiar with the first two properties, but the last one is new. The target strength is the maximum opacity that it achievable through constant painting. Its value is a percentage, with 1 being 100%. Use this as a control to prevent painting your textures on too strongly.

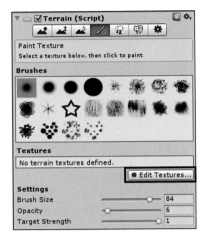

**FIGURE 4.9**
Terrain texture tool and properties.

To load a texture, follow these steps:

1. Click **Edit Textures > Add Texture**.

2. The Add Terrain Texture dialog will appear. Click **Select** in the Texture box (see Figure 4.10) and select **the Grass (Hill)** texture.

3. Click **Add**.

**FIGURE 4.10**
The Add Terrain Texture dialog.

At this point, your entire terrain should be covered in patchy grass. This looks better than the white terrain previously, but it is still far from realistic. Now, you will actually begin painting and making your terrain look better.

## Painting Textures onto Terrain

Let's apply a new texture to your terrain to give it a more realistic two-tone effect:

1. Using the steps listed earlier, add a new texture. This time, load the **Grass&Rock** texture. Once you have loaded it, be sure to select it by clicking it. (A blue bar appears under it if it is selected.)

2. Set your brush size to **30**, your opacity to **20**, and your target strength to **0.6**.

3. Sparingly, paint (click and drag) on the steep parts and crevices of your terrain. This gives the impression that grass isn't growing on the sides of steep grades and in between hills (see Figure 4.11).

4. Continue experimenting with texture painting. Feel free to load the texture **Cliff** and apply it to steeper parts or the texture **Sand** and make a path.

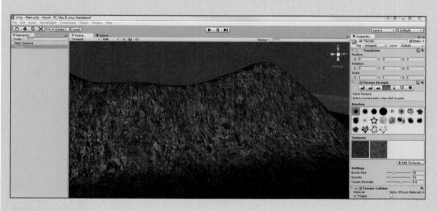

**FIGURE 4.11**
Example of a two-toned textured cliff.

You can load as many textures as you want in this fashion and achieve some realistic effects. Be sure to practice texturing to determine the best-looking patterns.

NOTE

**Creating Terrain Textures**

Game worlds are often unique and require custom textures to fit within the context of the games they are created for. You can follow some general guidelines when making your own textures for terrain. The first is to always try to make the pattern repeatable. This means that the textures can be tiled seamlessly. The larger the texture, the less obvious a repeating pattern is. The second guideline is to make the texture square. The last guideline is to try to make the texture dimension a power of two (32, 64, 128, 512, and so on). The last two guidelines effect the compression of the texture and the texture's efficiency. With a little practice, you will be making brilliant terrain textures in no time.

TIP

**Subtlety Is the Best Policy**

When texturing, remember to keep your effects subtle. Most of nature fades from one element to another without many harsh transitions. Your texturing efforts should also reflect that. If you can zoom out away from a piece of terrain and tell the exact point where one texture starts, your effect is too sudden. It is often better to work in many small and subtle applications of a texture rather than with one broad application.

# Summary

In this hour, you learned all terrains in Unity. You started by learning what terrains are and how to add them to your scene. From there, you looked at sculpting the terrain with both a heightmap and Unity's built-in sculpting tools. Finally, you learned how to make your terrains look more appealing by applying textures in a realistic fashion.

# Q&A

**Q. Does my game have to have terrain?**

**A.** Not at all. Many games take place entirely inside modeled rooms or in abstract spaces.

**Q. My terrain doesn't look very good. Is that normal?**

**A.** It takes a while to build up proficiency with the sculpting tools. With some practice, your levels will begin looking much better. True quality comes from play testing a level, which we cover in the next hour.

# Workshop

Take some time to work through the questions here to ensure that you have a firm grasp of the material.

## Quiz

1. True or False: You can make caves out of the Unity terrain.
2. What is a grayscale image containing terrain elevation information called?
3. True or False: Sculpting terrain in Unity is a lot like painting.
4. How do you access Unity's available terrain textures?

## Answers

1. False, Unity's terrain cannot overlap.
2. A heightmap.
3. True.
4. You import the terrain assets by going to **Assets > Import Package > Terrain Assets**.

# Exercise

Let's practice terrain sculpting and texturing. Sculpt a terrain that contains the following elements:

▶ Lakebed
▶ Beach
▶ Mountain range
▶ Flat plains

Once you have sculpted these, apply textures to your terrain in the following manner. You can find all textures listed here in the Terrain Assets package:

▶ The beach should use the texture Sand and should fade into Grass&Rock.
▶ Plains and all flat areas should be textured with Grass.
▶ The texture Grass should smoothly transition into Grass&Rock as the terrain gets steeper.
▶ The texture Grass&Rock should transition into Cliff at its steepest and highest points.

Be as creative as you want with this exercise. Build a world that makes you proud.

# Environments

---

**What You'll Learn in This Hour:**

▶ How to add trees and grass to your terrain

▶ How to add environment effects to your terrain

▶ How to navigate your world with a character controller

In the preceding hour, you learned to sculpt and texture terrain for your game. In this hour, you add environment effects that will really give character to your world. You start by learning how to add vegetation like trees and grass to your terrain. From there, you learn to apply environment effects like water, sky, fog, and lens flares. You finish by adding a character controller to your scene and moving around inside your world.

## Generating Trees and Grass

A world with only flat textures would be boring. Almost every natural landscape has some form of plant life. In this section, you learn how to add and customize trees and grass to give your terrain an organic look and feel.

### Painting Trees

Adding trees to your terrain works just like the sculpting and texturing from the preceding hour; the whole process is very similar to painting. The basic premise is to load a tree model, set the properties for the trees, and then paint the area you want the trees to appear in. Based on the options you choose, Unity will spread the trees out and vary them to give a more natural and organic look.

### Terrain Assets

To follow along with the rest of this section, you need the standard terrain assets loaded into your project. If you do not have them, refer to the preceding hour for instructions on how to import them into your project.

You use the Place Trees tool to spread trees out over the terrain. Once the terrain has been selected in the scene, the Place Trees tool is accessed in the Inspector view as part of the Terrain (Script) component. Figure 5.1 shows the Place Trees tool and its standard properties.

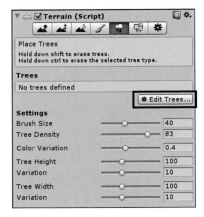

**FIGURE 5.1**
The Place Trees tool.

Table 5.1 describes the tree tool's properties.

**TABLE 5.1   The Place Tree Tool's Properties**

| Property | Description |
| --- | --- |
| Brush Size | The size of the area that trees are added to when painting. |
| Tree Density | How densely the trees will be able to be packed. |
| Color Variation, Tree Height/Width, and Variations | These properties allow all the trees to be slightly different from each other. This gives the impression of many different trees instead of the same tree repeated. |

## Placing Trees on a Terrain

Let's walk through the steps to place trees onto your terrain using the Paint Trees tool. This exercise assumes that you have created a new scene and have already added a terrain. The terrain should be set to a length and width of 100. It will look better of the terrain has some sculpting and texturing done already:

1. Click **Edit Trees > Add Tree** to pull up the Add Tree dialog (refer to Figure 5.1).

2. Clicking the **circle** icon to the right of the Tree text box on the Add Tree dialog pulls up the Tree Selector dialog (see Figure 5.2).

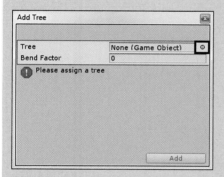

**FIGURE 5.2**
The Add Tree dialog.

3. Select the **Palm Tree** and click **Add**.

4. Set your brush size to **10**, your tree density to **70**, and your width and height to **50**. Choose whichever variation properties you want.

5. Paint trees on the terrain by clicking and dragging over the areas where you want trees. Holding the Shift key while click-dragging removes trees.

6. Continue to experiment with different brush sizes, densities, and tree sizes/variations.

NOTE

## Dark Trees

You might notice that some trees appear black. This can happen when smaller trees are placed close to larger trees. The reason is that whatever lighting exists in your scene is calculated as hitting the taller trees around the smaller tree. In effect, the smaller tree is in the shadow of the larger trees. You can resolve this issue with Unity Pro because the lighting is dynamically calculated and tends to be a little more accurate. If you don't have the Pro version, you can also simply remove and replace the tree.

NOTE

**Tree Warping**

As you move about your Scene view, you may see some trees bending and changing. What you are witnessing are built-in efficiencies to make the project run faster. When trees are far away from the viewer, they get rendered as a much lower-quality billboard. As the viewer gets closer, the trees are swapped with higher-quality versions. The effect is the warping that you are seeing. You can change when and how these transitions occur by changing some of the terrain settings. You get a chance to work with those later this hour.

# Painting Grass

Now that you have learned how to paint trees, you learn how to apply grass or other small plant life to your world. Grass and other small plants are called *details* in Unity. Therefore, the tool used to paint grass is the Paint Details tool. Unlike trees, which are 3D models, details are billboards (explained later). Just like you have seen over and over by now, details are applied to a terrain using a brush and a painting motion. Figure 5.3 illustrates the Paint Details tool and some of its properties.

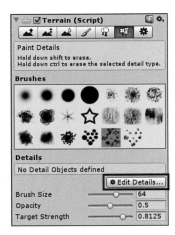

**FIGURE 5.3**
The Paint Details tool.

NOTE

**Billboards**

Billboards are a special type of visual component in a 3D world that give the effect of a 3D model without actually being a 3D model. Models exist in all three dimensions. Therefore, when moving around one, you can see the different sides. Billboards, however, are flat images that always face the camera. When you attempt to go around a billboard, the billboard turns to face your new position. Common uses for billboards are grass details, particles, and onscreen effects.

Applying grass to your terrain is a fairly straightforward process. You first need to add a grass texture. To add a grass texture:

1. Click **Edit Details** in the Inspector view and select **Add Grass Texture**.

2. In the Add Grass Texture dialog, click the **circle** icon next to the Texture text box (see Figure 5.4). Select the **Grass** texture (*not* the Grass (Hill) texture).

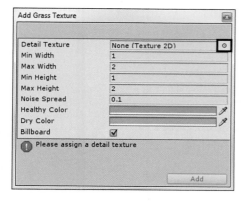

**FIGURE 5.4**
The Add Grass Texture dialog.

3. Set your texture properties to whatever values you want. Pay special attention to the color properties because those establish the range of natural colors for your grass.

4. When done, click **Apply**.

After you have your grass loaded, you just need to choose a brush and your brush properties. You are now ready to begin painting grass.

TIP

### Realistic Grass

You may notice that when you begin painting grass that it does not look realistic. You need to focus on a few things when adding grass to your terrain. The first is to pay attention to the colors you set for the grass texture. Try to keep them darker and more earth toned. The next thing you need to do is choose a nongeometric brush shape to help break up hard edges (see Figure 5.3 for a good brush to use). Finally, keep your opacity and target strength properties very low. A good setting to start with is .02 for each. If you need more grass, you can just keep painting over the same area.

CAUTION

**Vegetation and Performance**

The more trees and grass you have in a scene, the more processing is required to render it. If you are concerned with performance, you need to keep the amount of vegetation low. There are some properties that you look at later this hour that will help you manage this, but as an easy rule, try to add trees and grass only to areas where it is really needed.

TIP

**Disappearing Grass**

As with trees, grass is affected by its distance from the viewer. Whereas trees revert to a lower-quality when the viewer is far away, grass is just not rendered. The result is a ring around the viewer beyond which no grass is visible. Again, you can modify this distance by properties you look at later this hour.

## Terrain Settings

The last button on this list of terrain tools in the Inspector view is for the Terrain Settings tool. These settings control how the terrain, texture, trees, and details look and function overall. Figure 5.5 shows all the terrain settings.

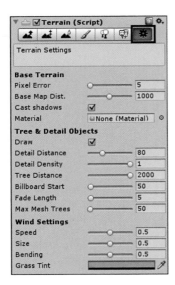

**FIGURE 5.5**
The Terrain Settings tool.

The first grouping of settings is for the overall terrain. Table 5.2 describes the various settings.

**TABLE 5.2   Base Terrain Settings**

| Setting | Description |
| --- | --- |
| Pixel Error | Number of allowable errors when displaying terrain geometry. The higher the value, the lower the detail of the terrain. |
| Base Map Dist. | The maximum distance that high-resolution textures will be displayed. When the viewer is farther than the given distance, textures degrade to a lower resolution. |
| Cast Shadows | Determines whether terrain geometry casts shadows. |
| Material | This slot is for assigning a custom material capable of rendering terrain. The material must contain a shader capable of rendering terrain. |

In addition, some settings directly affect the way trees and details (like grass) behave in your terrain. Table 5.3 describes these settings.

**TABLE 5.3   Tree and Detail Object Settings**

| Setting | Description |
| --- | --- |
| Draw | Determines whether trees and details are rendered in the scene. |
| Detail Distance | The distance from the camera where details will no longer be drawn to the screen. |
| Tree Distance | The distance from the camera where trees will no longer be drawn to the screen. |
| Billboard Start | The distance from the camera where 3D tree models will begin to transition into lower-quality billboards. |
| Fade Length | The distance over which trees will transition between billboards to higher-quality 3D models. The higher the setting, the smoother the transition. |
| Max Mesh Trees | The total number of trees able to be drawn simultaneously as 3D meshes and not billboards. |

The last settings you look at are for the wind. Because you haven't had a chance to actually run around inside your world yet (you will later this hour), you might be wondering what that means. Basically, Unity simulates a light wind over your terrain. This light wind causes the grass to bend and sway and livens up the world. Table 5.4 describes the wind settings.

**TABLE 5.4**   Wind Settings

| Setting | Description |
| --- | --- |
| Speed | The speed, and therefore the strength, of the wind effect. |
| Size | The size of the area of grass affected by the wind at the same time. |
| Bending | The amount of sway the grass will have due to wind. |
| Grass Tint | Although not a wind setting, this setting controls the overall coloration of all grass in your level. |

# Environment Effects

At this point, you have sculpted, textured, and added trees and grass to your terrain. It is safe to say that it is looking much better than when it was just a flat white square. In this section, you learn about adding environment details to really make your game world as complete as possible.

## Skyboxes

You might have noticed that while your terrain is full of texture and detail, the sky is a bland solid color. What you need to do is to add a skybox to your world. A skybox is a large box that goes around your world. Even though it is a cube consisting of six flat sides, it has inward-facing textures to make it look round and infinite. You can create your own skyboxes or use one of Unity's standard skyboxes. In this book, you will use the built-in ones.

To use the standard skyboxes, you need to import the assets into your project. To import the skyboxes, click **Assets > Import Package > Skyboxes**. This will open the Import Package dialog. Leave everything checked and click **Import**. After importing the assets, you can begin working with skyboxes.

There are two ways to add skyboxes to your world: You can add the skybox to your camera or add it to the scene.

### Adding a Skybox to the Camera

You can add a skybox to your camera so that whatever the camera sees beyond your game world will be replaced with sky. To add a skybox to your camera, follow these steps:

1. Select the **Main Camera** in the Hierarchy view.

2. Add a skybox component by clicking **Component > Rendering > Skybox**.

3. In the Inspector view, locate the Skybox component and click the **circle** icon next to the Custom Skybox field (see Figure 5.6). In the Select Material dialog, select the **Sunny2 Skybox**.

4. Run your scene to see the skybox applied to the camera.

**FIGURE 5.6**
The Skybox component.

---

NOTE

### Multiple Skyboxes

The reason there is an option to add the skybox to a specific camera is so that you can have different skyboxes (or no skyboxes) on different cameras. This enables you to make the world look different to different viewers. If you want to have flexibility in the way your world looks, add the skybox to the camera. If you want your world to look uniform to everyone, add it to the scene (as covered next).

---

## Adding a Skybox to the Scene

If you add a skybox to the scene, it will be present for all viewers. Another benefit of this method is that the skybox will be visible in the Scene view. This makes it easy to see how your world looks with all elements in place. To add a skybox to your scene, follow these steps:

1. Click **Edit > Render Settings** to open the render settings for the scene in the Inspector view.

2. Locate the Skybox Material field and click the **circle** icon to the right of it.

3. Choose the **Sunny1 Skybox**. Notice how the Scene view changes to contain the sky. If the Scene view doesn't change, turn on the skybox, fog, and lens flare scene setting (see Figure 5.7).

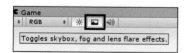

**FIGURE 5.7**
The environment effects toggle.

# Fog

In Unity, you can add fog to a scene. You can use this fog to simulate many different natural occurrences, such as haze, an actual fog, or the fading of objects over great distances. You can also use fog to give new and alien appearances to your world.

▼ TRY IT YOURSELF

## Adding Fog to a Scene

Let's add fog to your scene and learn about the different properties that affect it:

1. Click **Edit > Render Settings**. The render settings will open in the Inspector view.

2. Turn on fog by checking the **Fog** check box.

3. Experiment with the different fog densities and colors. Table 5.5 describes the various fog properties.

Several properties impact how fog looks in a scene. Table 5.5 describes these properties.

**TABLE 5.5**   Fog Properties

| Setting | Description |
| --- | --- |
| Fog Color | The color of the fog effect. |
| Fog Mode | This controls how the fog is calculated. The three modes are Linear, Exponential, and Exp2. Linear will be a smooth fog transition and is the default mode. |
| Fog Density | How strong the fog effect is. This property is used only if the fog mode is set to Exponential or Exp2. |
| Linear Fog Start Linear Fog End | These control how close to the camera the fog starts and how far from the camera it ends. These properties are only used in Linear mode. |

# Lens Flares

A lens flare is a visual deformity that occurs whenever a camera looks at a bright light source. It is the result of light bouncing around inside the glass of a lens. A lens flare can also be experienced when you attempt to look into a bright source like the sun (not recommended). In Unity, you can add flares to light sources to give them a more realistic effect and make it seem like they are very bright.

## Adding a Lens Flare to Your Scene

It will be easier to see how lens flares are placed in a scene if you follow along step by step. Adding a flare is pretty simple, but it uses some new items you might not be familiar with yet. Before you can add a flare to your scene, you need to have a light source and some flare assets. These will all be taken care of in the following steps:

1. Add a directional light to your scene by clicking **GameObject > Create Other > Directional Light**. Directional lights are covered in greater detail in a later hour. For now, just understand that a directional light is a parallel light, just like the sun.

2. Once the light is added to your scene, rotate it so that it gives the desired light effect on your terrain.

3. Next, you need light flare assets. Import the Unity light flare assets by clicking **Assets > Import Package > Light Flares**. In the Import dialog, leave everything checked and click **Import**.

4. Select the directional light in the Hierarchy view and locate the Flare property in the Inspector view.

5. Click the **circle** icon next to the Flare property and choose the **Sun** flare from the Select Flare dialog.

At this point, your flare is on the light and will be picked up by the camera. This is because the Main Camera of the scene has a Flare Layer component by default. Any cameras without that component will not be able to see the lens flares.

TIP

### Where's the Flare?

You might not be able to see the lens flare yet because your camera is not pointed at your directional light. Don't bother trying to make the camera point at the light just yet. Later this hour, you will move around your scene while it is running. At that point, you will be able to see it and make any needed adjustments.

# Water

The last environment effect you look at adding is water. Water is an effect that varies depending on whether you have the Pro or free version of Unity. The free version of Unity has access to basic water. The object is a little generic, but it is passable. The Pro version's water is much better looking. If you have Pro, that is definitely the version you opt for. Because this book is written to use the free version, that is the version that is used.

In Unity, water is an asset that needs to be imported. In the scene, water is a flat plane that looks like the top surface area of a pond or lake. Note that the water is just an effect. If a player jumps into a lake with water, the player will fall right through the water and down into the hole that was sculpted for it.

▼ TRY IT YOURSELF

### Creating a Lake and Adding Water

To add water, you need some part of your terrain to contain the water. In this exercise, you sculpt a lake and add water to it:

1. Create a new terrain or work with an existing terrain. Sculpt a lakebed down into the terrain.

2. Import the water assets by clicking **Assets > Import Package > Water (Basic)**. In the Import Package dialog, leave everything checked and click **Import**.

3. Locate the Water (Basic) folder in the Project view and locate the Daylight Simple Water asset (see Figure 5.8).

4. Drag the Daylight Simple Water asset onto the Scene view and into the lakebed you created. Scale and move the water as necessary until it fills up the lakebed properly.

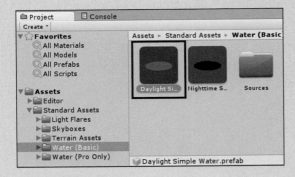

**FIGURE 5.8**
The Water (Basic) folder and assets.

# Character Controllers

At this point, you have finished your terrain. It has been sculpted and textured; had trees and grass added and has been given a sky; and it has a fog, lens flare, and water. It is now time to get into your level and "play" it. Unity provides two basic character controllers to easily get right into your scene without a lot of work on your end. Basically, you drop a controller into your scene and then move around with the control scheme common to most first-person games.

## Adding a Character Controller

To add a character controller to your scene, you first need to import the asset. Click **Assets > Import Package > Character Controller**. In the Import Package dialog, leave everything checked and click **Import**. A new folder named Character Controllers should have been added to your Project view under the Standard Assets folder. Because you don't have a 3D model to use as the player, we are going to use the first-person controller. Locate the **First Person** controller asset in the Character Controllers folder (see Figure 5.9) and drag it onto your terrain in the Scene view.

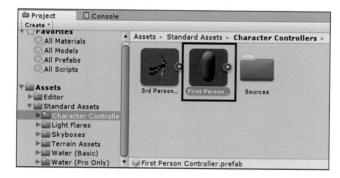

**FIGURE 5.9**
The First Person character controller.

Now that the character controller has been added to your scene, you can move around in the terrain you created. When you play your scene, you will notice that you can now see from where the controller was placed. You can use the WASD keys to move around, the mouse to look around, and the spacebar to jump. Play around with the controls if they feel a bit unusual to you and enjoy experiencing your world!

TIP
_____

## "2 Audio Listeners"

When you added the character controller to the scene, you might have noticed a message at the bottom of the editor that said, "There are 2 audio listeners in the scene." This is because the Main Camera (the camera that exists by default) has an audio listener component and so does the character controller that you added. Because the cameras represent the player's perspective, only one can listen for audio. You can fix this by removing the audio listener component from the Main Camera.
_____

TIP
_____

## Falling Through the World

If you find the camera falling through the world whenever you run your scene, chances are that your character controller is stuck partially in the ground. Try raising your character controller up a little bit above the ground. When the scene starts, the camera should fall just a little bit until it hits the ground and stops.
_____

NOTE
_____

## Importing Assets

In this hour, you imported a lot of asset packages. When you imported them, you left everything checked in the Import Package dialog. This caused every asset in that package to be added to your project. Doing this can make the project files very large. In a more realistic situation, you import only the assets that you need to use. You uncheck all the assets that you don't need. Remember, you can always import them later if needed!
_____

# Fixing Your World

Now that you can enter your world and see it close up, it is time to refine some of the smaller details. You might notice that some areas that you built to be a path are too steep to walk on. You may also see some areas where the textures are not placed quite right. Now is the time to smooth out the world and fix any errors you find. It can be difficult to see all the places that need fixed from the Scene view. It is not until you are on the ground moving around your world that you really get a chance to experience it.

One fix that is worth looking at is the lens flare added previously. If you look up at the sky, you notice a sun that is part of the skybox texture. You may also notice a lens flare. Chances are the lens flare that simulates the sun and the sun image itself do not line up. While looking at the sun and the flare, pause the scene. Note that it can be difficult to pause the scene with your mouse while looking at something specific. You can easily pause the scene while it is running by pressing **Shift+Ctrl+P** (which is **Shift+Cmd+P** on a Mac). In the Scene view, rotate the directional light until the sun image and the flare line up. Note the rotation information, because as soon as you stop the scene, any changes will be lost. Once the scene is stopped, simply rotate the directional light back to the direction that lined up with the sun image. Cross one more detail off your list.

# Summary

In this hour, you learned all about environment details in Unity. You started by learning to add trees and grass to your scene. Next, you added ambient effects like the sky, fog, and lens flares. From there, you worked with Unity's water assets. You finished this hour by adding a character controller to your scene and actually playing around in your world.

# Q&A

**Q. Do trees and grass greatly impact performance?**

**A.** It depends on how much of it you have on scene at once. It also depends on the power of the computer you are running it on. A good rule is to have grass and trees if they positively impact your scene.

**Q. Can I make my own skyboxes?**

**A.** Yes, you can. You should consider it mostly if you are building a custom world or a world with specific details not present in the available skyboxes.

**Q. There are a lot of properties to the character controller. Will I need to know them all?**

**A.** Not really. The character controllers are easy to use as they are. If you need to make easy changes to the movement, you can do that, but it shouldn't be necessary for most uses.

# Workshop

Take some time to work through the questions here to ensure that you have a firm grasp of the material.

## Quiz

**1.** What setting controls how much trees sway in the wind?

**2.** What's the name of the ambient effect that can simulate haze or fading of colors at a distance?

**3.** This object is a cube that fits around your world and is textured to look like a sky.

**4.** What character controller did you add to your scene: First Person or Third Person?

# Answers

1. That's a trick question. Trees don't sway in the wind, grass does. The setting that controls it is Bending (under Wind Settings).

2. Fog.

3. A skybox.

4. First Person.

# Exercise

In this exercise, you have a chance to finish the terrain you began making at the end of Hour 4, "Terrain." You will be adding the rest of the environmental effects to give your world a better level of realism.

Open the project or scene with the terrain you created in Hour 4. You need to add the following to it:

▶ Add water to the lakebed you created.

▶ Add some sparse grass around the edge of the lakebed and more grass over the flat plains.

▶ Add some palm trees to the grassy area where the grass texture meets the sand texture of the beach.

▶ Add a skybox to your scene.

▶ Add a fog effect to your scene. Change the settings so that it realistically makes the mountain range look cloudy.

▶ Add a directional light and a lens flare to the light. Ensure that the light lines up with a sun image if it is present in the skybox.

▶ Add a character controller and test drive your level. Ensure that everything is properly placed and looks realistic.

# HOUR 6
# Lights and Cameras

## What You'll Learn in This Hour:

▶ How to work with lights in Unity
▶ The core elements of cameras
▶ How to work with multiple cameras in a scene
▶ How to work with layers

In this hour, you learn to use lights and cameras in Unity. You start by looking at the main features of lights. You then explore the different types of lights and their unique uses. Once you are finished with lights, you begin working with cameras. You learn how to add new cameras, place them, and generate interesting effects with them. You finish by learning about layers in Unity.

## Lights

In any form of visual media, lights go a long way in defining how it is to be perceived. Bright, slightly yellow light can make a scene look sunny and warm. Take the same scene and give it a low-intensity blue light, and it will look eerie and disconcerting. Most scenes that strive for realism or dramatic effect implore at least one light (and often many). In the past, you have briefly worked with lights to highlight other elements. In this section, you work with lights more directly.

NOTE

### Repeat Properties

The different lights share many of the same properties. If a light has a property that has already been covered under a different light type, it won't be covered again. Just remember that if two different light types have properties with the same names, those properties do the same thing.

NOTE
_____

### What Is a Light?

In Unity, lights are not objects themselves. Instead, lights are a component. This means that when you add a light to a scene, you are really just adding a game object with the Light component. This light component can be any of the types of light you can use.
_____

# Point Lights

The first light type you will be working with is the point light. Think of a point light as a light bulb. All light is emitted from one central location out in every direction. The point light is also the most common type of light for illuminating interior areas.

To add a point light to a scene, click **GameObject > Create Other > Point Light**. Once in the scene, the point light game object can be manipulated just like any other. Table 6.1 describes the point light properties.

**TABLE 6.1**   Point Light Properties

| Property | Description |
| --- | --- |
| Type | The Type property is the type of light that the component gives off. Because this is a point light, the type should be Point. Changing the Type property changes the type of light it is. |
| Range | The Range property dictates how far the light shines. Illumination will fade evenly from the source of light to the range dictated. |
| Color | The color the light shines. Color is additive, which means that if you shine a red light on a blue object, it will end up purple. |
| Intensity | The Intensity property dictates how brightly a light will shine. Note that the light will still shine only as far as the Range property dictates. |
| Cookie | The Cookie property accepts a cubemap (like a skybox) that dictates a pattern for the light to shine through. Cookies are covered in more detail later. |
| Shadow Type | The Shadow Type property is how shadows are calculated for this source in a scene. Hard shadows are more accurate and more performance intensive. All shadows require Unity Pro to function. If you are using Unity Free, the only way to have shadows is if you manually bake them into your textures. |
| Draw Halo | The Draw Halo toggle determines whether a glowing halo will appear around your light. Halos are covered in more detail later. |
| Flare | The Flare property accepts a light flare asset and simulates the effect of a bright light shining into a camera lens. You have worked with light flares in previous hours to simulate a sun effect. |

| Property | Description |
|---|---|
| Render Mode | The Render Mode property determines the importance of this light. The three settings are Auto, Important, and Not Important. An important light is rendered in higher quality, whereas a less-important light is rendered more quickly. |
| Culling Mask | The Culling Mask property determines what layers are affected by the light. By default, everything is affected by the light. Layers are covered in detail later. |
| Lightmapping | The Lightmapping property determines whether the light is calculated in real time or baked into the lightmap. This is a more advanced setting that you are not going to need right now. Just leave this on Auto. |

NOTE

**Baking**

*Baking* refers to the process of adding light and shadow to textures and objects during creation. You can do this with Unity or with a graphical editor. For instance, if you were to make a wall texture with a dark spot on it that resembled a human shadow, and then put a human model next to the wall it was on, it would seem like the model was casting a shadow on the wall. The truth is, though, that the shadow was "baked" into the texture. Baking can make your games run much more quickly because the engine won't have to calculate light and shadow every single frame. That's a big deal!

TRY IT YOURSELF ▼

**Adding a Point Light to a Scene**

Let's build a scene with some dynamic point lighting. The completed version of this project is available as Hour6_PointLight in the book assets under Hour 6:

1. Create a new scene or project.

2. Add a plane to the scene (**GameObject > Create Other > Plane**). Ensure that the plane is positioned at (0, .5, 0) and it rotated (270, 0, 0). The plane should be visible to the camera.

3. Add two cubes to the scene. Position them at (−1.5, 1, -5) and (1.5, 1, −5).

4. Add a point light to the scene (**GameObject > Create Other > Point Light**). Position the point light at (0, 1, −5). Notice how the light illuminates the inner sides of the cubes and the background plane (see Figure 6.1).

5. Continue exploring the light properties. Be sure to experiment with the light color, range, and intensity.

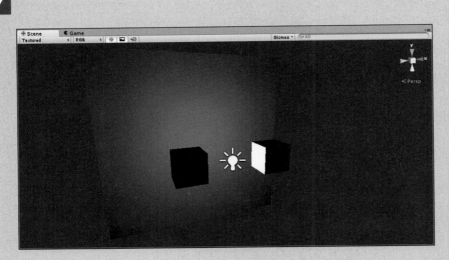

**FIGURE 6.1**
The results of the exercise.

## Spotlights

Spotlights work a lot like the headlights in a car or flashlights. The light of a spotlight begins in at a central spot and then radiates out in a cone. In other words, spotlights illuminate whatever is in front of them while leaving everything else in the dark. Unlike a point light, which sends light in every direction, you can aim spotlights.

To add a spotlight to your scene, click **GameObject > Create Other > Spotlight**. Alternatively, if you already have a light in your scene, you can change its type to **Spot**. It will then become a spotlight.

Spotlights have only one property not already covered: Spot Angle. The Spot Angle property determines the radius of the cone of light emitted by the spotlight.

### ▼ TRY IT YOURSELF

#### Adding a Spotlight to a Scene

You now have a chance to work with spotlights in Unity. For brevity, this exercise uses the project created in the previous Try It Yourself for point lights. If you have not completed that, do so to continue with this exercise. The completed version of this project is available as Hour6_SpotLight in the book assets under Hour 6:

   **1.** Open the previously created project.

2. Right-click the **Point Light** in the Hierarchy view and select **Rename**. Rename the object to **Spotlight**. In the Inspector, change the Type property to **Spot**. Place the light object at (0, 1, –13).

3. Experiment with the properties of the spotlight. Notice how the range, intensity, and spot angle shape and change the effect of the light.

# Directional Lights

The last light type you work with in this section is the directional light. The directional light is similar to the spotlight in that it can be aimed. Unlike the spotlight, though, the directional light illuminates the entire scene. You can think of a directional light as a sun. In fact, you used a directional light already as a sun in the previous hours working with terrain. The light from a directional light radiates evenly in parallel lines across a scene.

To add a directional light to your scene, click **GameObject > Create Other > Directional Light**. Alternatively, if you already have a light in your scene, you can change its type to Directional. It will then become a directional light.

Directional lights have one additional property that hasn't been covered yet: Cookie Size. Cookies are covered later, but basically this property controls how big a cookie is and thus how many times it is repeated across a scene.

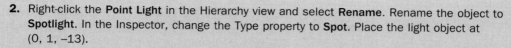

## TRY IT YOURSELF ▼

### Adding a Directional Light to a Scene

We will now add a directional light to a Unity scene. Once again, this exercise builds off of the previous project created in the Try It Yourself for spotlights. If you have not completed that, do so to continue with this exercise. The completed version of this project is available as Hour6_ DirectionLight in the book assets under Hour 6:

1. Open the previously created project.

2. Right-click the **Spotlight** in the Hierarchy view and select **Rename**. Rename the object to **Directional Light**. In the Inspector, change the Type property to **Directional**. Change the object's rotation to be (75, 0, 0).

3. Notice how the light looks on the objects in the scene. Now change the light's position to be (50, 50, 50). Notice how the light does not change. Because the directional light comes in parallel lines, the position of it does not matter. Only the rotation of a directional light matters.

4. Experiment with the properties of the directional light. There is no range (range is infinite), but see how the color and intensity affect the scene.

NOTE

**Honorable Mention: Area Light**

There is one more light type that is not being covered in this text: the area light. An area light is a Unity Pro-only feature that exists for a process called lightmap baking. These topics are more advanced than the aim of this text and aren't needed for basic game projects. If you want to learn more about this, Unity has a wealth of online documentation.

# Creating Lights out of Objects

Because lights in Unity are components, any object in a scene can be a light. To add a light to an object, first select the object. Then in the Inspector view, click the **Add Component** button. A new list should pop up. Select **Rendering** and then **Light**. Now your object has a light component. An alternative way to add a light to an object is to select the object and click **Component > Rendering > Light** in the menu.

Note a couple of things about adding lights to objects. The first is that the object will not block the light. This means that putting a light inside a cube will not stop the light from radiating. The second this is that adding a light to an object does not make it glow. The object itself will not look like it is giving off light, but it is.

# Halos

Halos are glowing circles that appear around lights in foggy or cloudy conditions (see Figure 6.2). They occur because light is bouncing off of small particles all around the light source. In Unity, you can easily add halos to your lights. Each light has a check box called Draw Halo. If it is checked, a halo will be drawn for the light.

CAUTION

**Unity Bug**

As of Unity 4.1, there is a bug when working with halos. As of the time of this writing, you need to perform a workaround to get the halo to appear around a light. If nothing appears when you check the Draw Halo check box on a light, you need to add a halo component. (If a halo appears, you do not need to follow these steps.) To do this, select your light and click **Component > Effects > Halo**. The halo for your light should now appear. At this point, you can remove the halo component you just added. You should also only have to do this once per scene. If the halo still isn't appearing, make sure to zoom out, because the halo will not appear when the camera is too close.

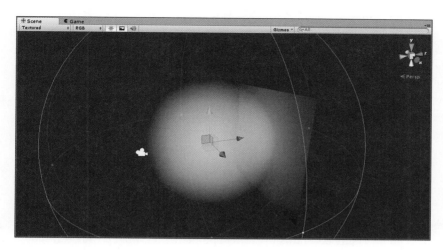

**FIGURE 6.2**
A halo around a light.

The size of a halo is determined by the light's range. The bigger the range, the bigger the halo. Unity also provides a few properties that apply to all halos in a scene. You can access these properties by clicking **Edit > Render Settings**. The render settings will then appear in the Inspector view (see Figure 6.3).

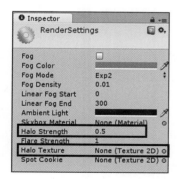

**FIGURE 6.3**
The render settings.

The Halo Strength property determines how big the halo will be based off of the light's range. For instance, if a light has a range of 10 and the strength is set to 1, the halo will extend out all 10 units. If the strength were set to .5, then the halo would extend out only 5 units (10 * .5 = 5). The Halo Texture property allows you to specify a different shape for your halo by providing a new texture. If you do not want to use a custom texture for your halo, you can leave it blank and the default circular one will be used.

## Cookies

If you have ever shone a light on a wall and then put your hand in between the light and the wall, you probably noticed that some of the light was blocked by your hand, leaving a hand-shaped shadow on the wall. You can simulate this effect in Unity with cookies. Cookies are special textures that you can add to lights to dictate how the light radiates. Cookies differ a little for point, spot, and directional lights. Spotlights and directional lights both use black-and-white flat textures for cookies. Spotlights don't repeat the cookies, but directional lights do. Point lights also use black-and-white textures, but they must be placed in a cubemap. A cubemap is six textures placed together to form a box (like a skybox).

Adding a cookie to a light is a fairly straightforward process. You simply apply a texture to the Cookie property of the light. The trick to getting a cookie to work is setting the texture up correctly ahead of time. To set up the texture correctly, select it in Unity, and then change its properties in the Inspector window. Figure 6.4 shows the correct properties for a point cookie, a spot cookie, and a directional cookie.

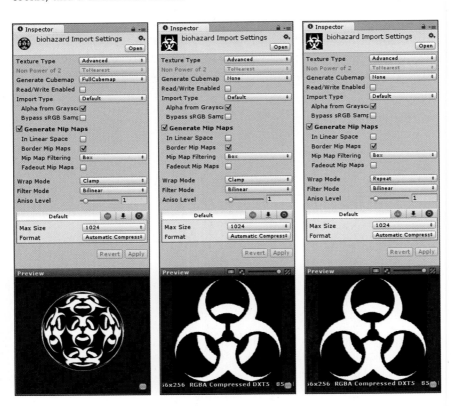

**FIGURE 6.4**
The texture properties of cookies for point, spot, and directional lights.

## Adding a Cookie to a Spotlight

Let's add a cookie to a spotlight so that you can see the process from start to finish. This exercise requires the biohazard.png image in the book assets for Hour 6:

1. Create a new project or scene. Add a plane to the scene and position it at (0, 1, 0) with a rotation of (270, 0, 0).

2. Add a spotlight to the Main Camera by selecting the **Main Camera** and then clicking **Component > Rendering > Light** and changing the type to **Spot**. Set the range to **18**, the spot angle to **40**, and the intensity to **3**.

3. Drag the biohazard.png texture from the book assets into your Project view. Select the texture, and in the Inspector view change the texture type to **Advanced**. Check the **Alpha from Grayscale** check box. Check the **Border Mip Maps** check box. Finally, change the wrap mode to **Clamp**. Click **Apply**. If you are unsure whether you have the correct settings, check the spot settings in Figure 6.4.

4. With the Main Camera selected, click and drag the biohazard texture into the Cookie property of the light component. You should see the biohazard symbol projected onto the plane (see Figure 6.5).

5. Experiment with different ranges and intensities of the light. Rotate the plane and see how the symbol warps and distorts.

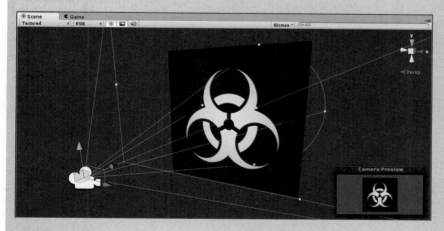

**FIGURE 6.5**
Spotlight with a cookie.

# Cameras

The camera is the player's view into the world. It provides their perspective and controls how things appear to them. All games in Unity have at least one camera. In fact, a camera is always added for you whenever you create a new scene. The camera always appears in the hierarchy as Main Camera. In this section, you learn all about cameras and how to use them for interesting effects.

## Anatomy of a Camera

All cameras share the same set of properties that dictate how they behave. Table 6.2 describes all the camera properties.

**TABLE 6.2**  Camera Properties

| Property | Description |
| --- | --- |
| Clear Flags | The Clear Flags property determines what the camera displays in the areas where there are no game objects. The default is Skybox. If there is no skybox, the camera defaults to a solid color. Depth Only should be used only when there are multiple cameras. Don't Clear causes streaking and should be used only if writing a custom shader. |
| Background | The Background property dictates the background color if there is no skybox present. |
| Culling Mask | The Culling Mask property determines what layers are picked up by the camera. By default, the camera sees everything. You can uncheck certain layers (more on layers later), and they won't be visible to the camera. |
| Projection | The Projection property determines how the camera sees the world. The two options are Perspective and Orthographic. Perspective cameras perceive the world in 3D, where closer objects are larger and farther objects are smaller. This is the setting to use if you want depth in your game. The Orthographic camera setting ignores depth and treats everything as flat. |
| Field of View | The Field of View property specifies how wide of an area the camera can see. |
| Clipping Planes | The Clipping Planes property dictates the range where objects are visible to the camera. Objects that are closer than the near plane or farther than the far plane will not be seen. |
| Normalized View Port Rect | The Normalized View Port Rect property establishes what part of the actual screen the camera is projected on. By default, the X and Y are both set to 0, which causes the camera to start in the upper left of the screen. The width and height are both set to 1, which causes the camera to cover 100% of the screen vertically and horizontally. This is covered in more detail later. |

| Property | Description |
|---|---|
| Depth | The Depth property dictates the priority for multiple cameras. Lower numbers are drawn first, which means that higher numbers may be drawn on top and effectively hide them. |
| Rendering Path | The Rendering Path property determines how the camera renders. It should be left as Use Player Settings. |
| Target Texture | The Target Texture property enables you to specify a texture for the camera to draw to instead of the screen. Render textures are a Unity Pro feature. |
| HDR | The HDR (Hyper-Dynamic Range) property determines whether Unity's internal light calculations are limited to the basic color range. The property allows for advanced visual effects. For now, leave this unchecked. |

Cameras have many properties, but you can set most and forget about them. Cameras also have a few extra components. The GUI Layer allows the camera to see GUI elements (as covered later in this book). The Flare Layer allows the camera to see the lens flares of lights. Finally, the audio listener allows the camera to pick up sound. If you add more cameras to a scene, you need to remove their audio listeners. There can be only one audio listener per scene.

## Multiple Cameras

Many effects in modern games would not be possible without multiple cameras. Thankfully, you can have as many cameras as you want in a Unity scene. To add a new camera to a scene, click **GameObject > CreateOther > Camera**. Alternatively, you can add the camera component to a game object already in your scene. To do that, select the object and click **Add Component** in the Inspector. Select **Rendering > Camera** to add the camera component. Remember that adding a camera component to an existing object will not automatically give you the GUI Layer, Flare Layer, or audio listener.

CAUTION

### Multiple Audio Listeners

As mentioned earlier, a scene can have only a single audio listener. In older versions of Unity, having two or more listeners would cause an error and prevent a scene from running. In Unity 4, having multiple listeners will just display a warning message, although audio might not be heard correctly. This topic is covered in detail in a later hour.

▼ TRY IT YOURSELF

**Working with Multiple Cameras**

The best way to understand how multiple cameras interact is to work with them hands on. This exercise focuses on basic camera manipulation:

1.  Create a new project or scene and add two cubes. Place the cubes at (–2, 1, –5) and (2, 1, 5). Add a directional light to the scene.

2.  Move the Main Camera to (–3, 1, –8) and change its rotation to (0, 45, 0).

3.  Add a new camera to the scene (click **GameObject > CreateOther > Camera**) and position it at (3, 1, –8). Change its rotation to (0, 315, 0). Be sure to disable the audio listener for the camera by unchecking the box next to the component.

4.  Run the scene. Notice how the second camera is the only one displayed. This is because the second camera has a higher depth than the Main Camera. The Main Camera is drawn to the screen first, and then the second camera is drawn overtop of it. Change the Main Camera to **1** and then run the scene again. Notice how the Main Camera is now the only one visible.

# Split Screen and Picture in Picture

As you saw earlier, having multiple cameras in a scene doesn't do much good if one simply draws over the other. In this section, you learn to use the Normalized View Port Rect property to achieve split screen and picture-in-picture effects.

The normalized view port basically treats the screen as a simple rectangle. The upper-left corner of the rectangle is (0, 0), and the lower-right corner is (1, 1). This does not mean that the screen has to be a perfect square. Instead, think of the coordinates as percentages of the size. So, a coordinate of 1 means 100%, and a coordinate of .5 means 50%. With this in mind, placing cameras on the screen becomes easy. By default, cameras project from (0, 0) with a width and height of 1 (or 100%). This causes them to take up the entire screen. If you were to change those numbers, however, you would get a different effect.

▼ TRY IT YOURSELF

**Creating a Split-Screen Camera System**

Let's walk through creating a split-screen camera system. This type of system is common in two-player games where the players have to share the same screen. This exercise builds off of the previous Try It Yourself for multiple cameras earlier this hour:

1.  Open the previously created project.

2. Ensure that the Main Camera has a depth of −1. Ensure that the X and Y properties of the camera's Normalized View Port Rect property are both **0**. Set the W and H properties to **1** and **.5**, respectively (100% of the width and 50% of the height).

3. Ensure that the second camera also has a depth of −1. Set the X and Y properties of the view port to (0, .5). This will cause the camera to begin drawing halfway down the screen. Set the W and H properties to **1** and **.5**, respectively.

4. Run the scene and notice how both cameras are now projecting on the screen at the same time (see Figure 6.6). You can split the screen like this as many times as you want.

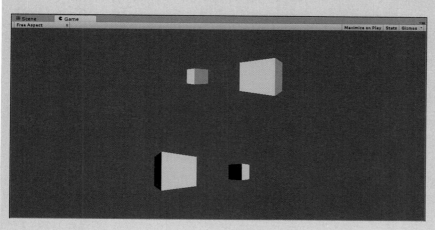

**FIGURE 6.6**
The split-screen effect.

## Creating a Picture-in-Picture Effect

Picture in picture is a common way to create effects like minimaps. With this effect, one camera is going to draw over another one in a specific area. This exercise will build off of the previous Try It Yourself for multiple cameras earlier in this hour:

1. Open the previously created project.

2. Ensure that the Main Camera has a depth of −1. Ensure that the X and Y properties of the camera's Normalized View Port Rect property are both **0** and the W and H properties both **1**.

3. Ensure that the depth of the second camera is 0. Set the X and Y property of the view port to (.75, .75) and set the W and H values to **.2** each.

4. Run the scene. Notice how the second camera appears in the upper-right corner of the screen (see Figure 6.7). Experiment with the different view port settings to get the camera to appear in the different corners.

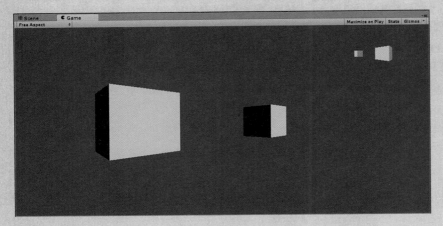

**FIGURE 6.7**
The picture-in-picture effect.

# Layers

With so many objects in a project and in a scene, it can often be difficult to organize them. Sometimes you want items to be viewable by only certain cameras or illuminated by only certain lights. Sometimes you want collision to occur only between certain types of objects. Unity's answer to this organization is layers. Layers are groupings of similar objects so that they can be treated a certain way. By default, there are 8 built-in layers and 24 layers for the user to define.

CAUTION

**Layer Overload!**

Adding layers can be a great way to achieve complex behaviors without doing a lot of work. A word of warning, though: Do not create layers for items unless you need to. Too often, people arbitrarily create layers when adding objects to a scene with the thinking that they might need them later. This approach can lead to an organizational nightmare as you try to remember what each layer is for and what it does. In short, add layers when you need them. Don't try to use layers just because you can.

# Working with Layers

Every game objects starts in the Default layer. That is, the object has no specific layer to belong to and so it is lumped in with everything else. You can easily add an object to a layer in the Inspector view. With the object selected, click the **Layer** drop-down in the Inspector and choose a new layer for the object to be a part of (see Figure 6.8). By default, there are four layers to choose from: Default, TransparentFX, Ignore Raycast, and Water. You can safely ignore most of these for now because they are not very useful to you at this point.

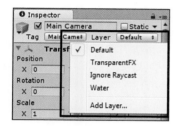

**FIGURE 6.8**
The Layer drop-down menu.

Although the current built-in layers aren't exactly useful to you, you can easily add new layers. You add layers in the Tag Manager, and there are three ways to open the Tag Manager:

- ▶ With an object selected, click the **Layer** drop-down and select **Add Layer** (see Figure 6.8).

- ▶ In the menu at the top of the editor, click **Edit > Project Settings > Tags**.

- ▶ Click the **Layers** selector in the scene toolbar and choose **Edit Layers** (see Figure 6.9).

**FIGURE 6.9**
The Layers selector in the scene toolbar.

Once in the Tag Manager, just click to the right of one of the user layers to give it a name. Figure 6.10 illustrates this process and shows two new layers being added. (They are added for this picture, and you won't have them unless you add them yourself.)

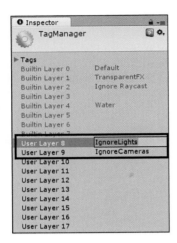

**FIGURE 6.10**
Adding new layers to the Tag Manager.

# Using Layers

There are many uses for layers. The usefulness of layers is limited only by what you can think to do with them. This section covers three common uses.

The first is the ability to hide layers from the Scene view. By clicking the Layers selector in the Scene view toolbar (see Figure 6.9), you can choose which layers appear in the Scene view and which don't. By default, the scene is set up to show everything.

---

TIP

**Invisible Scene Items**

One common mistake for people who are new to Unity is accidentally changing the layers visible in the Scene view. If you are not familiar with the ability to make layers invisible, this can be quite confusing. Just note that if at any time items are not appearing in the Scene view when they should, check the Layers selector to ensure that it is set to show everything.

---

The second utility of layers is to use them to exclude objects from being illuminated by light. This can prove useful if you are making a custom user interface, shadowing system, or are using a complex lighting system. To prevent a layer from being illuminated by a light, select the light. Then, in the Inspector view, click the **Culling Mask** property and deselect any layers that you want ignored (see Figure 6.11).

**FIGURE 6.11**
The Culling Mask property.

The last thing to know about layers is that you can use them to determine what a camera can and cannot see. This is useful if you want to build a custom visual effect using multiple cameras for a single viewer. Just as previously described, to ignore layers simply click the **Culling Mask** drop-down on the camera component and deselect anything you don't want to appear.

▼ **TRY IT YOURSELF**

**Ignoring Light and Cameras**

Let's take a moment to work with layers for both lights and cameras:

1. Create a new project or scene. Add two cubes to the scene and position them at (–2, 1, (–5) and (2, 1, (–5).

2. Enter the Tag Manager using any of the three methods listed earlier and add two new layers: **IgnoreLights** and **IgnoreCameras** (see Figure 6.10).

3. Select one of the cubes and add it to the IgnoreLights layer. Select the other cube and add it to the IgnoreCameras layer.

4. Add a point light to the scene and place it at (0, 1, (–7). In the Culling Mask property for the light, deselect the **IgnoreLights** layer. Notice now how only one of the cubes is illuminated. The other one has been ignored because of its layer.

5. Select the Main Camera and remove the IgnoreCameras layer from its Culling Mask property. Run the scene and notice how only one nonilluminated cube appears. The other one has been ignored by the camera.

# Summary

In this hour, you learned about lights and cameras. You worked with the different types of lights. You also learned to add cookies and halos to the lights you had in the scene. From there, you got hands on with cameras. You learned all about the basics of cameras and about adding multiple cameras to create a split-screen and picture-in-picture effect. You wrapped up the hour by learning about layers in Unity.

# Q&A

**Q. I noticed we skipped lightmapping. Is it important to learn?**

**A.** Lightmapping is a useful technique for optimizing the performance of a scene. That said, it is a more advanced topic and is not necessary for the projects you will be making at this stage. It will be more important for you when you get into more advanced game projects.

**Q. How do I know if I want a perspective or orthographic camera?**

**A.** As mentioned in the text, a general rule of thumb is that you want perspective for 3D games and effects and orthographic for 2D games and effects.

# Workshop

Take some time to work through the questions here to ensure that you have a firm grasp of the material.

## Quiz

1. If you want to illuminate an entire scene with one light, which type should you use?
2. How many cameras can be added to a scene?
3. How many user defined layers can you have?
4. What property determines which layers are ignored by lights and cameras?

## Answers

1. A directional light is the only light that is applied evenly to an entire scene.
2. You can have as many as you want.
3. 24.
4. The Culling Mask property.

# Exercise

In this exercise, you have a chance to work with multiple cameras and lights. You have a bit of leeway in the construction of this exercise, so feel free to be creative:

1. Create a new scene or project. Add a sphere to the scene and place it at (0, 0, 0).

2. Add four point lights to your scene. Place them at (–4, 0, 0), (4, 0, 0), (0, 0, –4), and (0, 0, 4). Give each of them their own color. Set the ranges and intensities to create the visual effect on the sphere that you want.

3. Delete the Main Camera from your scene (by right-clicking the **Main Camera** and selecting **Delete**). Add four cameras to the scene. Disable the audio listener on three of them. Position them at (2, 0, 0), (–2, 0, 0), (0, 0, 2), and (0, 0, –2). Rotate each of them about the y axis until they are facing the sphere.

4. Change the view port settings on the four cameras so that you achieve a split-screen effect with all four cameras. You should have a camera displaying in each corner of the screen taking up a quarter of the screen's size (see Figure 6.12). This step is left for you to complete. If you get stuck, a completed version of this exercise called Hour6_Exercise is available in the Hour 6 assets.

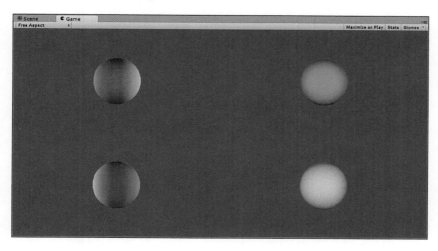

**FIGURE 6.12**
The completed exercise.

# Game 1: *Amazing Racer*

---

**What You'll Learn in This Hour:**

▶ How to design a basic game

▶ How to apply your knowledge of terrains to build a game-specific world

▶ How to add objects to a game to provide interactivity

▶ How to playtest and tweak a finished game

In this hour, you take what you have learned so far and use it to build your first Unity game. You start by covering the basic design elements of the game. From there, you build the world that the game will take place in. Then you add some interactivity objects to make the game playable. You finish by playing the game and making any necessary tweaks to improve the experience.

---

TIP

**Completed Project**

Be sure to follow along in this hour to build the complete game project. If you get stuck, you can find a completed copy of the game in the book assets for Hour 7. Take a look at it if you need help or inspiration!

---

# Design

The design portion of game development is where you plan ahead of time all the major features and components of a game. You can think of it as laying down the blueprint so that the actual construction process is much smoother. When making a game, a lot of time is normally spent working through the design. Because the game you are making in this hour is fairly basic, the design phase will go faster. You need to focus on three areas of planning to make this game: the concept, the rules, and the requirements.

# The Concept

The idea behind this game is simple. You start at one end of an area and run quickly to the other side. There will be hills, trees, and obstacles in your path. Your goal is to see how fast you can make it to the finish zone. This game concept was chosen for your first game because it highlights all the sections you have worked on so far. Also, because you have not learned scripting in Unity yet, you cannot add very elaborate interactions. Future games will be more complex.

# The Rules

Every game must have a set of rules. The rules serve two purposes. First, they tell you how the player will actually play the game. Second, because software is a process of permission (see the Process of Permission note), the rules dictate the actions available to the players to overcome challenges. The rules for *Amazing Racer* are as follows:

▶ There is no win or loss condition; only a completed condition. The game is completed when the player enters the finish zone.

▶ The player will always spawn in the same spot. The finish zone will always be in the same spot.

▶ There will be water hazards present. Whenever the player falls into a water hazard, that player is moved back to the spawn point.

▶ The objective of the game is to try to get the fastest time possible. This is an implicit rule and is not specifically built in to the game. Instead, cues will be built in to the game as hints to the player that this is the goal. The idea is that the players will intuit the desire for a faster time based on the signals given to them.

NOTE

**Process of Permission**

Something to always remember when making a game is that software is a process of permission. What this means is that unless you specifically allow something, it will be unavailable to the player. For instance, if the player wants to climb a tree, but you have not created any way for the player to climb a tree, that action will not be permitted. If you do not give players the ability to jump, they can't jump. Everything that you want the player to be able to do must be explicitly built in. Remember that you cannot assume any action and must plan for everything!

**Terminology**

Some new terms are used in this hour:

- **Spawn:** Spawning is the process by which a player or entity enters a game.
- **Spawning point:** A spawning point is the place where a player or entity spawns. There can be one or many of these. They can be stationary of moving around.
- **Condition:** A condition is a form of trigger. A win condition is the event that will cause the player to win the game (such as accumulating enough points). A loss condition is the event that will cause the player to lose the game (such as losing all of your click points).
- **Game Controller:** The game controller dictates the rules and flow of a game. It is responsible for knowing when the game is won or lost (or just over). Any object can be designated as the game controller as long as it is always in the scene. Often, an empty object or the Main Camera is designated as the game controller.

# The Requirements

Another important step in the design process is determining which assets will be required for the game. Generally speaking, a game development team is made up of several individuals. Some will be designing, and others program or make art. Every member of the team needs something to do to be productive during every step of the development process. If everyone waited until something was needed to begin working, there would be a lot of starting and stopping. Instead, you determine your assets ahead of time so that things can be created before they are needed. Here is a list of all of the requirements for *Amazing Racer*:

- A piece of rectangular terrain. The terrain needs to be big enough to present a challenging race. The terrain should have obstacles built in as well as a designated spawn and finish point (see Figure 7.1).
- Textures and environment effects for the terrain. These are provided in the Unity standard assets.
- A spawn point object, a finish zone object, and a water hazard object. These will be generated in Unity.
- A character controller. This is provided by the Unity standard assets.
- A graphical user interface (GUI). This will be provided for you in the book assets.
- A game controller. This will be created in Unity.

Spawn Point       Water Hazards       Finish Zone

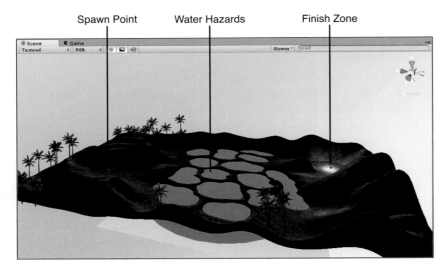

**FIGURE 7.1**
The general terrain layout for the game *Amazing Racer*.

# Creating the Game World

Now that you have the basic idea of the game on paper, it is time to start building it. There are many places to begin building a game. For this project, you begin with the world. Because this is a linear racing game, the world will be longer than it is wide (or wider than it is long, depending on how you look at it). Many of the Unity standard assets will be used to rapidly create the game.

## Sculpting the World

There are many ways you can create this terrain. Everyone will probably have a different vision for it in his or her head. To streamline the process, a heightmap has been provided for you. This is to ensure that everyone will have the same experiences during this hour. To sculpt the terrain, follow these steps:

1. Create a new project in a folder named Amazing Racer. Add a terrain to the project.

2. Set the resolution of the terrain to **200** wide by **100** long and **100** tall (in the Resolution section of the Terrain Settings).

3. Locate the file terrain.raw in the book assets for Hour 7. Import the terrain.raw file as a heightmap for the terrain (by clicking **Import Raw** in the Heightmap section of the Terrain Settings).

4. Create a **Scenes** folder under assets and save the current scene as **Main**.

The terrain should now be sculpted to match the world in the book. Feel free to make minor tweaks and changes to your liking.

CAUTION

**Building Your Own Terrain**

In this hour, you are building a game based on a heightmap given to you. The heightmap has been prepared for you so that you can quickly get through the process of game development. You may, however, choose to build your own custom world to make this game truly unique and yours. If you do that, however, be warned that some of the coordinates and rotations provided for you might not match up. If you want to build your own world, pay attention to intended placement of objects and position them in your world accordingly.

# Adding the Environment

At this point, you can begin texturing and adding the environment effects to your terrain. You need to import the following packages (click **Assets > Import Package**):

▶ Terrain Assets

▶ Skyboxes

▶ Water

You now have a bit of freedom to decorate the world however you would like. The following suggestions are guidelines. Feel free to do things in a manner that looks good to you:

▶ Add a directional light to the scene. Rotate the directional light to suit your preference.

▶ Texture the terrain. The sample project uses the following textures: Grass (Hill) for flat parts, Cliff (Layered Rock) for the steep parts, and Grass&Rock for the areas in between.

▶ Add a skybox to the scene (click **Edit > Render Settings**). The sample project uses the Sunny1 Skybox for its skybox.

▶ Add trees to your terrain. Trees should be placed sparsely and mostly on flat surfaces.

▶ Add some basic water to your scene (drag the **Daylight Simple Water** from the Assets\ Standard Assets\Water (Basic)) folder in the Project view). Place the water (at 88, 29, 49) and scale it (50, 1, 50).

The terrain should now be prepared and ready to go. Be sure to spend a good amount of time on texturing to make sure that you have a good blend and a realistic look. There are some additional things not present in the sample project but that you may want to add, including the following:

▶ Fog.

▶ Grass around the water hazards. This may obscure them a bit and add to the difficulty.

▶ Light flares for the directional light to simulate the sun. You need to rotate the directional light to match the sun image of the skybox if one is present.

## The Character Controller

At this stage of development, you want to add a character controller to your terrain:

1. Import the standard character controllers by clicking **Assets > Import Package > Character Controller.**

2. Drag a **First Person** controller asset from the Assets\Character Controllers folder into your scene.

3. Position the First Person controller (it will be named Player and be blue) at (160, 32, 64). Rotate the controller 260 on the y axis so that it faces the correct direction.

Once the character controller is in your scene and positioned, play the scene. Be sure to move around and look for any areas that need fixed or smoothed. Pay attention to the borders. Look for any areas where you are able to escape the world. Those places will need to be raised so that the player cannot fall off of the map. This is the stage where you generally fix any basic problems with your terrain.

TIP
_____

### Falling Off of the World

Generally, game levels will have walls or some other obstacle in place to prevent the player from exiting the developed area. If the game employs gravity, the player may fall off of the side of the world. You always want to create some way to prevent players from going somewhere they shouldn't. This game project uses a tall berm to keep the players in the play area. The heightmap provided to you in the book's assets for Hour 7 intentionally has a few places where the player can climb out. See if you can find and correct them.
_____

# Gamification

You now have a world in which your game can take place. You can run around and experience the world to an extent. The piece that is missing is the game itself. Right now, what you have is considered a toy. It is something that you can play with. What you want is a game, which is a toy that has rules and a goal. The process of turning something into a game is called *gamification*, and that's what this section is all about. If you followed the previous steps, your game project should now look something like Figure 7.2. The next few steps are to add game control objects for interaction, apply game scripts to those objects, and connect them to each other.

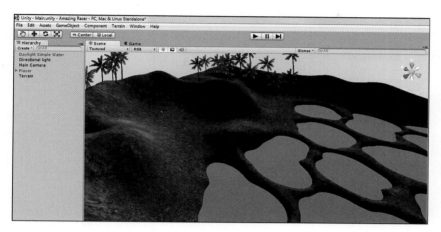

**FIGURE 7.2**
The current state of the *Amazing Racer* game.

---

NOTE

### Scripts

Scripts are pieces of code that define behaviors for game objects. You have not yet learned about scripting in Unity. To make an interactive game, however, scripts are a must. With this in mind, the scripts needed to make this game have been provided for you. An effort has been made to make the scripts as minimal as possible so that you can understand most of this project. Feel free to open the scripts in a text editor and read what they are doing. Scripts are covered in greater detail in Hour 8, "Scripting Part 1," and Hour 9, "Scripting Part 2."

---

## Adding Game Control Objects

As defined in your requirements section earlier, you need four specific game control objects. The first object will be a spawning point. This will be a simple game object that exists solely to tell the game where to spawn the player. To create the spawning point, follow these steps:

**1.** Add an empty game object to the scene (click **GameObject > Create Empty**) and position it (at 160, 32, 64).

**2.** Rename the empty object to **SpawnPoint** in the Hierarchy view.

Next, you want to create the water hazard detector. This will be a simple plane that will sit just below the water. The plane will have a trigger collider (as covered in more detail later in this book), which will detect when a player has fallen in the water. To create the detector, follow these steps:

1. Add a plane to the scene (click **GameObject > Create Other > Plane**) and position it (at 86, 27, 51). Scale the plan (10, 1, 10).

2. Rename the plane to **WaterHazardDetector** in the Hierarchy view.

3. Check the **Is Trigger** check box on the Mesh Collider component in the Inspector view (see Figure 7.3).

**FIGURE 7.3**
The Inspector view of the WaterHazardDetector object.

Next you want to add the finish zone to your game. This zone will be a simple object with a point light on it so that the player knows where to go. The object will have a capsule collider attached to it so that it will know when a player can enter the zone. To add the finish zone object, follow these steps:

1. Add an empty game object to the scene and position it at (26, 32, 24).

2. Rename the object to **Finish** in the Hierarchy view.

3. Add a light component to the finish object. (With the object selected, click **Component > Rendering > Light**.) Change the type to **Point** if it isn't already and set the range to **35** and intensity to **3**.

4. Add a capsule collider to the finish object by selecting the object and clicking **Component > Physics > Capsule Collider**. Change the Radius property to **9** and check the **Is Trigger** check box in the Inspector view (see Figure 7.4).

**FIGURE 7.4**
The Inspector view of the Finish object.

The final object you need to create is the game control object. This object doesn't technically need to exist. You could instead just apply its properties to some other persistent object in the game world such as the Main Camera. You generally create its own object to prevent any accidental deletion, though. During this phase of development, the game control object is very basic. It will be used more later. To create the game control object, follow these steps:

1. Add an empty game object to the scene.

2. Rename the game object to **GameControl** in the Hierarchy view.

# Adding Scripts

As mentioned earlier, scripts specify behaviors for your game objects. In this section, you apply scripts to your game objects. At this point, it is not important for you to understand what these scripts do. The first thing you need to do is add the scripts to your project:

1. Create a **Scripts** folder under Assets in the Project view.

2. Locate the Scripts folder in the book assets for Hour 7.

3. Click and drag the scripts from the book asset's Scripts folder into the Scripts folder in Unity. There should be three scripts: FinishScript, GameControlScript, and RespawnScript.

Once the scripts are in your project, applying them is easy. To apply a script, simply drag it from the Project view onto whatever object you want to apply it to (see Figure 7.5). Apply the following scripts:

▶ Apply the FinishScript to the Finish game object.

▶ Apply the GameControlScript to the GameControl object.

▶ Apply the RespawnScript to the WaterHazardDetector object.

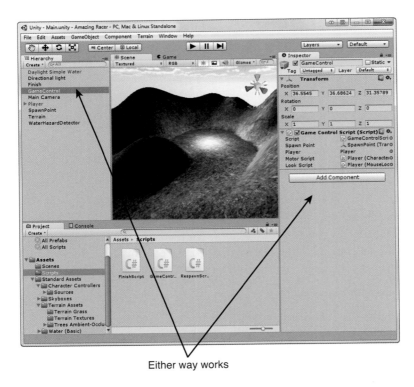

Either way works

**FIGURE 7.5**
Applying scripts by dragging them onto game objects.

# Connecting the Scripts Together

If you read through the scripts, you noticed that they all have placeholders for other objects. These placeholders allow one script to talk to another script. You see that for every placeholder that existed in the scripts, there is a property in the component for that script in the Inspector view. Just like with scripts, you apply the objects to the placeholders by clicking and dragging (see Figure 7.6).

**FIGURE 7.6**
Moving game objects onto placeholders.

You start connecting objects with the WaterHazardDetector first. Select the **WaterHazardDetector** in the Hierarchy view and notice how it has the Respawn Script component. This is the result of applying the respawn script in the previous section. You also notice that the respawn component has a Respawn Point property. This property is a placeholder for the SpawnPoint game object you made previously. With the WaterHazardDetector object selected, click and drag the **SpawnPoint** object from the Hierarchy view onto the Respawn Point property of the Respawn Script component. Now, whenever players fall into the water hazard, they will get moved back to the spawn point at the beginning of the level.

The next object to set up is the Finish game object. With the Finish game object selected, click and drag the **GameControl** object from the Hierarchy view onto the Game Control Script property of the Finish Script component in the Inspector view. Now, whenever the player enters the finish zone, the game control will be notified.

The last object you need to set up is the GameControl. To set this control up correctly, follow these steps:

1. Click and drag the **SpawnPoint** object onto the Spawn Point property of the Game Control Script component of the GameControl.

2. Click and drag the **Player** object (this is the character controller) onto the Player property, the Motor Script property, and the Look Script property of the Game Control Script of the GameControl.

3. You need to disable the mouse-look script of the camera on the Player character controller. To do this, expand the **Player** object in the Hierarchy view (click the arrow to the left of Player to expand), and then select the **Main Camera** that is nested under Player. Locate the **Mouse Look (Script)** component in the Inspector view and uncheck it (see Figure 7.7).

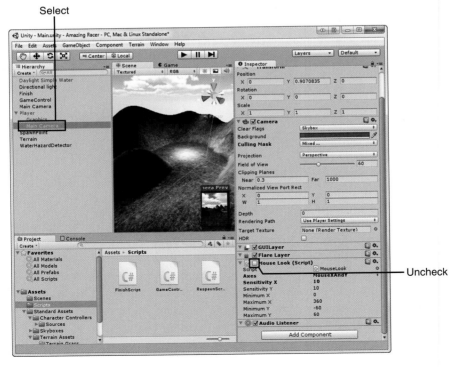

**FIGURE 7.7**
Unchecking the Mouse Look on the player's camera.

That's all there is to connecting the game objects. Your game is now completely playable! Some of this might not make sense right now, but the more you study it and work with it, the more intuitive it becomes.

# Playtesting

Your game is now done, but it is not time to rest just yet. Now you have to begin the process of playtesting. Playtesting is where you play a game with the intention of finding errors or things that just aren't as fun as you thought they would be. A lot of times it can be beneficial to have other people playtest your games so that they can tell you what makes sense to them and what they found enjoyable.

If you followed all the steps previously described, there shouldn't be any errors (commonly called *bugs*) for you to find. The process of determining what parts are fun, however, is completely at the discretion of the person making the game. Therefore, this part will be left up to you. Play the game and see what you don't like. Take notes on the things that aren't enjoyable to you. Don't just focus on the negative, though. Also find the things that you like. Your ability to change these things may be limited at the moment, so write them down. Plan on how you would change the game for the better if given the opportunity.

One simple thing you can tweak right now to make the game more enjoyable is the player's speed. If you have played the game a couple of times, you might have noticed that the character moves too slowly, and that can make the game feel very long and drawn out. To make the character fast, you need to modify the Character Motor (Script) component on the Player object. Expand the **Movement** property in the Inspector view and change the max forward speed (see Figure 7.8). The sample project has this set at 12. Try that and see how you like it. Try faster or slower speeds and pick one you enjoy.

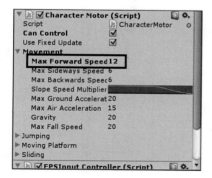

**FIGURE 7.8**
Changing the player's speed.

# Summary

In this hour, you made your first game in Unity. You started by designing the various aspects of the games concept, rules, and requirements. From there, you built the game world and added environment effects. Then, you added the game objects required for interactivity. You applied scripts to those game objects and connected them together. Finally, you playtested your game and noted the things you liked and didn't like.

# Q&A

**Q. This seems over my head. Am I doing something wrong?**

**A.** Not at all! This process can feel very alien to someone who is not used to it. Keep reading and studying the materials and it will all begin to come together. The best thing you can do is pay attention to how the objects connect to each other through the scripts.

**Q. You didn't cover how to build and deploy the game. Why not?**

**A.** Building and deployment is its own hour later on. There are many things to consider when building a game, and at this point you should just focus on the concepts required to develop it.

**Q. Why couldn't we make a game without scripts?**

**A.** As mentioned earlier, scripts define the behavior of objects. It is very difficult to have a coherent game without some form of interactive behavior. The only reason you are building a game in Hour 7 before learning scripting in Hours 8 and 9 is that you should reinforce the topics you have already learned before moving on to something different.

# Workshop

Take some time to work through the questions here to ensure that you have a firm grasp of the material.

## Quiz

1. What are a game's requirements?
2. What is the win condition of this game?
3. How many textures are recommended for a natural blended look in this terrain?
4. Which object is responsible for controlling the flow of the game?
5. Why do we playtest a game?

# Answers

1. The requirements are the list of assets that will need to be created to make the game.

2. Trick question! There is no explicit win condition for this game. It is assumed that the player wins when he or she gets a better time than previous attempts. This is not built in to the game in any way, though.

3. Three: grass, grass and rock, and rock.

4. The game controller. In this game, it was called GameControl.

5. To discover bugs and determine what parts of the game work the way we want them to.

# Exercise

The best part about making games is that you can get to make them the way you want. Following a guide can be a good learning experience, but you don't get the satisfaction of making a custom game. In this exercise, you have an opportunity to modify the game a little to make something more unique. Exactly how you want to change the game is up to you. Some suggestions are listed here:

▶ Try to add multiple finish zones. See whether you can place them in a way that offers the players more choice.

▶ Modify the terrain to have more or different hazards. As long as the hazards are built like the water hazard (including the script), they will work just fine.

▶ Try having multiple spawn locations. Make it so some of the hazards move you to a second or third spawn point.

▶ Modify the sky and textures to create an alien world. Make the world experience unique.

# HOUR 8
# Scripting Part 1

## What You'll Learn in This Hour:

▶ The basics of scripts in Unity
▶ How to use variables
▶ How to use operators
▶ How to use conditionals
▶ How to use loops

You have so far learned how to make objects in Unity. However, those objects have been a bit boring. How useful is a cube that just sits there? It would be much better to give the cube some custom action to make it interesting in some way. What you need are scripts. Scripts are files of code that are used to define complex or nonstandard behaviors for objects. In this hour, you learn about the basics of scripting. You begin by looking at how to start working with scripts in Unity. You learn how to create scripts and use the scripting environment. Then, you learn about the various components of a scripting language. These components include variables, operators, conditionals, and loops.

TIP

### Sample Scripts

Several of the scripts and coding structures mentioned in this hour are available in the book assets for Hour 8. Be sure to check them out for additional learning.

CAUTION

### New to Programming

If you have never programmed before, this might all seem strange and confusing. As you work through this hour, try your best to focus on how things are structured and why they are structured that way. Remember that programming is purely logical. If a program is not doing something you want it to, it is because you have not told it how to do it correctly. Sometimes it is up to you to change the way you think. Take this hour slowly, and be sure to practice.

# Scripts

As mentioned earlier, scripts are a way to define behavior. They attach to objects in Unity just like other components and give them interactivity. There are generally three steps to working with scripts in Unity:

**1.** Create the script.

**2.** Attach the script to one or more game objects.

**3.** If the script requires it, populate any properties with values or other game objects. (This step is talked about later.)

## Creating Scripts

Before creating scripts, it is best to create a Scripts folder under the Assets folder in the Project view. Once you have a folder to contain all of your scripts, simply right-click the folder and select **Create > C# Script**. Once created, you need to give your script a name before continuing.

NOTE
_____

### Scripting Language

Unity allows you to write scripts in C#, JavaScript, or Boo. This book uses the C# language for all scripts. Note that there is no real reason to select one language over the other. If you have a preference for a different language, feel free to work in that language.
_____

Once the script is created, you can view and modify it. Clicking the script in the Project view will enable you to see the contents of the script in the Inspector view (see Figure 8.1). Double-clicking the script in the Project view opens your default editor, which will enable you to add code to the script. Assuming that you have installed the default components and haven't changed anything, double-clicking a file will open the MonoDevelop development software (see Figure 8.2).

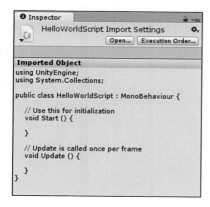

**FIGURE 8.1**
The Inspector view preview of a script.

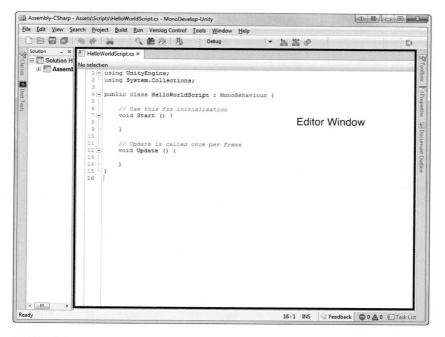

**FIGURE 8.2**
The MonoDevelop software with the editor window highlighted.

▼ TRY IT YOURSELF

## Creating a Script

Let's create a script for you to use in this section:

1. Create a new project or scene. Add a **Scripts** folder to the Project view.

2. Right-click the Scripts folder and choose **Create > C# Script**. Name the script **HelloWorldScript**.

3. Double-click the new script file and wait for MonoDevelop to open. In the editor window of MonoDevelop (refer to Figure 8.2 for the editor window), erase all the text and replace it with the code from this listing:

```
using UnityEngine;
using System.Collections;

public class HelloWorldScript : MonoBehaviour {

    // Use this for initialization
    void Start () {
        print ("Hello World");
    }

    // Update is called once per frame
    void Update () {

    }
}
```

4. Save your script by clicking **File > Save** or by pressing **Ctrl+S** (**Command+S** on a Mac). Back in Unity, confirm in the Inspector view that the script has been changed and run the scene. Notice how nothing happens. The script was created, but it does not work until it is attached to an object. That is covered next.

NOTE

## MonoDevelop

MonoDevelop is a robust and complex piece of software that is bundled with Unity. It is not actually a part of Unity. Therefore, we do not cover it in any depth. The only part of MonoDevelop you need to be familiar with right now is the editor window. If there is anything else you need to know about MonoDevelop, it is covered in the hour where it is needed.

# Attaching a Script

To attach a script to a game object, just click the script in the Project view and drag it onto the object (see Figure 8.3). You can drag the script onto the object in the Hierarchy view, Scene view, or the Inspector view (assuming the object is selected). Once attached to an object, the script will become a component of that object and will be visible in the Inspector view.

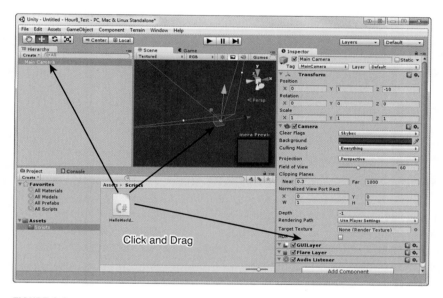

**FIGURE 8.3**
Click and drag the script onto the desired object.

To see this in action, attach the HelloWorldScript you created earlier to the Main Camera. You should now see a component named Hello World Script (Script) in the Inspector view. If you run the scene, you see Hello World appear at the bottom of the screen (see Figure 8.4).

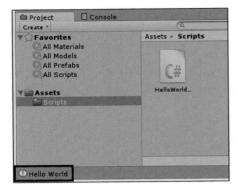

**FIGURE 8.4**
The words Hello World output when running the scene.

## Anatomy of a Basic Script

In the preceding section, you modified a script to output some text to the screen, but the contents of the script were not explained. In this section, you look at the default template that is applied to every new C# script. Note that scripts written in JavaScript or Boo will have the same components even if they look a little different. Listing 8.1 contains the full code that is generated for you by Unity when you make a new script. Listing 8.1 assumes that the script file created was named HelloWorldScript.

### Listing 8.1   Default Script Code

```
using UnityEngine;
using System.Collections;

public class HelloWorldScript : MonoBehaviour {

    // Use this for initialization
    void Start () {

    }

    // Update is called once per frame
    void Update () {

    }
}
```

This code can be broken down into three parts.

## The Using Section

The first part lists the libraries that this script will be using. It looks like this:

```
using UnityEngine;
using System.Collections;
```

Generally speaking, you won't be changing this section and should just leave it alone for the time being.

## The Class Declaration Section

The next part is called a class declaration. Every script contains a class that is named after the script. It looks like the following:

```
public class HelloWorldScript : MonoBehaviour { }
```

All the code in between the opening bracket { and closing bracket } will be a part of this class and therefore a part of the script. All of your code should go between these brackets. Once again, as above, you rarely change this and should just leave it alone for now.

## The Class Contents

The section in between the opening and closing brackets of the class is considered to be "in" the class. All of your code will go here. By default, a script contains two methods inside the class, Start and Update:

```
// Use this for initialization
void Start () {

}
 // Update is called once per frame
void Update () {
 }
```

Methods are covered in greater detail next hour. For now, just know that any code put inside the Start method will run when a scene first starts. Any code put inside the Update method will run every time the game updates (about 60 times a second on average depending on the computer).

TIP

### Comments

Programming languages have a way for the author of the code to leave messages for those who read the code later. These messages are called comments. Any words that follow two forward slashes (//) will be "commented out." This means that the computer will skip over them and not attempt to read them as code. You can see an example of commenting in the "Creating a Script" Try It Yourself.

NOTE

## The Console

There is another window in the Unity editor that has not been mentioned until now: the Console. Basically, the Console is a window that contains text output from your game. Often, when there is an error or output from a script, messages will get written to the Console. Figure 8.5 shows you the Console and how to access it. If the Console window isn't visible, you can also access it by clicking **Window > Console.**

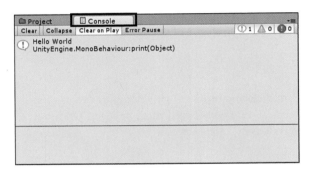

**FIGURE 8.5**
The Console window.

▼ TRY IT YOURSELF

## Using the Built-In Methods

Let's try out the built-in methods `Start` and `Update` and see how they work. The completed ImportantFunctions script is available in the book assets for Hour 8. Try to complete the exercise that follows on your own, but if you get stuck, refer to the book assets:

1. Create a new project or scene. Add a script to the scene named **ImportantFunctions**. Double-click the script to open MonoDevelop.

2. Inside the script, add the following line of code to the `Start` method:

   ```
   print("Start runs before an object Updates");
   ```

3. Save the script, and in Unity attach it to the Main Camera. Run the scene and notice the message that appears in the Console window.

4. Back in MonoDevelop, add the following line of code to the `Update` method:

   ```
   print("This is called once a frame");
   ```

5. Save the script and quickly start and stop the scene in Unity. Notice how, in the Console, there is a single line of text from the `Start` method and a bunch of lines from the `Update` method.

# Variables

Sometimes you want to use the same bit of data more than once in a script. What you need is a placeholder for data that can be reused. These placeholders are called *variables*. Unlike traditional math, variables in programming can contain more than just numbers. They can hold words, complex objects, or other scripts.

## Creating Variables

Every variable has a name and a type. These are given to the variable when it is created. You create a variable with the following syntax:

```
<variable type> <name>;
```

So, to create an integer named num1, you type the following:

```
int num1;
```

Table 8.1 contains all the primitive (or basic) variable types and the types of data they can hold.

---

NOTE

**Syntax**

The term *syntax* refers to the rules of a programming language. The syntax dictates how things are structured and written so that the computer knows how to read them. You may have noticed that every statement, or command, in our scripts ends with a semicolon. This is also a part of the C# syntax. Forgetting the semicolon will cause your script to not work. If you want to know more about the syntax of C#, check out the C# wiki at http://en.wikipedia.org/wiki/C_Sharp_syntax.

---

**TABLE 8.1    C# Variable Types**

| Type | Description |
| --- | --- |
| int | Short for integer, the int stores positive or negative whole numbers. |
| float | The float stores floating point data (such as 3.4) and is the default number type in Unity. |
| double | The double also stores floating point numbers; however it is not the default number type in Unity. It can generally hold bigger numbers than floats. |
| bool | Short for Boolean, the bool stores true or false (actually written in code as true or false). |
| char | Short for character, the char stores a single letter, space, or special character (such as a, 5, or !). Char values are written out with single quotes ('T'). |
| string | The string type holds entire words or sentences. String values are written out with double quotes ("Hello World"). |

# Variable Scope

The variable scope refers to where a variable is able to be used. As you have seen in scripts, classes and methods use open and close brackets to denote what belongs to them. The area between the two brackets can often be referred to as a *block*. The reason that this is important is that variables are only able to be used in the blocks in which they are created. So if a variable is created inside the `Start` method of a script, it will not be available in the `Update` method. Attempting to use a variable where it is not available will result in an error. They are two different blocks. If a variable is created in the class, but outside of a method, it will be available to both methods because both methods are in the same block as the variable (the class block). Listing 8.2 demonstrates this.

**Listing 8.2    Demonstration of Class and Local Block Level**

```
//This is in the "class block" and will
//be available everywhere in this class
private int num1;

void Start () {
    //this is in a "local block" and will
    //only be available in the Start method
    int num2;
}
```

# Public and Private

If you look in Listing 8.2, you see the keyword `private` appear before `num1`. This is called an *access modifier*, and it is needed only for variables declared at the class level. There are two access modifiers you need to use: `private` and `public`. A lot that can be said about the two access modifiers, but what you need to know is how they affect variables at this level. Basically, private variables (variables with the word *private* before them) are only usable inside the file they are created in. Other scripts and the editor cannot see them or modify them in any way. They are intended for internal use only. Public variables, in contrast, are visible to other scripts and even the Unity editor. This makes it easy for you to change the values of your variables on-the-fly within Unity.

### Modifying Public Variables in Unity

Let's see how public variables are visible in the Unity editor:

1. Create a new C# script and in MonoDevelop add the following line in the class but above the `Start` method:

   ```
   public int runSpeed;
   ```

2. Save the script and then in Unity attach it to the Main Camera.

3. Select the Main Camera and look in the Inspector view. Notice the script you just attached as a component. Now notice that the component has a new property: Run Speed. You can modify that property in the Inspector view and the change will be reflected in the script at runtime. See Figure 8.6 to see the component with the new property. This figure assumes that the script created was named ImportantFunctions.

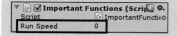

**FIGURE 8.6**
The new Run Speed property of the script component.

# Operators

All the data in variables is worthless if you have no way of accessing or modifying it. Operators are special symbols that enable you to perform modifications on data. They generally fall into one of four categories: arithmetic operators, assignment operators, equality operators, and logical operators.

## Arithmetic Operators

Arithmetic operators perform some standard mathematic operation on variables. They are generally used only on number variables, although a few exceptions exist. Table 8.2 describes the arithmetic operators.

**TABLE 8.2   Arithmetic Operators**

| Operator | Description |
|---|---|
| + | Addition. Adds two numbers together. In the case of strings, the + sign concatenates, or combines, them together.<br>`"Hello" + "World"; //produces "HelloWorld"` |
| - | Subtraction. Reduces the number on the left by the number on the right. |
| * | Multiplication. Multiplies two numbers together. |
| / | Division. Divides the number on the left by the number on the right. |
| % | Modulus. Divides the number on the left by the number on the right but does not return the result. Instead, the modulus returns the remainder of the division.<br>`10 % 2;  //returns 0`<br>`6 % 5;   //returns 1`<br>`24 % 7;  //returns 3` |

Arithmetic operators can be cascaded together to produce more complex math strings:

```
x + (5 * (6 - y) / 3);
```

Arithmetic operators work in the standard mathematic order of operations. Math is done left to right, with parentheses done first, multiplication and division done second, addition and subtraction done third.

## Assignment Operators

Assignment operators are just what they sound like. They assign a value to a variable. The most notable assignment operator is the equals sign, but there are more that combine multiple operations together. All assignment in C# is right to left. That means that whatever is on the right side gets moved to the left:

```
x = 5;  //This works. It sets the variable x to 5.
5 = x;  //This does not work. You cannot assign a variable to a value (5).
```

Table 8.3 describes the assignment operators.

**TABLE 8.3**   Assignment Operators

| Operator | Description |
|---|---|
| = | Assigns the value on the right to the variable on the left. |
| +=, -=, *=, /= | Shorthand assignment operator that performs some arithmetic operation based on the symbol used and then assigns the result to whatever is on the left.<br><br>```x = x + 5; //Adds 5 to x and then assigns it to x```<br>```x += 5;    //Does the same as above, only shorthand``` |
| ++, -- | Another shorthand operator. These are called the increment and decrement operators. They increase or decrease a number by 1.<br><br>```x = x + 1; //Adds 1 to x and then assigns it to x```<br>```x++;        //Does the same as above, only shorthand``` |

# Equality Operators

Equality operators compare two values. The result of an equality operator will always be either true or false. Therefore, the only variable type that can hold the result of an equality operator is a Boolean. (Remember that Booleans can only contain true or false.) Table 8.4 describes the equality operators.

**TABLE 8.4**   Equality Operators

| Operator | Description |
|---|---|
| == | Not to be confused with the assignment operator (=), this returns true only if the two values are equal. Otherwise, it returns false.<br><br>```5 == 6; //Returns false```<br>```9 == 9; //Returns true``` |
| >, < | These are the "greater than" and "less than" operators.<br><br>```5 > 3; //Returns true```<br>```5 < 3; //Returns false``` |
| >=, <= | These are similar to the "greater than" and "less than" except that they are the "greater than or equal to" and "less than or equal to" operators.<br><br>```3 >= 3; //Returns true```<br>```5 <= 9; //Returns true``` |
| != | This is the "not equal" operator and returns true if the two values are not the same. Otherwise, it returns false.<br><br>```5 != 6; //Returns true```<br>```9 != 9; //Returns false``` |

TIP
_____

**Additional Practice**

In the book assets for Hour 8, there is a script called EqualityAndOperations.cs. Be sure to look through it for some additional practice with the various operators.

_____

## Logical Operators

Logical operators enable you to combine two or more Boolean values (true or false) into a single Boolean value. They are useful for determining complex conditions. Table 8.5 describes the logical operators.

**TABLE 8.5**   Logical Operators

| Operator | Description |
|---|---|
| && | Known as the AND operator, this compares two Boolean values and determines whether they are both true. If either, or both, of the values is false, this returns false: |
| | ```
true && false;   //Returns false
false && true;   //Returns false
false && false; //Returns false
true && true;    //Returns true
``` |
| \|\| | Known as the OR operator, this compares two Boolean values and determines whether either of them are true. If either, or both, of the values is true, this returns true: |
| | ```
true && false;   //Returns true
false && true;   //Returns true
false && false; //Returns false
true && true;    //Returns true
``` |
| ! | Known as the NOT operator, this returns the opposite of a Boolean value: |
| | ```
!true;   //Returns false
!false; //Returns true
``` |

# Conditionals

Much of the power of a computer lies within its ability to make rudimentary decisions. At the root of this power lies the Boolean true and false. You can use these Boolean values to build conditionals and steer a program down a unique course. As you are building your flow of logic through code, just remember that a machine can only make a single, simple decision at a time. Put enough of those decisions together, though, and you can build complex interactions.
```

# The `if` **Statement**

The basis of conditionals is the `if` statement. And it is structured like this:

```
if( <some Boolean condition>)
{
    //do something
}
```

The `if` structure can be read as "if this is true, do this." So, if you want to output "Hello World" to the Console if the value of x is greater than 5, you could write the following:

```
if(x > 5)
{
    print("Hello World");
}
```

Remember that the contents of the `if` statement condition must evaluate to either a true or a false. Putting numbers, words, or anything else in there will not work:

```
if( "Hello" == "Hello")  //Correct
{}
```

```
if( x + y)  //Incorrect
{}
```

Finally, any code that you want to run if the condition evaluates to true must go inside the opening and closing brackets that follow the `if` statement.

---

TIP

### Odd Behavior

Conditional statements use a specific syntax and can give you strange behaviors if you don't follow it exactly. You may have an `if` statement in your code and notice that something isn't quite right. Maybe the condition code runs all the time even when it shouldn't. You may also notice that it never runs, even if it should. You want to be aware of two common causes for this. First, the `if` condition does not have a semicolon after it. If you write an `if` statement with a semicolon, the code following it will always run. Second, be sure that you are using the equality operator (`==`) and not the assignment operator (`=`) inside the `if` statement. Doing otherwise will lead to bizarre behavior:

```
if(x > 5);  //Incorrect
if(x = 5);  //Incorrect
```

---

# The `if` / `else` **Statement**

The `if` statement is nice for conditional code, but what if you want to diverge your program down two different paths? The `if` / `else` statement will enable you to do that. The `if` / `else` is the same basic premise of the `if` statement, except it can be read more like "if this is true do this, else do this other thing." The `if / else` statement is written like this:

```
if( <some Boolean condition>)
{
    //Do something
}
else
{
    //Do something else
}
```

For example, if you want to print "X is greater than Y" to the Console if the variable *x* is larger than the variable *y*, or you want to print "Y is greater than X" if *x* isn't bigger than *y*, you could write the following:

```
if(x > y)
{
    print("X is greater than Y");
}
else
{
    print("X is greater than Y");
}
```

## The `if / else if` Statement

Sometimes you want your code to diverge down one of many paths. You might want the user to be able to pick from a selection of options (such as a menu for example). The `if /else if` is structured in much the same way as the previous two structures, except that it has multiple conditions:

```
if( <some Boolean condition>)
{
    //Do something
}
else if( <some other Boolean condition>)
{
    //Do something else
}
else //The else is optional in the IF / ELSE IF statement
{
    //Do something else
}
```

For example, if you want to output a person's letter grade to the console based on his percentage, you could write the following:

```
if(grade >= 90)
{
    print("You got an A");
}
else if(grade >= 80)
{
    print("You got a B");
}
else if(grade >= 70)
{
    print("You got a c");
}
else if(grade >= 60)
{
    print("You got a D");
}
else
{
    print("You got an F");
}
```

TIP

**Single-Line** if **Statements**

If your if statement code is only a single line, you do not need to have the open and close brackets. Therefore, your code, which may look like this:

```
if(x > y)
{
    print("X is greater than Y");
}
```

can also be written as follows:

```
if(x > y)
    print("X is greater than Y");
```

# Iteration

You have so far seen how to work with variables and make decisions. This is certainly useful if you want to do something like add two numbers together. But what if you want to add all the numbers between 1 and 100 together? What about between 1 and 1,000? You definitely would not want to type all of that redundant code out. Instead, you can use something called *iteration* (commonly referred to as *looping*). There are two primary types of loops for you to work with: the while loop and the for loop.

# The `while` Loop

The `while` loop is the most basic form of iteration. It follows a similar structure to an `if` statement:

```
while(<some Boolean condition>)
{
    //do something
}
```

The only difference is that an `if` statement only runs its contained code once, whereas a loop will run the contained code over and over until the condition becomes false. Therefore, if you want to add together all the numbers between 1 and 100 and then output them to the console, you could write something like this:

```
int sum = 0;
int count = 1;

while(count >= 100)
{
    sum += count;
    count++;
}

print(sum);
```

As you can see, the value of `count` will start at 1 and increase by 1 every iteration, or execution of the loop, until it equals 101. When `count` equals 101, it will no longer be less than or equal to 100, and the loop will exit. Omitting the `count++` line will result in the loop running infinitely (so be sure it's there). During each iteration of the loop, the value of `count` is added to the variable `sum`. Once the loop exits, the sum is written to the console.

In summation, a `while` loop will run the code it contains over and over as long as its condition is true. Once its condition becomes false, it stops looping.

# The `for` Loop

The `for` loop follows the same idea as the `while` loop, except it is structured a bit differently. As you saw in the previous code for the `while` loop, you had to create a `count` variable, you had to test the variable (as the condition), and you had to increase the variable all on three separate lines. The `for` loop condenses that syntax down to a single line. It looks like this:

```
for(<create a counter> ; <Boolean conditional> ; <increment the counter >)
{
    //Do something
}
```

The for loop has three special *compartments* for controlling the loop. Notice the semicolons, not commas, in between each section in the for loop header. The first compartment creates a variable to be used as a counter (a common name for the counter is i, short for iterator). The second compartment is the conditional statement of the loop. The third compartment handles increasing or decreasing the counter. The previous while loop example can be rewritten using a for loop. It would look like this:

```
int sum = 0;

for(int count = 1; count <= 100; count++)
{
    sum += count;
}

print(sum);
```

As you can see, the different parts of the loop get condensed down and take up less space. You can see that the for loop is really good at things like counting.

## Summary

In this hour, you took your first steps into video game programming. You started by looking at the basics of scripting in Unity. You learned how to make and attach scripts. You also looked at the basic anatomy of a script. From there, you studied the basic logical components of a program. You worked with variables, operators, conditionals, and loops.

## Q&A

Q. **How much programming is required to make a game?**

A. Most games use some form of programming to define complex behaviors. The more complex the behaviors need to be, the more complex the programming needs to be. If you want to make games, you should definitely become comfortable with the concepts of programming. This is true even if you don't intend to be the primary developer for a game. With that in mind, know that this book will show you everything you need to know to make your first few simple games.

Q. **Is this all there is to scripting?**

A. Yes and no. Presented in this text are the fundamental blocks of programming. They never really change; they just get applied in new and unique ways. That said, a lot of what is presented here is simplified because of the complex nature of programming in general. If you want to learn more about programming, you should read books or articles specifically on the subject.

# Workshop

Take some time to work through the questions here to ensure that you have a firm grasp of the material.

## Quiz

1. What three languages does Unity allow you to program with?

2. True or False: The code in the Start method runs at the start of every frame.

3. Which variable type is the default floating point number type in Unity?

4. Which operator returns the remainder of division?

5. What is a conditional statement?

6. Which loop type is best suited for counting?

## Answers

1. C#, JavaScript, and Boo.

2. False. The `Start` method runs at the beginning of the scene. The `Update` method runs every frame.

3. `float`.

4. The modulus.

5. A code structure that allows the computer to choose a code path based on a simple decision.

6. The `for` loop.

# Exercise

It can often be helpful to view coding structures as building blocks. Alone, each piece is simple. Put together, however, they can build complex entities. In what follows you find multiple programming challenges. Use the knowledge you have gained this hour to build a solution to the problems. Put each solution in its own script and attach the scripts to the Main Camera of a scene to ensure that they work. You can find the solution to this exercise in the book assets for Hour 8:

1. Write a script that adds together all the even numbers from 2 to 499. Output the result to the console.

2. Write a script that outputs all of the numbers 1–100 to the console. Don't output multiples of 3 or 5, though. Instead, output "Programming is Awesome!" (Hint: You can tell whether a number is a multiple of another number if the result of a modulus operation is 0.)

3. In the Fibonacci sequence, you determine a number by adding the two previous numbers together. The sequence starts with 0, 1, 1, 2, 3, 5.... Write a script that determines the first 20 places of the Fibonacci sequence and outputs them to the console.

# HOUR 9
# Scripting Part 2

## What You'll Learn in This Hour:

▶ How to write methods
▶ How to capture user input
▶ How to work with local components
▶ How to work game objects

In the preceding hour, you learned about the basics of scripting in Unity. In this hour, you take what you have learned and use it to complete more meaningful tasks. You begin by examining methods. You learn what they are, how they work, and how to write them. Then you get hands on with user input. After that, you examine how to access components from scripts. You wrap up the hour by learning how to access other game objects and their components with code.

TIP

### Sample Scripts

Several of the scripts and coding structures mentioned in this hour are available in the book assets for Hour 9. Be sure to check them out for additional learning.

## Methods

Methods, often called *functions*, are modules of code that can be called and used independently of each other. Each method generally represents a single task or purpose, and often many methods can work together to achieve complex goals. Consider the two methods you have seen so far: Start and Update. Each represents a single and concise purpose. The Start method contains all the code that is run for an object when the scene first begins. The Update method contains the code that is run every frame of the scene.

NOTE

## Method Shorthand

You have seen so far that whenever the Start method is mentioned, the word *method* has followed it. It can become cumbersome to always have to specify that a word used is a method. You
can't write just *Start*, though, because people wouldn't know if you meant the word or a method.
A shorter way of handling this is to use parentheses with the word. So, the method Start can be
rewritten as just Start(). If you ever see something written like SomeWords(), you can know instantly
that the writer is talking about a method named SomeWords.

# Anatomy of a Method

Before working with methods, you should look at the different parts that compose them. What
follows is the general format of a method:

```
<return type> <name>(<parameters>)
{
    <Inside the method's block>
}
```

## Method Name

Every method must have a unique name. Though the rules that govern proper names are determined by the language used, good general guidelines for method names include the following:

▶ Make a method name descriptive. It should be an action and preferably a verb.

▶ Avoid spaces in method names. Spaces are not allowed.

▶ Avoid special characters (!@*%$, etc.) in method names. Different languages allow differ-
ent characters. By not using any, you don't run the risk of there being a problem.

Method names are important because that is both how you identify them and also how you use
them.

## Return Type

Every method has the ability to return a variable back to whatever code called it. The type of
this variable is called the *return type*. If a method returns an integer, the return type is an int.
Likewise, if the method returned a true or false, the return type is bool. If a method doesn't
return any value, it still has a return type. In that instance, the return type is void (meaning
nothing). Any method that returns a value will do so with the keyword return.

## Parameter List

Just as methods can pass a variable back to whatever code called it, the calling code can pass
variables in. These variables are called *parameters*. The variables sent into the method are

identified in the parameter list section of the method. An example of a method named Attack that takes an integer called enemyID would look like this:

```
void Attack(int enemyID)
{}
```

As you can see, when specifying a parameter, you must provide both the variable type as well as the name. Multiple parameters are separated with a comma.

## Method Block

This is where the code of the method actually goes. Every time a method is used, the code inside the method block will run in its entirety.

TRY IT YOURSELF ▼

### Identifying Method Parts

Take a moment to review the different parts of a method. Given the following method:

```
int TakeDamage(int damageAmount)
{
    int health = 100;
    return health - damageAmount;
}
```

Can you identify the following pieces?

1. What is the method's name?
2. What variable type does the method return?
3. What are the methods parameters? How many are there?
4. What code is in the method's block?

TIP

### Methods as Factories

The concept of methods can be confusing for someone who is new to programming. Often, mistakes will be made regarding the parameters and return of methods. A good way to keep it straight is to think of a method as a factory. Factories receive raw materials and use that to make products. Methods are the same way. The parameters are the materials you are passing in to the "factory," and the return is the final product of that factory. Just think of methods that don't take parameters as factories that don't require raw goods. Likewise, think of methods that don't return anything as factories that don't produce final products. By imagining method as little factories, you can work to keep the flow of logic straight in your head.

# Writing Methods

Now that you understand the components of a method, writing them is easy. Before you begin writing your methods, take a moment ask yourself three main questions:

1. What specific task will the method achieve?

2. Does the method need any outside data to achieve it?

3. Does the method need to give any data back?

Answering these questions will help you determine the method's name, parameters, and return data.

Consider this example: A player has been hit with a fireball. You need to write a method to simulate this by removing 5 health points. You know what the specific task of this method is. You also know that the task doesn't need any data (because you know it takes 5 points) and should probably give the new health value back. You could write the method like this:

```
int TakeDamageFromFireball()
{
    int playerHealth = 100;
    return playerHealth - 5;
}
```

As you can see in this method, the player's health is 100 and 5 is taken away from it. The result (which is 95) is passed back. Obviously, this can be improved. For starters, it is said above that the fireball does 5 points of damage, but what if you want it to do more? You would then need to know exactly how much damage a fireball was supposed to do at any given time. You would need a variable, or in this case a parameter. Your new method could be written as follows:

```
int TakeDamageFromFireball(int damage)
{
    int playerHealth = 100;
    return playerHealth - damage;
}
```

Now you can see that the damage is read in from the method and applied to the health. Another place where this can be improved is with the health itself. Currently, players can never lose because their health will always refresh back to 100 before having damage taken out. It would be better to store the player's health elsewhere so that its value was persistent. You could then read it in and remove the damage appropriately. Your method would then look like:

```
int TakeDamageFromFireball(int damage, int playerHealth)
{
    return playerHealth - damage;
}
```

By examining your needs, you can build better, more robust methods for your game.

NOTE

## Simplification

In the preceding example, the resulting method simply performs basic subtraction. This is oversimplified for instruction's sake. In a more realistic environment, there are many ways to handle this task. A player's health could be stored in a variable belonging to a script. Doing so would mean that it did not need to be read in. Another possibility is a complex algorithm in the TakeDamageFromFireball method where the incoming damage is reduced by some armor value, a player's dodging ability, or a magical shield. If the examples here seem silly, just bear in mind that they are that way to demonstrate various elements of the topic.

## Using Methods

Once a method is written, all that is left is to use it. Using a method is often referred to as *calling* or *invoking* the method. To call a method, you just need to write the method's name following by parentheses and any parameters. So, if you were trying to use a method that was named SomeMethod, you would write the following:

```
SomeMethod();
```

If SomeMethod() requires a integer parameter, you call it like this:

```
//Method call with a value of 5
SomeMethod(5);
```

```
//Method call passing in a variable
int x = 5;
SomeMethod(x); //do not write "int x" here.
```

Note that when you call a method, you do not need to supply the variable type with the variable you are passing in. If SomeMethod() returns a value, you want to *catch* it in a variable. The code could look something like this (with a Boolean return type is assumed; in reality, it could be anything):

```
bool result = SomeMethod();
```

Using this basic syntax is all there is to writing methods.

▼ TRY IT YOURSELF

## Calling Methods

Let's work further with the TakeDamageFromFireball method described in the previous section. In this exercise, you call the various forms of the method. You can find the solution for this exercise as FireBallScript in the book assets for Hour 9:

1.  Create a new project or scene. Locate the FireBallScript in the book assets for Hour 9 and import it into your project. Alternatively, create a C# script called **FireBallScript** and enter in the three TakeDamageFromFireball methods described earlier.

2.  In the Start method, call the first TakeDamageFromFireball() by typing the following:

    ```
    int x = TakeDamageFromFireball();
    print ("Player health: " + x);
    ```

3.  Attach the script to the Main Camera and run the scene. Notice the output in the Console. Now call the second TakeDamageFromFireball() in Start() by typing the following (placing it below the first bit of code you typed, no need to remove it):

    ```
    int y = TakeDamageFromFireball(25);
    print ("Player health: " + y);
    ```

4.  Again, run the scene and note the output in the console. Finally, call the last TakeDamageFromFireball() in Start() by typing the following:

    ```
    int z = TakeDamageFromFireball(30, 50);
    print ("Player health: " + z);
    ```

5.  Run the scene and note the final output. See how all three methods behave a little differently. Notice how you called each one specifically.

# Input

Without player input, *video games* would just be *video*. Player input can come in many different varieties. Inputs can be physical like gamepads, joysticks, keyboards, and mice. There are capacitive controllers such as the relatively new touch screens that are found in modern mobile devices. There are also motion devices like the Wii Remote, the PlayStation Move, and the Microsoft Kinect. Rarer is the audio input that uses microphones and a player's voice to control a game. In this section, you learn all about writing code to allow the player to interact with your game with physical devices.

# Input Basics

With Unity (like most game engines), you can detect specific key presses in code to make it interactive. It is a good idea, however, to avoid doing that. Doing so makes it difficult to allow players to remap the controls to their preference. Thankfully, Unity has a simple system for generically mapping controls. With Unity, you look for a specific *axis* to know whether a player intends a certain action. Then, when the player runs the game, he can choose to make different controls mean different axes.

You can view, edit, and add different axes using the Input Manager. To access the Input Manager, click **Edit > Project Settings > Input**. In the Input Manager, you can see the various axes associated with different input actions. By default, there are 15 input axes, but you can add your own if you want. Figure 9.1 shows the default Input Manager with the horizontal axis expanded.

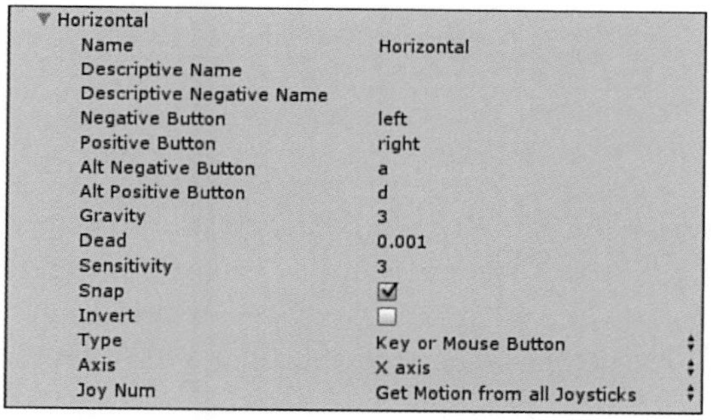

**FIGURE 9.1**
The Input Manager.

While the horizontal axis doesn't directly control anything (we will write scripts to do that later), it represents that player going sideways. Table 9.1 describes the properties of an axis.

**TABLE 9.1** Axis Properties

| Property | Description |
| --- | --- |
| Name | The name of the axis. This is how you reference it in code. |
| Descriptive Name / Descriptive Negative Name | A verbose name for the axis that will appear to the player in the game configuration. The negative is the opposite name. For example: "Go left" and "Go right" would be a name and negative name pair. |
| Negative Button / Positive Button | The buttons that pass negative and positive values to the axis. For the horizontal axis these are the left arrow and the right arrow. |
| Alt Negative Button / Alt Positive Button | Alternate buttons to pass values to the axis. For the horizontal axis, these are the A and D keys. |

| Property | Description |
| --- | --- |
| Gravity | How fast the axis will return to 0 once the key is no longer pressed. |
| Dead | Any input smaller than this value will be ignored. This helps prevent jittering with joystick devices. |
| Sensitivity | How quickly the axis responds to input. |
| Snap | When checked, this will cause the axis to immediately go to 0 when the opposite direction is pressed. |
| Invert | This will invert the controls when checked. |
| Type | The type of input. The types are keyboard / mouse buttons, mouse movement, and joystick movement. |
| Axis | The corresponding axis from an input device. This doesn't apply to buttons. |
| Joy Num | Which joystick to get input from. By default this gets input from all joysticks. |

## Input Scripting

Once your axes are set up in the Input Manager, working with them in code is simple. To access any of the player's input, you will be using the Input object. More specifically, you will be using the GetAxis method of the input object. GetAxis() reads the name of the axis in as a string and returns back the value of that axis. So, if you want to get the value of the horizontal axis, you type the following:

```
float hVal = Input.GetAxis("Horizontal");
```

In the case of the horizontal axis, if the player is pressing the left arrow (or the A key), GetAxis() will return a negative number. If the player is pressing the right arrow (or D key), the method will return a positive value.

▼ TRY IT YOURSELF

### Reading in User Input

Let's work with the vertical and horizontal axes to get a better idea of how to use player input:

1. Create a new project or scene. Add a script to the project named **PlayerInput** and attach it to the Main Camera.

2. Add the following code to the Update method in the PlayerInput script:

```
float hVal = Input.GetAxis("Horizontal");
float vVal = Input.GetAxis("Vertical");

if(hVal != 0)
    print("Horizontal movement selected: " + hVal);
if(vVal != 0)
    print("Vertical movement selected: " + vVal);
```

**3.** Save the script and run the scene. Notice what happens when you press the arrow keys. Now try out the W, A, S, and D keys.

# Specific Key Input

Although you generally want to deal with the generic axes for input, sometimes you do want to determine whether a specific key has been pressed. To do so, you will again be using this input object. This time, however, you use the GetKey method. This method reads in a special code that corresponds to a specific key. It then returns back a true of the key is currently down and a false if the key is not currently down. To determine whether the K key is currently pressed, you type the following:

```
bool isKeyDown = Input.GetKey(KeyCode.K);
```

TIP
_____

### Finding Key Codes

Each key has a specific key code. You can determine the key code of the specific key you want by reading the Unity documentation. Alternatively, you can use the built-in tools of MonoDevelop to find it. Whenever you are working on a script in MonoDevelop, you can always type in the name of an object followed by a period. Doing so will result in a menu popping up with all of the possible options. Likewise, if you type an open parenthesis after typing a method name, the same menu will pop-up showing you the various options. Figure 9.2 illustrates using the auto menu to find the key code for the Esc key.

_____

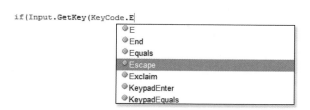

**FIGURE 9.2**
The automatic pop-up in MonoDevelop.

### Reading in Specific Key Presses

Let's write a script that will determine whether a specific key is pressed:

1. Create a new project or scene. Add a script to the project named **PlayerInput** and attach it to the Main Camera.

2. Add the following code to the Update method in the PlayerInput script:

```
if(Input.GetKey(KeyCode.M))
    print("The 'M' key is pressed down");
```

3. Save the script and run the scene. Notice what happens when you press the M key.

## Mouse Input

Besides key presses, you want to capture mouse input from the user. There are two components to mouse input: mouse buttons and mouse movement. Determining whether mouse buttons are pressed is much like key presses covered earlier. Again you will be using the Input object. This time you use the GetMouseButtonDown method. This method takes an integer between 1 and 3 to dictate which mouse button you are asking about. The method returns a Boolean value indicating if the button is pressed. The code to get the mouse button presses looks like this:

```
bool isButtonDown;
isButtonDown = Input.GetMouseButtonDown(0);   //left mouse button
isButtonDown = Input.GetMouseButtonDown(1);   //right mouse button
isButtonDown = Input.GetMouseButtonDown(3);   //center mouse button
```

Mouse movement is only along two axis: x and y. To get the mouse movement, you use the GetAxis method of the input object. You can use the names Mouse X and Mouse Y to get the movement along the x and y axis, respectively. The code to read in the mouse would look like this:

```
float value;
value = Input.GetAxis("Mouse X");   //x axis movement
value = Input.GetAxis("Mouse Y");   //y axis movement
```

Unlike button presses, the mouse movement is measured by the amount the mouse has moved since the last frame only. Basically, holding a key will cause a value to increase until it maxes out at –1 or 1 (depending on whether is it positive or negative). The mouse movement, however, will generally have smaller numbers because it is measured and reset every frame.

**Reading Mouse Movement**

In this exercise, you read in mouse movement and output the results to the Console:

1. Create a new project or scene. Add a script to the project named **PlayerInput** and attach it to the Main Camera.

2. Add the following code to the Update method in the PlayerInput script:

```
float mxVal = Input.GetAxis("Mouse X");
float myVal = Input.GetAxis("Mouse Y");
if(mxVal != 0)
    print("Mouse X movement selected: " + mxVal);
if(myVal != 0)
    print("Mouse Y movement selected: " + myVal);
```

3. Save the script and run the scene. Read through the console to see the output when you move the mouse around.

# Accessing Local Components

As you have seen numerous times in the Inspector view, objects are composed of various components. You can interact with these components at runtime through scripts. Every component differs a little, but the general syntax for editing components is to type the component's name followed by a period and ending with the name of the property you want to change. For instance, if you want to change the type of a point light component, you could write the following:

```
light.type = LightType.Directional;
```

This syntax changes the type property of the light component to be directional. Notice how the light component and type property are capitalized in the Inspector but lowercase in code. Just remember that when you are attempting to access a specific thing ("this light," for example) you use lowercase letters.

The most common component you work with is the transform component. By editing this, you can make objects move around the screen. Remember that an object's transform is made up of its translation (or position), its rotation, and its scale. Although you can modify those directly, it is easier to use some built-in options called the Translate method, the Rotate method, and the localScale variable:

```
//Moves the object along the positive x axis.
//The '0f' means 0 as a float. It is the way Unity reads floats
transform.Translate(.05f, 0f, 0f);

//Rotates the object along the z axis
transform.Rotate(0f, 0f, 1f);

//Scales the object to double its size in all directions
transform.localScale = new Vector3(1.5f, 1.5f, 1.5f);
```

Because Translate() and Rotate() are methods, if the preceding code were to be put in Update(), the object would continually move along the positive x axis while being rotated along the y axis.

▼ TRY IT YOURSELF

### Transforming an Object

Let's see the previous code in action by applying it to an object in a scene:

1. Create a new project or scene. Add a cube to the scene and position it at (0, –1, 0).

2. Create a new script and name it **CubeScript**. Place the script on the cube. In MonoDevelop, enter the following code to the Update method:

```
transform.Translate(.05f, 0f, 0f);
transform.Rotate(0f, 0f, 1f);
transform.localScale = new Vector3(1.5f, 1.5f, 1.5f);
```

3. Save the script and run the scene. Notice how the effects of the Translate and Rotate methods are cumulative and the variable localScale is not; it does not keep growing.

# Accessing Other Objects

Many times, you want a script to be able to find and manipulate other objects and their components. Doing so is simply a matter of finding the object you want and calling on the appropriate component. There are a few basic ways to find objects that aren't local to the script or to the object the script is attached to.

## Finding Other Objects

The first and easiest way to find other objects to work with is to use the editor. By creating a public variable on the class level of type GameObject, you can simply drag the object you want onto the script component in the Inspector view. The code to set this up looks like this:

```
//This is here for reference
public class SomeClassScript : MonoBehaviour {

    //This is the game object you want to access
    public GameObject objectYouWant;

    //This is here for reference
    Void Start() {
    }
}
```

After you have attached the script to a game object, you see a property in the Inspector called Object You Want (see Figure 9.3). Just drag any game object you want onto this property to have access to it in the script.

Drag Other Game Object Here

**FIGURE 9.3**
The new Object You Want property in the Inspector.

Another way to find a game object is by using the Find method. To find it this way, you need to know the object's name. The object's name is what it is called inside the Hierarchy view. Assuming that you are looking for an object named Cube, the code would look like this:

```
//This is here for reference
public class SomeClassScript : MonoBehaviour {

    //This is the game object you want to access
    public GameObject target;

    //This is here for reference
    void Start() {
        target = GameObject.Find("Cube");
    }
}
```

The shortcoming of this method is that it just returns the first item it finds with the given name. If you have multiple Cube objects, you won't know which one you are getting.

The final way to find an object is by its tag. An object's tag is much like its layer (which was covered previously). The only different is semantics. The layer is used for broad categories of interaction, whereas the tag is used for basic identification. You create tags using the Tag Manager (click **Edit > Project Settings > Tags**). Figure 9.4 shows how to add a new tag to the Tag Manager.

Type Tag Name Here

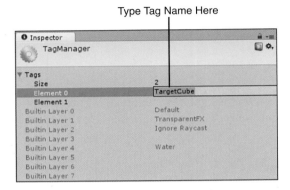

**FIGURE 9.4**
Adding a new tag.

Once a tag is created, simply apply it to an object using the Tag drop-down list in the Inspector view (see Figure 9.5).

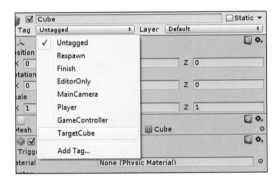

**FIGURE 9.5**
Selecting a tag.

Now that a tag is added to an object, you can find it using the FindWithTag method:

```
//This is here for reference
public class SomeClassScript : MonoBehaviour {

    //This is the game object you want to access
    public GameObject target;

    //This is here for reference
    void Start() {
```

```
            target = GameObject.FindWithTag("TargetCube");
    }
}
```

### Finding Efficiency

In the previous examples, the target game object has been stored in a class variable (often called a *member*). The code to find the target object has then been placed in the Start method. You could always simply create the variable and find the target audience in the Update method (or wherever else you need it), but you should avoid doing that. Finding an object over and over is inefficient and can slow down a game's performance. Remember, performance is good. Doing the same thing over and over is bad.

## Modifying Object Components

Once you have a reference to another object, working with the components of that object is almost 100% exactly the same. The only difference is that now, instead of simply writing the component name, you need to write the object variable and a period in front of it:

```
//This accesses the local component, not what you want
transform.Translate(0, 0, 0);

//This accesses the target object, what you want
targetObject.transform.Translate(0, 0, 0);
```

**TRY IT YOURSELF**

### Transforming a Target Object

Let's take a moment to modify a target object using scripts:

1. Create a new project or scene. Add a cube to the scene and position it at (0, –1, 0).

2. Create a new script and name it **TargetCubeScript**. Place the script on the Main Camera. In MonoDevelop, enter the following code to the TargetCubeScript:

```
//This is the game object you want to access
public GameObject target;

//This is here for reference
void Start() {
    target = GameObject.Find("Cube");
}

void Update() {
```

```
        target.transform.Translate(.05f, 0f, 0f);
        target.transform.Rotate(0f, 0f, 1f);
        target.transform.localScale = new Vector3(1.5f, 1.5f, 1.5f);
    }
```

3. Save the script and run the scene. Notice how the cube is moving around even though the script was applied to the Main Camera.

# Summary

In this hour, you explored more scripting in Unity. You learned all about methods and looked at some ways to write your own. Then, you worked with player inputs from the keyboard and mouse. After that you learned about modifying object components with code. You finished the hour by learning how to find and interact with other game objects via scripts.

# Q&A

**Q.** **How many methods should I write?**

**A.** A method should be a single, concise function. You don't want to have too few methods because that would cause each method to do more than one thing. You also don't want to have too many small methods because that defeats the purpose. As long as each process has its own specific method, you have enough.

**Q.** **Why don't we learn more about gamepads?**

**A.** The problem with gamepads is that they all differ. In addition, different operating systems treat them differently. The reason they weren't covered in detail this hour is because they are too varied and wouldn't allow for a consistent reader experience (plus not everyone has gamepads).

**Q.** **Is every component editable by script?**

**A.** Yes, at least all of the built-in ones.

# Workshop

Take some time to work through the questions here to ensure that you have a firm grasp of the material.

## Quiz

1. True or False: Methods can also be referred to as functions.

2. True or False: Not every method has a return type.

3. Why is it a bad thing to map player interactions to specific buttons?

4. In the Try It Yourself exercises in the sections on local and target components, the cube was translated along the positive x axis and rotated along the z axis. This caused the cube to move around in a big circle. Why?

## Answers

1. True.

2. False. Every method has a return type. If the method returns nothing, the type is void.

3. The players will have a much harder time remapping the controls to meet their preferences. By mapping your controls to generic axes, the player can change which buttons map to those axes easily.

4. Transformations happen on the local coordinate system (remember Hour 2, "Game Objects"). Therefore, the cube did move along the positive x axis. The direction that axis was facing relative to the camera, however, kept changing.

# Exercise

It is a good idea to combine each hour's lessons together to see them interact in a more realistic way. In this exercise, you write scripts to allow the player directional control over a game object. You can find the solution to this exercise in the book assets for Hour 9 if needed:

1. Create a new project or scene. Add a cube to the scene and position it at (0, 0, –5). Add a direction light to your scene.

2. Create a new folder called **Scripts** and create a new script called **CubeControlScript**. Attach the script to the cube.

Try to add the following functionality to the script. If you get lost, check the book assets for Hour 9 for help:

▶ Whenever the player presses the left or right arrow, move the cube along the x axis negatively or positively, respectively. Whenever the player presses the down or up arrow, move the cube along the y axis negatively or positively, respectively.

▶ When the player moves the mouse along the y axis, rotate the cube about the x axis. When the player moves the mouse along the x axis, rotate the cube about the y axis.

▶ When the player presses the M key, scale the cube up. When the player presses the N key, scale the cube down.

# Collision

---

## What You'll Learn in This Hour:

▶ The basics of rigidbodies

▶ How to use colliders

▶ How to script with triggers

▶ How to raycast

In this hour, you learn to work with the most prevalent physics concept in video games: collision. *Collision*, simply put, is knowing when the border of one object has come into contact with another object. You begin by learning what rigidbodies are and what they can do for you. After that, you experiment with Unity's powerful built-in physics engine by colliding objects together. From there, you learn the more subtle uses of collision with triggers. You end the hour by learning to use a raycast to detect collisions.

## Rigidbodies

For objects to take advantage of Unity's built-in physics engine, they must include a component called a *rigidbody*. Adding a rigidbody component makes an object behave like a real-world solid entity. To add a rigidbody component, simply select the object that you want and click **Component > Physics > Rigidbody**. You will notice the new rigidbody component added to the object in the Inspector (see Figure 10.1).

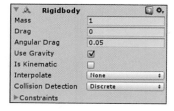

**FIGURE 10.1**
The rigidbody component.

The rigidbody component has several new properties that you have not seen yet. Table 10.1 describes these properties.

**TABLE 10.1**   Rigidbody Properties

| Property | Description |
| --- | --- |
| Mass | The mass of the object in arbitrary units. A heavier object will have a higher mass. |
| Drag | How much air resistance is applied to the object when moving. Higher drag will make an object require more force to move and will stop a moving object more quickly. A drag of 0 will apply no air resistance. |
| Angular Drag | Much like drag, this is air resistance applied when turning. |
| Use Gravity | Determines whether Unity's gravity calculations are applied to this object. Gravity will affect an object more or less depending on its drag. |
| Is Kinematic | If an object is kinematic, it will not be affected by Unity's physics. This is for times where you want a rigidbody, but you don't want to use Unity's stock physics. |
| Interpolate | Determines how and if motion for an object is smoothed. By default, this is set to Smooth. Interpolate bases the smoothing on the previous frame, whereas Extrapolate is based on the next assumed frame. It is recommended to turn this on for the player object and turn it off for everything else. This will give you the best performance and quality. |
| Collision Detection | Determines how collision is calculated. Discrete is the default and is how all objects test against each other. The Continuous setting can help if you are having trouble detecting collisions with very fast objects. Be aware, though, that Continuous can have a large impact on performance. The Continuous Dynamic setting will use discrete detection against other discrete objects and continuous detection against other continuous objects. |
| Constraints | Constraints are movement limitations that a rigidbody enforces on an object. By default, these are turned off. Freezing a position axis will prevent the object from moving along that axis, and freezing a rotation axis will prevent an object from rotating about that axis. |

ariables

**TRY IT YOURSELF** ▼

## Using Rigidbodies

Let's take a moment to see a rigidbody in action:

1. Create a new project or scene. Add a cube to the scene and place it at (0, 1, –5). You may optionally want to add a directional light to the scene.

2. Run the scene. Notice how the cube floats in front of the camera.

3. Add a rigidbody to the object (click **Components > Physics > Rigidbody**).

4. Run the scene. Notice how the object now falls due to gravity.

5. Continue experimenting with the drag and constraints properties.

# Collision

Now that you have your objects moving around, it is time to start getting them to crash into each other. For objects to detect collision, they need a component called a collider. A *collider* is a perimeter that is projected around your object that can detect when other objects enter it.

NOTE

## Collision Requirements

It is worth mentioning that objects don't need rigidbodies to collide. All that is needed for collision is for both objects involved to have a collider object. Rigidbodies are included in this chapter because they help demonstrate topics by enabling objects to fall. Also, rigidbodies are required for trigger collision, which is covered later in this chapter.

# Colliders

Geometric objects like spheres, capsules, and cubes already have collider components on them when created. You can add a collider to an object without one by clicking **Component > Physics** and then choosing the collider shape you want from the menu. Figure 10.2 illustrates the different collider shapes you can choose from.

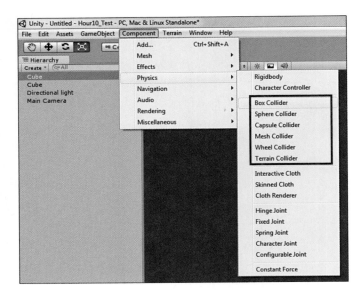

**FIGURE 10.2**
The different colliders.

Once a collider is added to an object, the collider object appears in the Inspector. Table 10.2 describes the collider properties.

**TABLE 10.2** Collider Properties

| Property | Description |
| --- | --- |
| Is Trigger | Determines whether the collider is a physical collider or a trigger collider. Triggers are covered in greater detail later this hour. |
| Material | Colliders enable you to apply physics materials to objects to change the way in which they behave. You can make an object behave like wood, metal, or rubber, for instance. Physics materials are covered later this hour. |
| Center | The center point of the collider relative to the containing object. |
| Size | The size of the collider. |
| Geometric properties | If the collider is a sphere or capsule, you might have an additional property, such as Radius. These behave exactly as you would expect them to. |

TIP

## Mix and Match Colliders

Using different-shaped colliders on objects can have some interesting effects. For instance, making the collider on a cube much bigger than the cube makes the cube look like it is floating above a surface. Likewise, a smaller collider will allow an object to sink into a surface. Furthermore, putting a sphere collider on a cube will allow the cube to roll around like a ball. Have fun experimenting with the various ways to make colliders for objects.

### TRY IT YOURSELF ▼

## Experimenting with Colliders

It's time to try out some of the different colliders and see how they interact. Be sure to save this exercise; you use it again later in the hour:

1. Create a new project or scene. Add two cubes and a directional light to the scene. Place one cube at **(0, 1, −5)** and put a rigidbody on it. Place the other cube at **(0, −1, −5)** and scale it to **(4, .1, 4)** with a rotation of **(0, 0, 15)**. Put a rigidbody on the second cube, as well, but uncheck the **Use Gravity** property.

2. Run the scene and notice how the top cube falls onto the other cube. They then both fall away from the screen. Now, on the bottom cube, under the constraints of the rigidbody component, freeze all three axes for both position and rotation.

3. Run the scene and notice how the top cube now falls and stops on the bottom cube. Remove the box collider from the top cube (right-click the **Box Collider** component and select **Remove Component**). Add a sphere collider to the top cube (click **Component > Physics > Sphere Collider**). Give the bottom cube a rotation of **(0, 0, 350)**.

4. Run the scene. Notice how the box rolls off of the ramp like a sphere even though it is a cube.

5. Continue experimenting with the different colliders. Another fun experiment is to change the constraints on the bottom cube. Try only freezing the y axis position and unfreezing everything else. Try out the different ways to make the boxes collide.

TIP

## Complex Colliders

You may have noticed a collider called the Mesh Collider. This collider is specifically left out of the text because it is more a practice in modeling than anything. Basically, a *mesh collider* is a collider that has the exact shape of a 3D model. This sounds useful, but in practice can greatly reduce the performance of your game. Furthermore, Unity puts a severe limit to the number of polygons allowed in a mesh collider. A better habit to get into is to compose your complex object with several basic colliders. If you have a humanoid model, try spheres for the head and hands and capsules for the torso, arms, and legs. You will save on performance and still have some very sharp collision detection.

# Physics Materials

Physics materials can be applied to colliders to give objected varied physical properties. For instance, you can use the rubber material to make an object bouncy or an ice material to make it slippery. You can even make your own to emulate a specific material of your choosing.

To import the materials Unity makes available, click **Assets > Import Package > Physic Materials**. In the Import screen, leave everything selected and click **Import**. This will bring a Standard Assets folder into your project that contains materials for Bouncy, Ice, Metal, Rubber, and Wood. To create a new physics material, right-click the Assets folder in the Project view and select **Create > Physic Material**.

A physics material has a set of properties that determine how it behaves on a physical level (see Figure 10.3). Table 10.3 describes the physics material's properties. You can apply a physics material to an object by dragging it from the Project view onto an object.

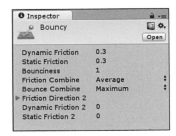

**FIGURE 10.3**
The properties of physics materials.

**TABLE 10.3    Physics Material Properties**

| Property | Description |
| --- | --- |
| Dynamic Friction | The friction applied when an object is already moving. Lower numbers make an object more slippery. |
| Static Friction | The friction applied when an object is stationary. Lower numbers make an object more slippery. |
| Bounciness | The amount of energy retained from a collision. A value of 1 causes the object to bounce without any loss of energy; it will bounce forever. A value of 0 prevents the object from bouncing. |
| Friction Combine | Determines how friction of two colliding objects is calculated. The friction can be averaged, the smallest or largest can be used, or they can be multiplied. |

| Property | Description |
|---|---|
| Bounce Combine | Determines how the bounce of two colliding objects is calculated. The bounce can be averaged, the smallest or largest can be used, or they can be multiplied. |
| Friction Direction 2 | Specify this property if you want the object to have different friction in a specific direction. (Think of an ice skate.) |
| Dynamic Friction 2 | Like Dynamic Friction, only applied to the specified direction. Only used if a Friction Direction 2 is supplied. |
| Static Friction 2 | Like Static Friction, only applied to the specified direction. Only used if a Friction Direction 2 is supplied. |

The effects of the physics material can be as subtle or as distinct as you like. Try it out for yourself and see what kind of interesting behaviors you can create.

# Triggers

So far, you have seen physical colliders, colliders that react in a positional and rotational fashion using Unity's built-in physics engine. If you think back to Hour 7, "Game 1: *Amazing Racer*," however, you probably can remember using another type of collider. Remember how the game detected when the player entered the water hazards and finish zone? That was the trigger collider at work. A trigger detects collision just like normal colliders do, but it doesn't do anything specific about it. Instead, triggers call three specific methods that allow you, the programmer, to determine what the collision means:

```
void OnTriggerEnter(Collider other)      //is called when an object enters the
➥trigger
void OnTriggerStay(Collider other)       //is called when an object stays in the
➥trigger
void OnTriggerExit(Collider other)       //is called when an object exits the trigger
```

Using these methods, you can define what happens whenever an object enters, stays in, or leaves the collider. For example, if you want to write a message to the console whenever an object enters the perimeter of a cube, you could add a trigger to the cube. Then attach a script to the cube with the following code:

```
void OnTriggerEnter(Collider other)
{
    print("Object has entered collider");
}
```

NOTE

**Triggers Not Working**

For trigger colliders to work, a rigidbody must be involved. If an object without a rigidbody enters a trigger collider, nothing will happen. If you are noticing in your scene that some objects aren't triggering the way you want, ensure that they have rigidbodies on them.

You might notice the one parameter to the trigger methods: the variable other of type collider. This is a reference to the object that entered the trigger. Using that variable, you can manipulate the object however you want. For instance, if you want to modify the preceding code to write the name of the object that enters the trigger to the console, you could write the following:

```
void OnTriggerEnter(Collider other)
{
    print(other.gameObject.name + " has entered the trigger");
}
```

You could even go so far as to destroy the object entering the trigger with some code like this:

```
void OnTriggerEnter(Collider other)
{
    Destroy(other.gameObject);
}
```

▼ TRY IT YOURSELF

**Working with Triggers**

In this exercise, you get a chance to build an interactive scene with a functioning trigger. You can find the completed project for this exercise, called Hour10_TriggerExercise, in the book assets for Hour 10:

1. Create a new project or scene. Add a directional light to the scene. Add a cube and sphere to the scene. Place the cube at (–1, 1, –5) and place the sphere at (1, 1, –5).

2. Create two scripts named **TriggerScript** and **MovementScript**. Place the trigger script on the cube and the movement script on the sphere.

3. On the cube's collider, check **Is Trigger**. Add a rigidbody to the sphere and uncheck **Use Gravity**.

4. Add the following code to the Update method of the movement script:

```
float mX = Input.GetAxis("Mouse X") / 10;
float mY = Input.GetAxis("Mouse Y") / 10;
transform.Translate(mX, mY, 0);
```

**5.** Add the following code to the trigger script. Be sure to place the code outside of any methods but inside of the class:

```
void OnTriggerEnter(Collider other)
{
    print(other.gameObject.name + " has entered the cube");
}

void OnTriggerStay(Collider other)
{
    print(other.gameObject.name + " is still in the cube");
}

void OnTriggerExit(Collider other)
{
    print(other.gameObject.name + " has left the cube");
}
```

**6.** Run the scene. Notice how the mouse moves the sphere. Collide the sphere with the cube and pay attention to the console output. Notice how the two objects don't physically react, but they still interact.

# Raycasting

*Raycasting* is the act of sending out an imaginary line, a ray, and seeing what it hits. Imagine, for instance, looking through a telescope. Your line of sight is the ray, and whatever you can see at the other end is what your ray hits. Game developers use raycasting all the time for things like aiming, determining line of sight, gauging distance, and more. There are a few Raycast methods in Unity. The two most common uses are laid out here. The first Raycast method looks like this:

```
bool Raycast(Vector3 origin, Vector3 direction, float distance, LayerMask mask) ;
```

Notice that this method takes quite a few parameters. Also notice that it uses a variable called a Vector3. A Vector3 is a variable type that holds three floats inside of it. It is a great way to specify an x, y, and z coordinate without requiring three separate parameters. The first parameter, origin, is the position the ray starts at. The second, direction, is which direction the ray travels. The third parameter, float, determines how far out the ray will go, and the final variable, mask, determines what layers will be hit. You can omit both the distance and mask variables. If you do, the ray will travel and infinite distance and hit all object types.

As mentioned earlier, there are many things you can do with rays. For instance, if you want to determine whether something is in front of the camera, you could attach a script with the following code:

```
void Update() {

    //cast the ray from the camera's position in the forward direction
    if (Physics.Raycast(transform.position, transform.forward, 10))
        print("There is something in front of the camera!");
}
```

Another way we can use this method is to find the object that the ray collided with. This version of the method uses a special variable type called a RaycastHit. Many versions of the Raycast method utilize distance (or don't) and layer mask (or don't). The most basic way to use this version of the method, though, looks something like this:

```
bool Raycast(Vector3 origin, Vector3 direction, out Raycast hit, float distance);
```

There is one new interesting thing about this version of the method. You might have noticed that it uses a new keyword that you have not scene before: out. This keyword means that when the method is done running, the variable hit will contain whatever object was hit. The method effectively sends the value back *out* when it is done.

▼ TRY IT YOURSELF

## Casting Some Rays

Let's create an interactive "shooting" program. This program will send a ray from the camera and destroy whatever objects it comes into contact with. You can find the completed project for this exercise, called Hour10_RaycastExercise, in the book assets for Hour 10–

1. Create a new project or scene. Add four spheres to the scene and change their names to be **Sphere1** through **Sphere4**. Place the spheres at (–1, 1, –5), (1, 1.5, –5), (–1, –2, 5), and (1.5, 0, 0).

2. Create a new script called **RaycastScript** and attach it to the Main Camera. Inside the Update method for the script, add the following:

```
float dirX = Input.GetAxis("Mouse X");
float dirY = Input.GetAxis("Mouse Y");

//opposite because we rotate about those axes
transform.Rotate(dirY, -dirX, 0);

CheckForRaycastHit(); //this will be added in the next step
```

**3.** Now, add the method CheckForRaycastHit() to your script by adding the following code outside of a method but inside the class:

```
void CheckForRaycastHit()
{
    RaycastHit hit;
    if(Physics.Raycast(transform.position, transform.forward, out hit))
    {
        print (hit.collider.gameObject.name + " destroyed!");
        Destroy(hit.collider.gameObject);
    }
}
```

**4.** Run your scene. Notice how moving the mouse moves the camera. Try to center the camera on each sphere. Notice how the sphere is destroyed and the message is written to the console.

# Summary

In this hour, you learned about object interactions through collision. You learned about the basics of Unity's physics capabilities with rigidbodies. Then, you worked with various types of colliders and collision. From there, you learned that collision is more than just stuff bouncing around when you got hands on with triggers. Finally, you learned to find objects by raycasting.

# Q&A

**Q. Should all my objects have rigidbodies?**

**A.** Rigidbodies are useful components that serve largely physical roles. That said, adding rigidbodies to every object can have strange side effects and may reduce performance. A good rule of thumb is to add components only when they are needed, not preemptively.

**Q. There are several colliders we didn't talk about. Why not?**

**A.** Most colliders either behave the same way as the ones we covered or are beyond the scope of this text. For that reason, they are omitted. Suffice to say that this text still provides what you will need to know to make some very fun games.

# Workshop

Take some time to work through the questions here to ensure that you have a firm grasp of the material.

# Quiz

1. This component is required on an object if you want it to exhibit physical traits like falling.
2. True or False: An object can only have a single collider on it.
3. Tue or False: For a trigger to work, the trigger object also needs a rigidbody.
4. What sorts of things are raycasts useful for?

# Answers

1. Rigidbody.
2. False. An object can have many, and varied, colliders on it.
3. False. Whatever collides with the trigger needs to have a rigidbody.
4. Determining what an object can see and finding objects along line of site as well as finding distances between objects.

# Exercise

In this exercise, you create an interactive application that utilizes motion and triggers. The exercise requires you to creatively determine a solution (because one is not presented here). If you get stuck and need help, you can find the solution to this exercise, called Hour10_Exercise, in the book assets for Hour 10.

1. Create a new project or scene. Add a directional light to the scene. Add a cube to the scene and position it at (− **1.5, 0,** − **5**). Scale the cube (**.1, 2, 2**) and rename it **LTrigger**.
2. Duplicate the cube. (Right-click the cube in the Hierarchy view and select **Duplicate**.) Name the new cube **RTrigger** and place it at (**1.5, 0,** − **5**).
3. Add a sphere to your scene and place it at (**0, 0,** − **5**). Add a rigidbody to the sphere and uncheck **Use Gravity**.
4. Create a script named **TriggerScript** and place it on both the LTrigger and the RTrigger. Create a script called **MotionScript** and place it on the sphere.

Now comes the fun part. You will need to create the following functionality in your application:

▶ The player should be able to move the sphere with the arrow keys.
▶ When the sphere enters, exits, or stays in either of the triggers, the corresponding message should be written to the console.

The name of the trigger that the sphere enters (LTrigger or RTrigger) should also be written to the console with the above message.

Good luck!

# Game 2: *Chaos Ball*

---

**What You'll Learn in This Hour:**

▶ How to design the game Chaos Ball

▶ How to build the ChaosBall arena

▶ How to build the ChaosBall entities

▶ How to build the ChaosBall control objects

▶ How to further improve ChaosBall

It is time once again to take what you have learned and make another game. In this hour, you make the game *Chaos Ball*, which is a faster-paced arcade-style game. You start by covering the basic design elements of the game. From there, you build arena and game objects. Each object type will be made unique and given special collision properties. Then, you add interactivity to make the game playable. You finish by playing the game and making any necessary tweaks to improve the experience.

TIP

**Completed Project**

Be sure to follow along in this hour to build the complete game project. In case you get stuck, you can find a completed copy of the game in the book assets for Hour 11. Take a look at it if you need help or inspiration!

---

# Design

You have already learned what the design elements are in Hour 7, "Game 1: *Amazing Racer*." This time, you get right into them.

# The Concept

This is a game slightly akin to *Pinball* or *Breakout*. The player will be in an arena. Each of the four corners will have a color, and four balls with corresponding colors will be floating around. Amid the four colored balls, there will be several yellow balls, called *chaos balls*. Chaos balls exist solely to get in your way and make the game challenging. They are smaller than the four colored balls, but they also move faster. Players will have a flat surface with which they will attempt to knock the colored balls into the correct corners.

# The Rules

The rules for this game will state how to play, but will also allude to some of the properties of the objects. The rules for *Chaos Ball* are as follows:

▶ The player wins when all four balls are in the correct corners. There is no loss condition.

▶ Hitting the correct corner causes a ball to become inert.

▶ All objects in the game are super bouncy. (They lose no momentum on impact.)

▶ No ball (or player) can leave the arena.

▶ Ball speeds and chaos ball speeds are randomized.

# The Requirements

The requirements for this game are simple. This is not a graphically intense game and instead relies on scripting and interaction for its entertainment. The requirements for *Chaos Ball* are as follows:

▶ A walled piece of terrain to act as the arena.

▶ Textures for the terrain and game objects. These are provided in the Unity standard assets.

▶ Several colored balls and chaos balls. These will be generated in Unity.

▶ A character controller. This is provided by the Unity standard assets.

▶ A game controller. This will be created in Unity.

▶ A bouncy physics material. This will be created in Unity.

▶ Colored corner indicators. These will be generated in Unity.

▶ Interactive scripts. These will be written in MonoDevelop.

# The Arena

The first thing you want to create is an area for the action to take part in. The term *arena* is chosen to give the idea that the terrain is quite small and also walled in. Neither the player, nor any balls, should be able to leave the arena. Otherwise, the arena is quite simple (see Figure 11.1).

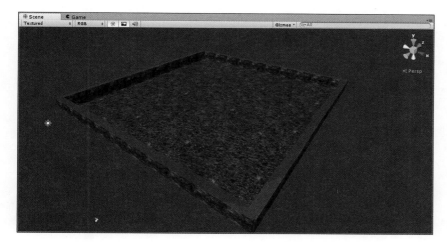

**FIGURE 11.1**
The arena.

## Creating the Arena

As mentioned earlier, this is going to be a simple process because of the simplicity of a basic arena map. To create the arena, follow these steps:

1. Create a new project in a folder called **ChaosBall**. This time at the Create New Project dialog, check the boxes next to **Character Controller.unityPackage** and **Terrain Assets. unityPackage** (see Figure 11.2). Add a terrain to the project.

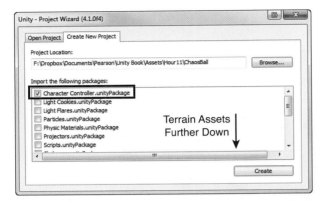

**FIGURE 11.2**
The Create New Project dialog.

2. Set the resolution of the terrain to **50 by 50**. (Remember, this is in the Resolution section of the Terrain Settings.) Add a directional light to the scene. Delete the Main Camera.

3. Add a cube to your scene. Place the cube at (0, 1.5, 25) and scale it to (1.5, 3, 51). Notice how it becomes a side wall for the arena. Rename the cube to **Wall**.

4. Save the scene as **Main** in a Scenes folder.

---

TIP

### Consolidating Objects

You might be wondering to yourself why you created only a single wall when the arena will obviously need four. The idea is that you want to do as little redundant, tedious work as possible. Often, if you require several objects that are very similar, you can create the object one and then duplicate it multiple times. In this instance, you set up a single wall with its materials and properties and then simply copy it three times. You repeat the same process for the corner nodes, the chaos balls, and the colored balls. Hopefully, you can see how a little planning can save you a fair bit of time.

---

# Texturing

Right about now the arena is looking pretty pitiful and bland. Everything is white, and there is only a single wall. The next step is to add some textures to liven the place up. You need to texture two objects specifically: the wall and the ground. Feel free to experiment with the texturing as you complete this step. You can make it more interesting if you'd like!

1. Create a new folder called **Materials** under Assets in the Project view. Add a material to the folder (right-click the folder and select **Create > Material**). Name the material **WallMaterial**.

2. Set the x axis tiling to **10** (see Figure 11.3).

3. Apply the **Cliff (Layered Rock)** texture to the wall material in the Inspector view (see Figure 11.3).

4. Click and drag the wall material onto the wall object in the Scene view.

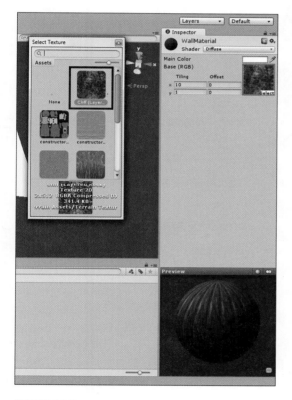

**FIGURE 11.3**
Adding cliff texture to material.

Next, you need to texture the ground. Recall that because the ground is a terrain, it is textured a little differently:

1. With the terrain selected, choose the terrain texturing tool in the Inspector (see Figure 11.4).

2. Click **Edit Textures** > **Add Texture**. In the Add Terrain Texture dialog, select the **Grass (Hill)** texture and click **Add**.

3. Your terrain will now be textured with grass.

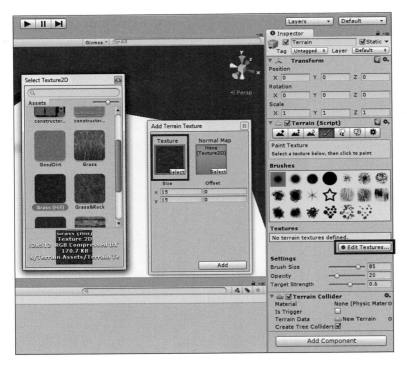

**FIGURE 11.4**
Adding terrain texture.

## Super Bouncy Material

You want objects to bounce off of the walls without losing any momentum. What you need is a super bouncy material. If you recall, Unity has a set of physics materials available. The bouncy material they provide, however, is not quite bouncy enough for your needs. Therefore, you need to create a new material, as follows:

1. Right-click the **Materials** folder and select **Create** > **Physic Material**. Name the material **SuperBouncyMaterial**.

2. Set the properties for the super bouncy material as they appear in Figure 11.5. Basically, you want everything that reduces energy to be minimized.

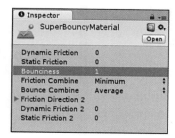

**FIGURE 11.5**
SuperBouncyMaterial settings

3. Click and drag the super bouncy material onto the wall object in the scene. It will automatically get applied as the physics material for the collider. You should see the material listed in the Material property of the Box Collider component.

## Finish the Arena

Now that the wall and ground is complete, you can finish the arena. The hard work has been done, and now all you need to do is duplicate the walls (right-click in the Hierarchy view and select **Duplicate**). The exact steps are as follows:

1. Duplicate the wall once. Place the new instance at (50, 1.5, 25).

2. Duplicate the wall again. Place it at (25, 1.5, 0) with a rotation of (0, 90, 0).

3. Duplicate the wall created in the previous step (the one that's turned) and place it at (25, 1.5, 50).

Your arena should now have four walls without any gaps or seams (refer to Figure 11.1).

# Game Entities

In this section, you create the various game objects required for playing the game. Just like with the arena wall, it will be easier for you to create one instance of each entity and then duplicate it.

## The Player

The player in this game will be a modified First Person character controller. When you created this project, you should have selected to import that character controller's package. Go ahead and click and drag a **First Person** character controller into the scene. Place the controller at (46, 1, 4) with a rotation of (0, 315, 0).

The first thing you want to do is to move the camera up and away from the controller. This will allow the player a greater field of vision while playing the game. To do this, follow these steps:

1. Expand the **First Person** controller in the Hierarchy view (click the arrow next to its name) and locate the Main Camera. You know you have the correct one because it will be blue.

2. After selecting the controller's camera, position it at (0, 5, –3.5) with a rotation of (43, 0, 0). The camera should now be above, behind, and slightly looking down on the controller.

The next thing to do is to add a bumper to the controller. The bumper will be the flat surface the player will bounce balls off of. To do this, follow these steps:

1. Add a cube to the scene. Rename the cube **Bumper**. Scale the bumper (3.5, 3, 1).

2. Click and drag your super bouncy material onto the bumper.

3. In the Hierarchy view, click and drag the bumper onto the First Person controller. This will nest the bumper onto the controller. After doing that, change the position of the bumper to (0, 0, .1) with a rotation of (0, 0, 0). The bumper will now be slightly in front of the controller.

The last thing to do is to speed the player up a bit. Select the **First Person** controller, and in the Inspector view expand the **Movement** property of the Character Motor (Script) component. Change the max forward speed to **11** and the max sideways speed to **10**.

## Chaos Balls

The chaos balls will be the fast and wild balls flying around the arena and disrupting the player. In many ways, they are similar to the colored balls, so you will be working to give them universally applicable assets. To create the first chaos ball, follow these steps:

1. Add a sphere to the scene. Rename the sphere **Chaos** and position it at (15, 2, 25) with a scale of (.5, .5, .5).

2. Click and drag the super bouncy material onto the sphere.

3. Create a new material (*not* a physics material) for the chaos ball called **ChaosBallMaterial**. In the color selector for the material, select a bright yellow color (see Figure 11.6). Click and drag the material onto the sphere.

4. Add a rigidbody to the sphere. Change the angular drag to **0** and uncheck **Use Gravity**. Change the Collision Detection property to **Continuous**. Under the Constraints property, freeze the y position. We don't want the balls to be able to go up or down.

5. Open the Tag Manager (click **Edit > Project Settings > Tags**), expand the **Tags** section by clicking the arrow next to Tags, and add the tag Chaos at Element 0. While you're here, go ahead and add the tags Green, Orange, Red, and Blue. These are used later.

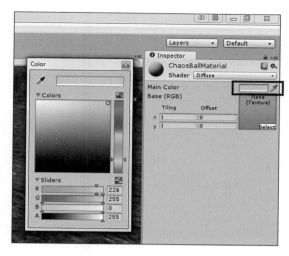

**FIGURE 11.6**
The ChaosBallMaterial settings.

6. Select the chaos sphere and change its tag to be **Chaos** in the Inspector view (see Figure 11.7).

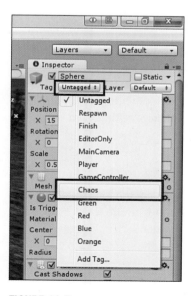

**FIGURE 11.7**
Choosing the Chaos tag.

The ball is now complete, but it still doesn't do anything. You need to create a script to move the ball all around the arena. You need to create a script called **VelocityScript** and attach it to the chaos ball. Listing 11.1 contains the full code for the velocity script.

**Listing 11.1   VelocityScript.cs**

```
using UnityEngine;
using System.Collections;

public class VelocityScript : MonoBehaviour {
    public float max = 50;

    // Use this for initialization
    void Start () {
        rigidbody.velocity = new Vector3(Random.Range(0, max), 0, Random.Range(0,
➡max));
    }

    // Update is called once per frame
    void Update () {

    }
}
```

As you can see in this listing, the Random.Range() method is used to give the ball an initial velocity between 0 and 50 along the x and z axis. Random.Range() takes two numbers as parameters and returns a random number in between them.

Run your scene and watch the ball begin to fly around the arena. At this point, the chaos ball is finished. In the Hierarchy view, duplicate the chaos ball four times. Scatter each ball around the arena (be sure to only change the x and z positions) and give each of them a random y axis rotation. Remember that movement along the y axis is locked, so make sure that each ball stays at a y position of 2.

## The Colored Balls

While the chaos balls are yellow, and that is a color, the colored balls are the four specific balls needed to win the game. They will be red, orange, blue, and green. As with the chaos balls, you can make a single ball and then duplicate it to make the creation easier.

To create the first ball, follow these steps:

1. Add a sphere to the scene. Rename the sphere **Blue**. Position the sphere somewhere near the middle of the arena, and make sure that the y position is **2**.

2. Create a new material called **BlueMaterial** and set its color to blue the same way you did for the chaos balls (refer to Figure 11.6). While you're at it, go ahead and create **RedMaterial**, **GreenMaterial**, and **OrangeMaterial** and set them to the appropriate color. Click and drag the BlueMaterial onto the sphere.

3. Click and drag the super bouncy material onto the ball.

4. Add a rigidbody to the sphere. Change its angular drag to **0**, uncheck **Use Gravity**, and freeze the y position under Constraints.

5. Previously, you created the Blue tag. Now, change the sphere's tag to Blue just like you did for the chaos ball (refer to Figure 11.7).

6. Attach the velocity script to the sphere. In the Inspector, locate Velocity Script (Script) component and change the Max property to **25** (see Figure 11.8). This causes the sphere to move slower than the chaos balls initially.

**FIGURE 11.8**
Changing the Max property.

If you run the scene now, you should see the blue ball moving rapidly around the arena. Now you need to create the other three balls. Each one will be a duplicate of the blue ball. To create the other balls, follow these steps:

1. Duplicate the blue ball. Rename the new ball to its color: **Red**, **Orange**, and **Green**.

2. Give the new ball the tag corresponding to its name. It is important for the name and the tag to be the same thing.

3. Drag the appropriate color material onto the new ball. It is important for the ball to be the same color as its name.

4. Give the ball a random location and rotation in the arena, but ensure that its y position is **2**.

At this point, the game entities are complete. If you run the scene you see all of the balls bouncing around the arena.

# The Control Objects

Now that you have all the pieces in place, it is time to gamify them. That is, it is time to turn these into a playable game. To do that, you need to create the four corner goals, the goal scripts, and the game controller. Once done, you have yourself a game.

## The Goals

Each of the four corners has a specific colored goal that corresponds with a colored ball. The idea behind the goal is that when a ball enters, the goal will check its tag. If the tag matches the color of the goal, there is a match. When a match is found, the ball is set to **Kinematic** (remember that makes it inert) and the goal is set to **Solved**. As with the ball objects earlier, you can configure a single goal and then duplicate it to match your needs.

To set up the initial goal, follow these steps:

1. Create an empty game object (click **GameObject > Create Empty**). Rename the game object **BlueGoal** and assign the tag Blue to it. Position the game object at (1.6, 2, 1.6).

2. Attach a box collider to the goal and check the **Is Trigger** property. Change the size of the box collider to be (1.5, 1.5, 1.5).

3. Attach a light to the goal (click **Component > Rendering > Light**). Make it a point light and make it the corresponding color of the goal (see Figure 11.9). Change the intensity of the light to 3.

**FIGURE 11.9**
The blue goal.

Next, you need to create a script called **GoalScript** and attach it to the blue goal. Listing 11.2 shows the contents of the script.

## Listing 11.2    GoalScript.cs

```
using UnityEngine;
using System.Collections;

public class GoalScript : MonoBehaviour {

    private bool solved = false;

    // Use this for initialization
    void Start () {

    }

    // Update is called once per frame
    void Update () {

    }

    void OnTriggerEnter(Collider other)
    {
        if(other.tag == tag)
        {
            solved = true;
            other.rigidbody.isKinematic = true;
        }
    }

    public bool IsSolved()
    {
        return solved;
    }
}
```

As you can see in the script, the OnTriggerEnter() method will check the tag of every object that contacts it against its own tag. If they match, the object is made inert, and that goal gets flagged as solved.

NOTE

**Private Variable**

You might notice that the GoalScript has a private solved variable and a public IsSolved() method. The method simply returns the variable. You may be wondering to yourself why that extra work was done when the variable could have simply been made public. The reason things were structured this way was to prevent any other objects or scripts from accidentally setting the goal to be solved. Because nothing has access to that variable besides the goal, nothing can mess it up. The method exists solely to tell the game control when if the goal is complete.

When the script is complete and attached to the goal, it is time to duplicate it. To create the other goals, follow these steps:

1. Duplicate the BlueGoal. Name the new goal corresponding to its color: **RedGoal**, **GreenGoal**, and **OrangeGoal**.

2. Change the tag of the goal to its corresponding color.

3. Change the color of the point light to the goal's corresponding color.

4. Position the goal. The colors can go in any corner as long as each goal gets its own corner. The three other corner positions are (1.6, 2, 48.4), (48.4, 2, 1.6), and (48.4, 2, 48.4).

All the goals should now be set up and operational.

# The Game Controller

The last element needed to finish the game is the game controller. This controller will be responsible for checking each goal every frame and determining when all four are solved. For this particular game, the game controller is very simple. To create the game controller, follow these steps:

1. Add an empty game object to the scene. Move it someplace out of the way. Rename it **GameController**.

2. Create a script called **GameControlScript** and add the code from Listing 11.3 to it. Attach the script to the game controller.

3. With the game controller selected, click and drag each goal to their corresponding property on the Game Control Script component (see Figure 11.10).

## Listing 11.3   Game Control Script

```
using UnityEngine;
using System.Collections;

public class GameControlScript : MonoBehaviour {

    public GoalScript red;
    public GoalScript blue;
    public GoalScript orange;
    public GoalScript green;

    private bool isGameOver = false;

    // Use this for initialization
    void Start () {

    }

    // Update is called once per frame
    void Update () {

        if(red.IsSolved() && blue.IsSolved() && orange.IsSolved() && green.
IsSolved())
        {
            isGameOver = true;
        }

    }

    void OnGUI()
    {
        if(isGameOver)
        {
            GUI.Box(new Rect(Screen.width / 2 - 100,
                    Screen.height / 2 - 50, 200, 75), "Game Over");

            GUI.Label(new Rect(Screen.width / 2 - 30,
                    Screen.height / 2 - 25, 60, 50), "Good Job!");
        }
    }
}
```

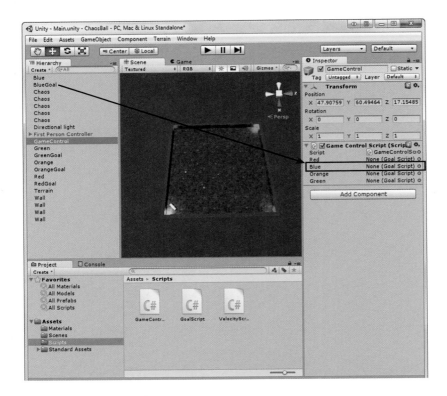

**FIGURE 11.10**
Adding the goals to the game controller.

As you can see in the preceding script, the game controller has a reference to each of the four goals. Every frame, the controller checks the goals to see if they are complete. If they are, the controller sets the variable isGameOver to true and displays the game over message on the screen.

Congratulations. *Chaos Ball* is now complete!

# Improving the Game

Even though *Chaos Ball* is a complete game, it is hardly as good as it could be. Several features that would greatly improve game play have been omitted. They were left out so that you could experiment with the game and make it better. In a way, you could say that *Chaos Ball* is now a complete prototype. It is a playable example of the game, but it lacks polish. You are encouraged to go back through this chapter and look for ways you can make the game better. Think to yourself as you play it:

▶ Is the game too easy or hard?

▶ What would make it easier or harder?

▶ What would give it that "wow" factor?

▶ What parts of the game are fun? What parts of the game are tedious?

In the exercise that follows, you have an opportunity to improve the game and add some of those features. Note that if you get any errors, it means you missed a step. Be sure to go back through and double-check everything to resolve any errors that might arise.

# Summary

In this hour, you made the game *Chaos Ball*. You started by designing the game. You determined the concept, the rules, and the requirements. From there, you sculpted the arena and learned that sometimes you can make a single object and duplicate it to save time. From there, you created the player, the chaos balls, the colored balls, the goals, and the game controller. You finished by playing the game and thinking of ways to improve it.

# Q&A

**Q. Why do we use continuous collision detection on the chaos balls? I thought that reduced performance.**

**A.** Continuous collision detection can, in fact, reduce performance. In this instance, it is needed, however. The chaos balls are small and fast enough that sometimes they can pass right through the walls.

**Q. The goals determined if the correct ball entered based on its tag. Could the same thing have been accomplished with just its name?**

**A.** Absolutely! The reason tags were used was for simplicity. Using tags and the editors, the scripts could be written generically. This allowed you to make it once and use it four times.

# Workshop

Take some time to work through the questions here to ensure that you have a firm grasp of the material.

## Quiz

**1.** True or False: Unity's bouncy physics material was used for this game.

**2.** How does the player lose the game?

3. What positional axis where all of the ball objects frozen on?

4. True or False: The goals utilized the method OnTriggerEnter() to determine whether an object was the correct ball.

5. Why were some basic features omitted?

## Answers

1. False. You created your own super bouncy physics material.

2. Trick question. The player cannot lose the game.

3. The y axis.

4. True.

5. To give the reader a chance to add them in.

# Exercise

The best part about making games is that you can get to make them the way you want. Following a guide can be a good learning experience, but you don't get the satisfaction of making a custom game. In this exercise, you have an opportunity to modify the game a little to make something more unique. Exactly how you want to change the game is up to you. Here are some suggestions:

▶ Try adding a button that allows the player to play again whenever the game is completed. (GUI elements haven't been covered yet, but this feature existed in the last game; see if you can figure it out.)

▶ Try adding a timer so that the player knows how long it took to win.

▶ Try adding variances of the chaos balls.

▶ Try adding a chaos goal that requires all of the chaos balls to be complete.

▶ Try changing the size or shape of the player's bumper. Try making a complex bumper out of many shapes.

# HOUR 12
# Prefabs

---

**What You'll Learn in This Hour:**

▶ The basics of prefabs

▶ How to work with custom prefabs

▶ How to instantiate prefabs in code

A prefab is a complex object that has been bundled up so that it can be re-created over and over with little extra work. In this hour, you learn all about prefabs. You start by learning about prefabs and what they do. From there, you learn how to create prefabs in Unity. You learn about the concept of inheritance. You finish by learning how to add prefabs to your scene both through the editor and through code.

## Prefab Basics

As mentioned earlier, a prefab is a special type of asset that bundles up game objects. Unlike simply nesting objects in the Hierarchy view, a prefab exists in the Project view and can be reused over and over across many scenes. This enables you to build complex objects, like an enemy, and use it to build an army. You can also create prefabs with code. This allows you to generate a nearly infinite number of objects during runtime. The best part is that any game object, or collection of game objects, can be put in a prefab. The possibilities are endless!

**Thought Exercise**

If you are having trouble understanding the importance of prefabs, consider this: In the preceding hour, you made the game *Chaos Ball*. When making that game, you had to make a single chaos ball and duplicate it four more times. What if you want to make more chaos balls on-the-fly during runtime? The fact is that you can't. Not without prefabs anyway. Now what if you have a game that uses an orc enemy type? Again, you could set a single orc up and then duplicate it many times, but what if you want to use the orc again in another scene? You would have to completely remake the orc in the new scene. If the orc were a prefab, though, it would be a part of the project and could be reused again in any number of scenes. Prefabs are an important aspect of Unity game development.

# Prefab Terminology

Some terms that are important to know when working with prefabs. If you are familiar with the concepts of object-oriented programming practices, you may notice some similarities:

▶ **Prefab:** The prefab is the base object. This exists only in the Project view. Think of it as the blueprint.

▶ **Instance:** An actual object of the prefab in a scene. If the prefab is a blueprint for a car, an instance is an actual car. If an object in the Scene view is referred to as a prefab, it is really meant that it is a prefab instance. The phrase *instance of a prefab* is synonymous with *object of a prefab*.

▶ **Instantiate:** The process of creating an instance of a prefab. It is a verb and is used like: "I need to instantiate an instance of this prefab."

▶ **Inheritance:** This does not mean the same thing as standard programming inheritance. In this case, the term *inheritance* refers to the nature by which all instances of a prefab are linked to the prefab itself. This is covered in greater detail later this hour.

# Prefab Structure

Whether you know it or not, you have already worked with prefabs. Unity's character controller is a prefab. To instantiate an object of a prefab into a scene, you only need to click and drag it into place in the Scene view or Hierarchy view (see Figure 12.1).

**FIGURE 12.1**
Add a prefab instance to a scene.

When looking at the Hierarchy view, you can always tell which objects are instances of prefabs because they will appear blue (see Figure 12.2). Just as with nonprefab complex objects, complex instances of prefabs also have an arrow that allows you to expand them and modify the objects inside.

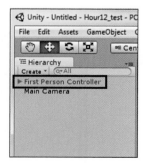

**FIGURE 12.2**
Prefab instances appear blue in the Hierarchy view.

Because a prefab is an asset that belongs to a project and not a particular scene, you edit the prefab in the Project view. Just like game objects, prefabs can be complex. Editing the children elements of the prefab is done by clicking the arrow on the right side of the prefab (see Figure 12.3). Clicking this arrow expands the object for editing. Clicking again condenses the prefab again.

**FIGURE 12.3**
Expanding the contents of a prefab in the Project view.

# Working with Prefabs

Using Unity's built-in prefabs is nice, but often you want to create your own. Creating a prefab is a two-step process. The first step is the creation of the prefab asset. The second step is filling the asset with some content.

Creating a prefab is really easy. Like all other assets, you want to start by creating a folder under Assets in the Project view to contain them. Then, just right-click the newly created folder and select **Create > Prefab** (see Figure 12.4). A new prefab will appear, which you can name whatever you want. Because the prefab is empty, it will appear as an empty white box.

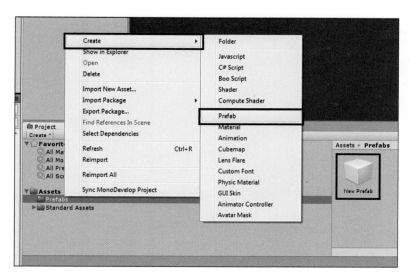

**FIGURE 12.4**
Creating a new prefab.

The next step is to fill the prefab with something. Any game object can go into a prefab. You simply need to create the object once in the Scene view and then click and drag it onto the prefab asset.

TRY IT YOURSELF ▼

## Creating a Prefab

Let's create a prefab asset and fill it with a complex game object. The prefab asset created here will be used later in this hour, so don't delete it:

1. Create a new project or scene. Add a cube and a sphere to the scene.

2. Position the cube at (0, 0, 0) with a scale of (.5, 2, .5). Add a rigidbody to the cube. Position the sphere at (0, 1.2, 0) with a scale of (.5, .5, .5). Put a point light component on the sphere.

3. Click and drag the sphere in the Hierarchy view onto the cube. This will nest the sphere into the cube (see Figure 12.5).

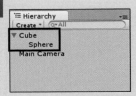

**FIGURE 12.5**
The sphere nested under the cube.

4. Create a new folder under the Assets folder in the Project view. Name the new folder **Prefabs**. Create a new prefab in the Prefabs folder (right-click and select **Create > Prefab**). Name the new prefab Lamp.

5. In the Hierarchy view, click and drag the cube (containing the sphere) onto the lamp prefab in the Project view (see Figure 12.6). You will notice that the prefab now looks like the lamp. You will also notice that the cube and sphere in the Hierarchy view turned blue. At this point, you can delete the cube and sphere from the scene. They are now contained in the prefab.

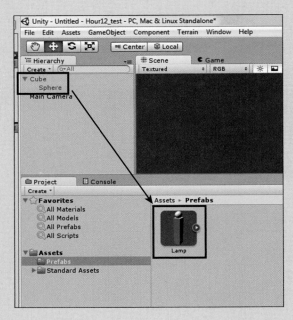

**FIGURE 12.6**
Adding an object to a prefab.

# Adding a Prefab Instance to a Scene

Once a prefab asset is created, it can be added as many times as you want to a scene or any number of scenes in a project. To add a prefab instance to a scene, all you need to do is click and drag the prefab from the Project view into place in the Scene view. You notice that when placing prefab instances into the scene, the instance can easily be placed on top of other objects. This makes positioning the new instances very simple.

## Creating Multiple Prefab Instances

In the last exercise, you made a Lamp prefab. This time, you will be using the prefab to create many lamps in a scene. Be sure to save the scene created here; it is used later this hour:

1. Create a new scene in the same project used for the last exercise.

2. Add a cube to the scene. Position the cube at (0, 0, 0) with a scale of (5, .1, 5).

3. Click and drag the prefab Lamp from the Prefabs folder onto the flattened cube (see Figure 12.7). Repeat this as many times as you want. Notice how the lamps are easily placed on the cube and positioning is fairly simple. Also notice how the object name is no longer Cube. It is now Lamp, just like the prefab.

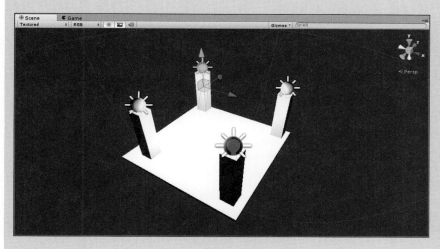

**FIGURE 12.7**
Placing lamps in the scene.

# Inheritance

When the term *inheritance* is used in conjunction with prefabs, it means the link by which the instances of a prefab are connected to the actual prefab asset. That is, if you change the prefab asset, all objects of the prefab are also automatically changed. This is incredibly useful. More often than not, you put a large number of prefab objects into a scene only to realize that they all need a minor change. Without inheritance, you would have to change each one independently.

There are two ways in which you can change a prefab asset. The first is by making changes in the Project view. Just selecting the prefab asset in the Project view will bring up its components and properties in the Inspector view. If you need to modify a child element, you can expand the prefab (described earlier) and change those objects in a similar fashion.

Another way you can modify a prefab asset is to drag an instance into the scene. From there, you can make any major modifications you would like. When finished, simply drag the instance back onto the prefab asset to update it.

▼ TRY IT YOURSELF

## Updating Prefabs

So far, you have created a prefab and added several instances to a scene. Now you get a chance to modify the prefab and see how it affects the assets already in the scene. This exercise uses the scene created in the previous exercise. If you have not done that one yet, you need to do so before continuing:

1. Open the scene with the lamps that you created previously.

2. Select the **Lamp** prefab from the Project view and expand it (click the arrow on the right side). Select the **Sphere** child component. In the Inspector, change the color of the light to orange (see Figure 12.8). Notice how the prefabs in the scene automatically change.

3. Select one of the lamp instances in the scene. Expand it by clicking the arrow to the left of its name in the Hierarchy view and select the Sphere child object. Change the sphere's light back to white. Notice how the other prefab objects don't change.

4. Click and drag the modified lamp instance back onto the prefab asset (see Figure 12.9). Notice how all of the instances change back to a white light.

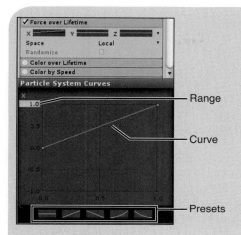

Range

Curve

Presets

**FIGURE 12.8**
The modified lamp instances.

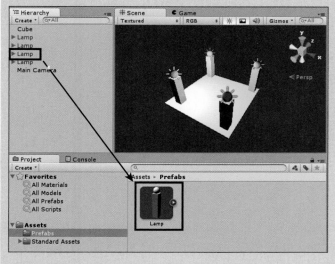

**FIGURE 12.9**
Updating the Lamp prefab with a modified instance.

## Breaking Prefabs

Sometimes, you need to break a prefab instance's link to the prefab asset. You might want to do this if you need an object of the prefab but you don't want the object to change if the prefab ever changes. Breaking an instance's link to the prefab does not change the instance in any way. It still maintains all of its objects, components, and properties. The only difference is that it is no longer an instance of the prefab and therefore is no longer affected by inheritance.

To break and object's link to the prefab asset, simply select the object in the Hierarchy view. After selecting it, click **GameObject > Break Prefab Instance**. You will notice that the object does not change, but its name turns from blue to black. Once the link is broken, it cannot be reapplied.

# Instantiating Prefabs Through Code

Placing prefab objects into a scene is a great way to build a consistent and planned level. Sometimes, however, you want to create instances at runtime. Maybe you want enemies to respawn, or you want them to be randomly placed. It is also possible that you need so many instances that placing them by hand is no longer feasible. Whatever the reason, instantiating prefabs through code is a good solution.

There are two ways to instantiate prefab objects in a scene and they both use the Instantiate() method. The first way is to use Instantiate() like this:

```
Instantiate(GameObject prefab);
```

As you can see, this method simply reads in a game object variable and makes a new object of it. The location, rotation, and scale of the new object are the same as the prefab in the Project view. The second way to use the Instantiate() method is like this:

```
Instantiate(GameObject prefab, Vector3 position, Quaternion rotation);
```

This method requires three parameters. The first is still the object to make a copy of. The second and third parameters are the desired position and rotation of the new object. You might have noticed that the rotation is stored in something called a Quaternion. Just know that this is how Unity stores rotation information. The true application of the Quaternion is beyond the scope of this hour. An example of the two methods of instantiating objects in code can be found in the exercise at the end of this hour.

# Summary

In this hour, you learned all about prefabs in Unity. You started by learning the basics of prefabs: the concept, the terminology, and the structure. From there, you learned to make your own prefabs. You explored how to create them, add them to a scene, modify them, and break them. Finally, you learned to instantiate prefabs objects through code.

# Q&A

**Q.** Prefabs seem a lot like classes in object oriented programming (OOP). Is that accurate?

**A.** Yes, there are many similarities between classes and prefabs. Both are like blueprints. Objects of both are created through instantiation. Objects of both are linked to the original.

**Q.** How many objects of a prefab can exist in a scene?

**A.** As many as you want. Be aware, though, that after you get above a certain number, the performance of the game will be impacted. Every time you create an instance, it is permanent until destroyed. Therefore, if you create 10,000, there will be 10,000 just sitting in your scene.

# Workshop

Take some time to work through the questions here to ensure that you have a firm grasp of the material.

## Quiz

1. What is the term for creating an instance of a prefab asset?

2. What are the two ways to modify a prefab asset?

3. What is inheritance?

4. How many ways can you use the Instantiate() method?

## Answers

1. Instantiation.

2. You can modify a prefab asset through the Project view or by modifying an instance in the Scene view and dragging it back onto the prefab asset in the Project view.

3. It is the link that connects the prefab asset to its instances. It basically means that when the asset changes, the objects change as well.

4. Two. You can specify just the prefab or you can also specify the position and rotation.

# Exercise

In this exercise, you work once again with the prefab you made earlier this hour. This time, you instantiate objects of the prefab through code and hopefully have some fun with it. You can find the complete project for this exercise as Hour12_Exercise in the book assets for Hour 12:

1. Create a new scene in the same project the Lamp prefab is in. Click the **Lamp** prefab in the Project view and give it a position of (−1, 1, −5).

**2.** Add an empty game object to your scene. Rename the game object **SpawnPoint** and position it at (1, 1, −5). Add a plane to your scene and position it at (0, 0, −4) with a rotation of (270, 0, 0).

**3.** Add a script to your project. Name the script **PrefabGenerator** and attach it to the spawn point object. Listing 12.1 has the complete code for the prefab generator script.

**Listing 12.1   PrefabGenerator.cs**

```
using UnityEngine;
using System.Collections;

public class PrefabGenerator : MonoBehaviour {
    //We will store a reference to the target prefab from the inspector
    public GameObject prefab;

    // Use this for initialization
    void Start () {

    }

    // Update is called once per frame
    void Update () {
        //Whenever we hit the B key, we will generate a prefab at the
        //position of the original prefab
        //Whenever we hit the space key, we will generate a prefab at the
        //position of the spawn object that this script is attached to
        if(Input.GetKeyDown(KeyCode.B))
            Instantiate(prefab);

        if(Input.GetKeyDown(KeyCode.Space))
            Instantiate(prefab, transform.position, transform.rotation);
    }
}
```

**4.** With the spawn point selected, drag the Lamp prefab onto the Prefab property of the Prefab Generator component. Now run the scene. Notice how pressing the **B** button creates a lamp at its default prefab position and how pressing the spacebar creates an object at the spawn point. Also notice how the prefabs collide with each other causing some unique interactions.

You might notice while running this scene that the lamps created continue to fall forever and never disappear from the scene. As a bonus challenge, see if you can create a plane with a trigger below the scene that will destroy the lamps when they enter. This way, the game cleans up the lamps no longer visible and the game has no long-term performance issues as a result.

# HOUR 13
# Graphical User Interfaces

**What You'll Learn in This Hour:**

▶ Unity GUI basics
▶ How to use the different GUI controls
▶ How to customize a GUI

A graphical user interface (GUI) is a special set of components responsible for sending information to, and reading information from, the user. In this hour, you learn all about using Unity's built-in GUI system. You start by examining the GUI basics. From there, you get to try out the various GUI controls. You finish by learning how to customize the look of the GUI using both styles and skins.

## GUI Basics

As mentioned previously, graphical user interfaces (commonly referred to as GUIs) are a special layer that sits between the player and the actual game. The role of the GUI is to display important information to the user and sometimes read data back from the user. In Unity, the GUI consists of several controls that are created in code. These controls are things like labels, buttons, text boxes, and sliders. The controls will be covered in greater detail later.

TIP

### GUI Design

As a general rule, you want to design your GUI ahead of time. A fair bit of thought needs to go into what data you display on the screen, where it will be displayed, and how. Too much information will cause the screen to feel cluttered. Too little information will leave the players confused or unsure. Always look for ways to condense information or make information more meaningful. Your players will thank you.

CAUTION

**Creating the GUI**

Because the GUI is created through code, it can be added to any script and any object. This can make for an organizational issue if you aren't careful. Placing bits of the GUI code in multiple scripts can make finding the parts that you want difficult. Furthermore, bugs become harder to track down and fix. Placing GUI parts on multiple objects also makes it difficult to define what object is responsible for the GUI. A good way to handle this is to put all of your GUI code together is a specifically designated object. Putting all your GUI stuff in the same spot makes for easier game development.

To add a GUI to your project, you need to add a special function to a script in your scene. It doesn't matter what script you put it in. Because long as the script is active and on a game object in a running scene, you see the GUI. The method that creates the GUI is OnGUI(), and it looks like this:

```
void OnGUI()
{
    //GUI code goes here
}
```

As you can see, the OnGUI() method takes no parameters and returns no data. The method gets called every frame, just like Update(), and draws your GUI components to the screen. As you will see later this hour, the GUI controls consist of simple lines of code. The code for those controls goes inside the OnGUI() method.

▼ TRY IT YOURSELF

**Creating a GUI**

Let's draw a basic GUI controls to the screen. In this exercise, you write a message to the screen with a label. Don't get too wrapped up in the label code; it is covered in greater detail later. Instead, just make sure that you can get a GUI to appear on your screen so that you are ready for the next section:

1. Create a new project or scene. Create a new script called **BasicGUIScript** and attach it to the Main Camera.

2. Add the following code outside of any method, but inside the class (see the book assets for Hour 13 if you need guidance):

   ```
   void OnGUI()
   {
       GUI.Label(new Rect(0, 0, 80, 20), "Hello World");
   }
   ```

3. Run the scene. Notice how Hello World is printed on the screen (see Figure 13.1).

**FIGURE 13.1**
Hello World printed to the screen.

# GUI Controls

In this section, you work with the more common built-in Unity GUI controls. Most of the controls are created and work in similar ways. Before getting into the specific controls, though, you need to become familiar with the Rect variable type. Rect is short for rectangle, and it is how all the components know their position on the screen. As mentioned previously in this book, GUI elements work only with 2D coordinates. Therefore, the exact position and size of any GUI element can be specified with a rectangle. You see many times in this hour the following code:

```
new Rect(<left>, <top>, <width>, <height>)
```

The previous code creates a new Rect that contains the value for the x axis position of the left side, the y axis position of the top side, and the width and height. Therefore, if you want to specify a rectangle that starts in the upper-left corner and is 100 units wide by 50 units tall, you could say the following:

```
new Rect(0, 0, 100, 50)
```

Aside from a Rect containing a position, each control will require some additional information that will be covered separately.

The last thing you need to know before working with each component is how the screen coordinates. As mentioned previously, the screen is only two dimensions. The upper-left corner is the origin (0, 0), and the lower-right corner is the maximum screen size. Because Unity can work with many different screen sizes at the same time, it is hard to know exactly what the maximum screen size is. Therefore, you can use two built-in variables, Screen.width and Screen.height, to know what the maximum size is on any screen. For example, the code to create a Rect with its upper-left corner in the exact center of the screen looks like this:

```
new Rect(Screen.width / 2, Screen.height / 2, 100, 50)
```

TIP

**Centering a Control**

Often you want a control to be in the exact center of the screen. You might notice that creating a Rect at the middle of the screen actually puts your Rect a little lower and to the right of the middle. This is because the upper-left corner of the Rect is in the middle and the rest of it extends past. To place the control in the actual middle requires a little more math. Basically, you need to place the Rect at the middle *minus* half of its width and height. This way, half is to the top left of the middle and half is to the lower right. Therefore, to place a Rect that is 100 wide and 50 tall in the middle of the screen, you write the following:

```
new Rect(Screen,width / 2 - 50, Screen.height / 2 - 25, 100, 50)
```

This might seem confusing at first, but play around with the numbers a bit and it will make sense in no time.

# Label

The label control is the most basic control. Its job is only to display data to the string. The code to create a label looks like this:

```
GUI.Label(new Rect(<x>, <y>, <w>, <h>), <Some String>);
```

Therefore, to create a label in the top-left corner that says Hello World, you write the following:

```
GUI.Label(new Rect(0, 0, 80, 20), "Hello World");
```

You can see this in action in the previous exercise.

# Box

The box control is similar to a label. The only difference is that a box also has a containing dark box around the label. The box is useful as a background for the various other controls. The syntax to create a box looks like this:

```
GUI.Box(new Rect(<x>, <y>, <w>, <h>), <Some String>);
```

So, if you want a box at the middle-top of the screen that says Box Label, you write the following:

```
GUI.Box(new Rect(Screen.width / 2 - 50, 0, 100, 50), "Box Label");
```

If you want an empty box at the same position with no label, you could also write this:

```
GUI.Box(new Rect(Screen.width / 2 - 50, 0, 100, 50), "");
```

Figure 13.2 illustrates the box created previously with the code.

**FIGURE 13.2**
The box control.

## Button

The button is a simple control that works in conjunction with a conditional statement. The button can either be false (not pressed) or true (pressed). A button control can also only be pressed once at a time. Continuing to hold the button will have no additional effect. The syntax for a button looks like this:

```
if(GUI.Button(new Rect(<x>, <y>, <w>, <h>), <Some String>))
{
    //whatever your button does when clicked.
}
```

So, to place a button in the upper-left corner of the screen that sets a variable to false when clicked, you could type the following:

```
if(GUI.Button(new Rect(0, 0, 40, 20), "Exit ?"))
{
    gameOver = true;
}
```

Note that if you actually try to run this it will fail because gameOver doesn't exist. It was just thrown in there for the example. Figure 13.3 shows the button created by the previous code.

**FIGURE 13.3**
The button control.

## Repeat Button

The repeat button is nearly identical to the button except that it can be pressed and held down. If you want to create a button that increases the value of some variable the whole time it is held down, you could type the following:

```
if(GUI.RepeatButton(new Rect(0, 0, 80, 20), "Increase"))
{
    someValue += 1;
}
```

Again, the variable someValue was just added for the example's sake.

## Toggle

The toggle is what you call a *stated* button. That means that the buttons retains a state that is either clicked or unclicked (think of a switch). The code for a toggle is the same as the other buttons with the exception that it takes in a Boolean parameter and returns a Boolean value. The parameter that it reads in determines whether it is currently clicked. The Boolean it returns tells you whether it is clicked. The syntax for a toggle looks like this:

```
<Some Boolean> = GUI.Toggle(new Rect(<x>, <y>, <w>, <h>), <Some Boolean>, <Some
➥String>);
```

A good idea when making a toggle is to create a Boolean variable outside of the OnGUI() method to store the toggle's state. To create a toggle, you say something like this:

```
bool toggleState = false;

void OnGUI()
{
    toggleState = GUI.Toggle(new Rect(5, 5, 80, 30), toggleState, "My Toggle");
}
```

Figure 13.4 illustrates a toggle button.

**FIGURE 13.4**
The toggle control.

## Toolbar

The toolbar is a row of buttons. The number of buttons that it contains is up to you. Just like a normal toolbar, only one button on the toolbar can be selected at a time, and you use an integer variable to keep track of which button is currently selected. The other new thing with toolbars is the use of an array of strings. However, many items are in the array will determine how many buttons appear in the toolbar. The syntax for the toolbar control looks like this:

```
<Some int> = GUI.Toolbar(new Rect(<x>, <y>, <w>, <h>), <Some Int>, <Array>);
```

So, if you want to make a toolbar with buttons that say Easy, Medium, and Hard, you could write the following:

```
int buttonInt = 0;
string[] list = {"Easy", "Medium", "Hard"};

void OnGUI()
{
    buttonInt = GUI.Toolbar(new Rect(5, 5, 200, 30), buttonInt, list);
}
```

### TRY IT YOURSELF ▼

### Toolbars

Let's take a moment to try out a toolbar in Unity:

1. Create a new project or scene. Create a script called **GUIScript** and attach it to the Main Camera.

2. Add the previous toolbar code to the script. Be sure to place the code outside of any method but inside the class.

3. Run the scene. You should see three buttons (see Figure 13.5). Try clicking the buttons and see how they interact.

**FIGURE 13.5**
The toolbar control.

## Textfield

The textfield control allows the user to type text into a scene. The control itself will appear as a box that can be selected and typed in. You have an option to put a string in the box as well. Just like with previous controls, you need to pass in a string as well as accept a string from the textfield to keep track of the user's interaction. The syntax for the textfield looks like this:

```
<Some String> = GUI.TextField(new Rect(<x>, <y>, <w>, <h>), <Some String>);
```

So, to create a textfield that says Enter Text Here, you could write the following:

```
string textString = "Enter Text Here";

void OnGUI()
{
    textString = GUI.TextField(new Rect(5, 5, 100, 30), textString);
}
```

Try it out! One thing to note is that no matter how tall the textfield is, it can contain only a single line of text. Figure 13.6 illustrates a textfield.

**FIGURE 13.6**
The textfield control.

## Textarea

The textarea is exactly like the textfield except that it can contain multiple lines. The syntax to create a textarea is as follows:

```
<Some String> = GUI.TextArea(new Rect(<x>, <y>, <w>, <h>), <Some String>);
```

Note that because the textarea can contain multiple lines, it is possible for the user to enter so many lines that the text goes beyond the vertical space of the area.

## Sliders

Sliders are controls that allow the user to select between a range of values by "sliding" the control. There are two slider types in Unity: horizontal and vertical. Besides a position Rect variable, sliders require three parameters. The slider reads in a float to denote the current value of the slider. The slider also reads in two additional parameters to denote the minimum and maximum slider value. The slider returns back a float containing the value of the slider. The syntax for the two sliders looks like this:

```
<Value> = GUI.HorizontalSlider(new Rect(<x>, <y>, <w>, <h>), <Value>, <Min>,
➥<Max>);
<Value> = GUI.HorizontalSlider(new Rect(<x>, <y>, <w>, <h>), <Value>, <Min>,
➥<Max>);
```

So, to create two sliders, each with a range of 0 to 100, you could write the following:

```
float hValue = 0;
float vValue = 0;

void OnGUI()
{
    vValue = GUI.VerticalSlider(new Rect(5, 5, 20, 150), vValue, 0, 100);
    hValue = GUI.HorizontalSlider(new Rect(30, 30, 150, 20), hValue, 0, 100);
}
```

Figure 13.7 shows the two slider controls created by the previous code.

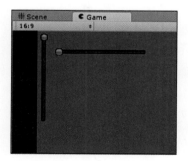

**FIGURE 13.7**
The slider controls.

# Customization

The GUI is an important and prominent part of any game. Unity's built-in GUI system is very powerful, but you will often want a more custom look and feel. Thankfully, customizing the way GUI controls works is a simple process. Controls can be changed using GUI styles and GUI skins.

# GUI Styles

A GUI style is something that you add to a control that dictates how it looks. These styles in Unity are built to emulate the Cascading Style Sheets (CSS) used in web pages and enable you to change text color, background textures, font, and more.

Every GUI control already has a default GUI style applied to it. The name of the style is the same as the name for the control. For instance, a button has a style named button applied to it. This becomes interesting when you realize that you can apply one control's style to another type of control. If you were to apply the button style to a toggle, for instance, you would get a control that looked like a button but acted like a toggle. Each control discussed earlier in this hour has the option of supplying an additional parameter. This parameter is the style parameter, and it can be either a GUIStyle object or a string with the name of a style.

▼ TRY IT YOURSELF

## Mix and Match Styles

In this exercise, you create a toggle that looks like a button:

1. Create a new project or scene. Add a script to the scene named **GUIScript** and attach it to the Main Camera.

2. Add the following code to the script. Notice how the toggle has an additional parameter that is just the name button:

```
bool value = false;

void OnGUI()
{
    value = GUI.Toggle(new Rect(5, 5, 100, 100), value, "toggle", "button");
}
```

3. Run the scene and notice the toggle that looks like a button. Notice what happens when you click it. Go ahead and experiment with different controls and styles. Remember that a controls style is simply the controls name.

If you don't want to reuse one of the built-in control styles, you can create your own. There is a way to create build a style in code, but it is much easier to use the editor. To use the editor to build a style, you first must add a GUIStyle variable to a script. Here are the steps in detail:

1. Add a script with an OnGUI() method to your scene if you don't already have one. If you do, you want to just use that. Make sure that the script is attached to an object.

2. Add a GUIStyle variable to your script. The syntax for doing this is:

```
public GUIStyle <variable name>;
```

This code goes inside the class, but outside of any methods.

3. In Unity, select the object with the script attached to it and notice the Style property on the script component (see Figure 13.8). You can click through the different properties of the style and change them how you like.

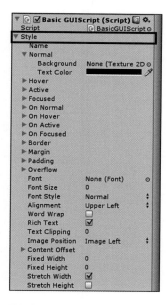

**FIGURE 13.8**
The Style property.

## Creating a Custom Style

In this exercise, you make a custom style and apply it to a button control:

1. Create a new project or scene. Add a script named **GUIScript** and attach it to the camera.

2. Add the following code to the script:

```
public GUIStyle style;

void OnGUI()
{
    if(GUI.Button(new Rect(5, 5, 100, 30), "Hello World", style);
}
```

3. In Unity, expand the Style and Normal properties in the Inspector view and change the Text Color property to orange (see Figure 13.9). Run the scene and see how the label looks.

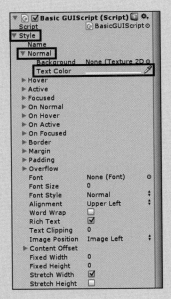

**FIGURE 13.9**
Changing the normal text color.

CAUTION

### Style Complexity

As you experiment with styles, you might notice some of the features not having any effect. You may also notice that applying a style to a button (or any other control) makes it look just like a label. This is because styles have a lot of complexity to them. For instance, the graphic that makes a button look like a button is just that: a graphic. If you don't supply a graphic in your style, your buttons won't look like buttons. The same thing applies to the button being clicked. The pressed button image is, in fact, another image. Therefore, if you are planning on making your own styles for your controls, spend some time thinking about all of the assets you need to make the controls look the way you want.

## GUI Skins

The GUI style dictates how a control will look when it is rendered. This is nice if you only need to manage a few controls. If you need to build the "look and feel" for an entire GUI with many different controls, however, it can be difficult to maintain all the different styles needed. That is where the GUI skin becomes useful. Basically, a GUI skin is just a collection of styles. By creating one skin, you have the ability to dictate how all of your various controls for a project will look.

To add a skin to your project, simply right-click a folder in Project view and select **Create > GUI Skin**. Selecting the newly created skin will show you a list of styles in the Inspector view. These are the styles for each of the GUI controls. There are also a few extra options available such as a universal font for all controls. Linking a skin to the GUI is handled in script. You need to create a GUISkin variable in the script. The syntax to do that looks like this:

```
public GUISkin <variable name>;
```

After you have given the variable a value in the editor, you simply assign it to the GUI. The syntax for the whole thing will look like this:

```
public GUISkin skin;

void OnGUI()
{
    GUI.skin = skin;
    //GUI code goes here
}
```

### TRY IT YOURSELF ▼

### Working with GUI Skins

Let's try out a GUI skin:

1. Create a new project or scene. Add a script named **GUIScript** and attach it to the camera.

2. Add the following code to the script:

```
public GUISkin skin;

void OnGUI()
{
    GUI.skin = skin;
    if(GUI.Button(new Rect(5, 5, 100, 30), "Hello World"))
    {}
}
```

3. In Unity, create a GUI skin (right-click the **Assets** folder and select **Create > GUI Skin**). Name the skin **NewSkin**. Expand the **Button** property, then the **Active** property, and change the Text Color property to red (see Figure 13.10).

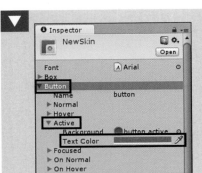

**FIGURE 13.10**
Changing the active text color.

4. With the camera selected, click and drag the NewSkin asset onto the Skin property of the GUI Script component (see Figure 13.11). Run the scene and click the button. Notice how the text color changes to red.

**FIGURE 13.11**
Applying the GUI skin.

---

NOTE

## A Word on Fonts

You can use both styles and skins to dictate fonts for your GUI controls. Font's in Unity work just like any other asset. Just drag the font you want into the Assets folder and Unity will automatically recognize it. Then you can simply apply it to any font property. The only requirement for fonts is that they be .ttf or .dfont file types.

---

# Summary

In this hour, you learned all about GUIs in Unity. You started by learning the basics of GUIs and how they are designed and created. From there, you learned about positioning GUI controls. You examined many of the common GUI controls and got to try them out. You wrapped up the hour by learning about GUI styles and skins.

# Q&A

**Q. Does every game need a GUI?**

**A.** Usually, a game benefits from having a well-thought-out GUI. It is rare for a game to have no GUI whatsoever. That said, it is always a good idea to go light with a GUI. You definitely don't want to overburden your players with too much clutter.

**Q. Are there any performance considerations to using a GUI?**

**A.** Yes, there are. The GUI system in Unity can be a very inefficient system if used too much. This is especially true on mobile platforms. That is not to say that the GUI system should not be used. It should just be used sparingly and appropriately. Again, it all comes back to only using the GUI to display what is needed without trying to put too much on the screen.

# Workshop

Take some time to work through the questions here to ensure that you have a firm grasp of the material.

## Quiz

1. What does GUI stand for?

2. What variable type stores an x and y position as well as a width and a height?

3. What is meant when it is said that a toggle is a stated button?

4. What is the difference between a GUI style and a GUI skin?

## Answers

1. Graphical user interface.

2. A Rect.

3. The toggle maintains a state. That is to say that the toggle knows whether it has been clicked.

4. A style dictates how one control looks. A skin is a collection of styles and is used for giving an entire GUI system a consistent look and feel.

# Exercise

In this exercise, you design your own GUI system. For the sake of creativity, you are allowed to style your GUI however you want. The completed exercise example in the book assets for Hour 13 (named Hour13_Exercise) uses only the default control styles. You will be tasked with giving it a unique style. The project itself is a simple program. See whether you can figure it out for yourself. If you are having difficulty, be sure to check the example:

- ▶ Add a textfield to the scene. It should contain no text.
- ▶ Add a button to the scene. It should say Click Me.
- ▶ Add a label to the scene. It should contain no text.
- ▶ When the button is clicked, take the text from the textfield and put it in the label.
- ▶ Using a GUI skin, give your textfield, button, and label a unique look. They should have a consistent color scheme and font. Feel free to be creative here. This is your chance to build something that is unique to you.

# Character Controllers

## What You'll Learn in This Hour:

▶ The basics of Unity's character controller
▶ How to create scripts for a character controller
▶ How to build a simple custom character controller

In this hour, you learn all about the character controller components in Unity. You start by learning about the basics of the character controller. You learn what it is and how it functions. From there, you learn how to write scripts to manipulate to utilize the abilities of the character controller. You finish the chapter by building your own character controller from scratch.

NOTE

### Why Learn About Controllers?

You might be wondering why you need to learn about character controllers when Unity provides two very robust controllers already (the First Person controller and the Third Person controller). Although it is true that those two controllers are very powerful, there are plenty of situations where they won't suffice. What if you want to make a controller for a 2D game? What if you want a controller that calculates gravity differently? It is important to understand the fundamental workings of the controller so that you can build specific solutions for your projects.

## The Character Controller

So far, you have seen many ways to interact with an object in a scene. You have explored ways to move them manually via scripts. You have also seen physical interactions with rigidbodies. Normally, these are acceptable ways to get movement in your game. If you are looking for more realistic and consistent gameplay, however, you need something a little more powerful. What you need is a character controller (often called just a *controller*). The character controller is a specialized component that allows you a high level of control over a game object without rigidbody physics. That is to say, a character controller enables to move an object along the ground and be constrained by walls and steep hills without pushing objects or being pushed by objects. At its heart, the character controller is a capsule collider with some additional functionality that will be examined later this hour.

# Adding a Character Controller

The character controller itself is a component and can be applied to any game object. Although the term *character* generally implies a player, it can be used to control all moving entities in a scene (players, enemies, cars, and so on). To apply a character controller to an object, just select the object and then click **Component > Physics > Character Controller**. A character controller should now appear under the object in the Inspector view.

---

NOTE

**Collider Quarrel**

Because a character controller has its own capsule collider, you may get a warning message when you attempt to add it to an object that already has a collider (see Figure 14.1). You have the option to cancel the character controller, replace the existing collider with the new capsule one, or keep both on the object. The effect you want to have will determine which option you choose. Generally speaking, if you are using your character controller for normal movement, you want to replace the existing collider with the capsule collider.

---

**FIGURE 14.1**
Message when adding controller to object with collider.

---

▼ TRY IT YOURSELF

**Adding a Character Controller to an Object**

In this exercise, you add a character controller to an object in a scene:

1. Create a new project or scene. Add a cube to the scene.

2. With the cube selected, add a character controller by clicking **Component > Physics > Character Controller**.

3. The cube should now have the character controller component in the Inspector view. Also, it may be faint, but you should be able to see a capsule collider present inside of the cube in the Scene view.

CAUTION

## Character Controllers and Rigidbodies

Because character controllers and rigidbodies are both components, they can both be added to the same object. This is not a good idea, though. Both the controller and the rigidbody will attempt to control the movement of the object in their own specific way. This can cause strange behaviors in the objects. A good general rule is to pick one or the other. Only use both if you are trying to accomplish a specific goal and know what you are doing.

# Character Controller Properties

The character controller has two sets of properties. There are the properties that are used via the Inspector view in the Unity editor (covered here), and there are the properties that are accessed via scripting (covered later). Figure 14.2 illustrates the different properties of the character controller component.

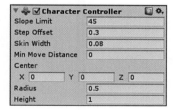

**FIGURE 14.2**
The character controller component.

Table 14.1 describes all the properties of the character controller.

**TABLE 14.1**   Character Controller Properties

| Property | Description |
| --- | --- |
| Slope Limit | Determines the steepest slope a controller can climb. Any slopes steeper than the value indicated here will be impassable to the controller. |
| Step Offset | Any steps closer to the ground than the specified value will be climbable. Any steps further than the value specified will be impassable. |
| Skin Width | Determines how deeply a collider can penetrate the controller's collider before a collision is detected. Too little width causes the controller to jitter. Too much causes the controller to get stuck. A good general setting is 10% of the controller's radius. |
| Min Move Distance | Determines the minimum distance a controller can be told to move. This can be used to reduce jitter, but setting it too high can cause the controls to feel unresponsive. A good rule is to set this at 0 and only increase it if needed. |

| Property | Description |
|----------|-------------|
| Center | The center of the capsule collider belonging to the character controller. |
| Radius | The radius of the capsule collider belonging to the character controller. |
| Height | The height of the capsule collider belonging to the character controller. |

# Scripting for Character Controllers

You might have noticed earlier that simply placing a controller on a game object didn't have much of an effect. In fact, if you had created a scene with any falling or moving items, you would have seen that they would collide with the object containing the controller, but the controller would not be moved by them. Most of the power of the character controller exists in scripting. Note that the character controller simply provides the foundations of control. Actual implementation is entirely up to you. This means that you have to do a little more work to make your controllers, but the result can be much more powerful, custom tailored, and refined.

## Controller Scripting

As mentioned earlier in this hour, the character controller has a series of properties (variables) that are accessible through scripting that really give it a lot of power. Before you can work with the controller in code, however, you have to acquire a reference to it:

```
CharacterController controller;

void Start () {
    controller = GetComponent<CharacterController>();
}
```

This bit of code will create a CharacterController variable. Then, in the Start() method, it will find the controller reference and save it to the variable. from that point on you will be able to use it in code. Table 14.2 describes the character controller scripting variables.

---

NOTE

### Common Functionality

The character controller component is a descendant of the collider component. We say the character controller "inherits" from the collider. Therefore, the controller has access to all the scripting capabilities that also belong to a collider. This section of the book, however, only covers the items that are unique to the character controller. It is just worth noting the relationship between controllers and colliders in case you notice some extra functionality in the code and wonder where it comes from.

---

**TABLE 14.2**   Character Controller Scripting Variables

| Property | Description |
|---|---|
| slopeLimit, stepOffset, center, radius, height | These are the same as the component properties mentioned in Table 14.1. |
| isGrounded | A Boolean value that tells you whether the controller is currently touching the ground. Is useful for jumping and flight mechanics. |
| velocity | A Vector3 variable that tells you how fast the controller is traveling along each axis. This is determined by calculating the position before and after a Move() or SimpleMove() call (discussed later). |
| collisionFlags | A CollisionFlags variable that tells you where collision has occurred on the controller (covered in more detail later). |
| detectCollisions | A Boolean variable that determines whether the character controller will detect collisions with other colliders and rigidbodies. By default, this is set to true. |

Along with a set of variables, the character controller provides you with two new methods: SimpleMove() and Move().These methods use the idea of motion to move an object around. This means that the objects aren't placed, nor are they pushed. They also aren't translated. The effect is instead based on the actual input controls set up in the Input Manager. The result is that the movement of the controller has a little bit of buildup and sliding to it. This makes it feel more realistic.

```
bool SimpleMove(Vector3 movement)
```

SimpleMove(), as its name implies, is a simple way to move an object around. This method reads in a Vector3 variable containing how much the object should move along each axis. The method returns a Boolean value indicating whether the object is grounded (touching the ground). Internally, the method applies gravity to the object automatically. As a result, the SimpleMove() method ignores any movement in the y axis that you give it. The result is that you cannot use your own gravity, nor can you apply any jumping or flying with SimpleMove(). If you would like to have those, you need to use Move() instead. Another thing to note is that SimpleMove() calculates move distances differently than Move(). Therefore, the amount that you need to move an object with SimpleMove() differs from the amount you need to move an object with Move() to go the same distance:

```
CollisionFlags Move(Vector3 movement)
```

Like SimpleMove(), Move() is responsible for moving an object around the scene. It takes in a Vector3 containing the amount of movement you want along each axis. Move() returns a CollisionFlags variable (covered later) containing any collisions that occurred during the move. The Move() method does not apply any gravity so you have to calculate and apply that yourself.

TIP

## Controlling Slide

Movement with a character controller can contain some amount of *slide*. That is, the object doesn't stop immediately when a key is pressed. Instead, the object slows down to a halt over time. You can increase or decrease the amount of slide an object has by changing the Gravity property for the input axis in the Input Manager (see Figure 14.3). To open the Input Manager, click **Edit > Project Settings > Input**.

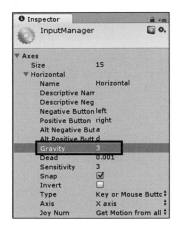

**FIGURE 14.3**
The gravity setting of the Input Manager.

# CollisionFlags

The CollisionFlags variable type is a complex variable that contains information about how collision occurred with a character controller. The variable is a *bitmask*, which means that the data is stored within the binary code itself. All that this means for you is that there is a different way to extract the information you need from it. A CollisionFlags variable can either *be a* value or *contain* a value. The difference is that if the flags are a certain value, all other values are excluded. Conversely, a CollisionFlags variable can contain many different values. This will make more sense with an example.

Suppose you want to determine if a variable is colliding only with an object below it. You write the following

```
if (controller.collisionFlags == CollisionFlags.Below)
    print("This is only colliding with an object below");
```

If the previous is true, you know that the object cannot be colliding in any other direction. If you want to determine if the object is colliding along the bottom, but could also be colliding in another direction, you write the following:

```
if (controller.collisionFlags & CollisionFlags.Below)
    print("This is colliding with an object below. Could be colliding elsewhere.");
```

The difference between the two is that in the first code sample the value was Below and in the second it simply contained Below. Obviously, a CollisionFlags variable can only be equal to None. It cannot contain the value of None and another value. It isn't possible for a collider to not be colliding and still also be colliding in a direction. The CollisionFlags variable type can contain values of None, Sides, Above, or Below. Those are written out like this:

```
CollisionFlags.None
CollisionFlags.Above
CollisionFlags.Sides
CollisionFlags.Below
```

Using these flags, you can determine exactly how an object is colliding with your controller.

## Colliding

The character controller automatically handles collision when moving, but sometimes you want a finer level of control. That is why the controller calls the method OnControllerColliderHit() whenever a collision is detected. Using this method, you can write your own custom collision effects (like pushing an object). To detect collisions, you need to add the following code to your script:

```
void OnControllerColliderHit(ControllerColliderHit hit) {
    //your collision code goes here
}
```

After you have added this method to your code, you can put whatever collision code you want inside. The parameter hit will contain information about the object that collided with the controller. A practical look at this method will be given later this hour.

# Building a Controller

Now that you have learned about the Character Controller component and seen how to work with it, you can begin to build your own controllers. Note that no two controllers are exactly the same. They are designed in such a way that they are easy to custom make to your exact needs. Therefore, the controller presented in this section of the text is not *the* way to make a controller. It is simply *a* way to make a controller.

There are many different controllers that could be presented here in this book. The type you will be making is a controller meant for 2D platformer-style game like *Super Mario Bros.* You can find the complete project and controller script as Hour14_Controller in the book assets for Chapter 14.

## Initial Setup

Before actually diving into the scripting of a custom controller, you want to set up a scene to try out the various aspects. This scene will be simple enough, containing a ground, a single platform, and a character to move around:

1. Create a new project or scene. Add a directional light, two cubes, and a capsule.

2. Because this is a 2D scene, you want to set your camera up correctly. With the camera selected, change the Projection property to **Orthographic** and the Size property to **8** in the Inspector (see Figure 14.4). Change the position of the camera to be (0, 2.4, –10).

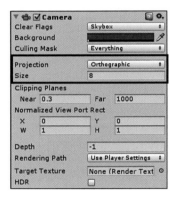

**FIGURE 14.4**
The camera properties.

3. Place one of the cubes at (0, 0, –5) with a scale of (20, .5, 2). This will act as the floor. Place the other cube at (3, 3, –5) with a scale of (3, .5, 1).

4. Place the capsule at (0, 2, –5). Add a character controller to the capsule (click **Component > Physics > Character Controller**). When prompted, go ahead and replace the existing collider with the new one.

5. Add a **Scripts** folder to your scene. Add a script to the folder named **ControllerScript**. Attach the script to your capsule. This will be the object controlled by the character controller. Modify the controller script to contain the following:

```
    CharacterController controller;

void Start () {
    controller = GetComponent<CharacterController>();
}
```

If you run the scene, you will see something similar to Figure 14.5. Now that the scene is set up, you can begin working through the various functionalities.

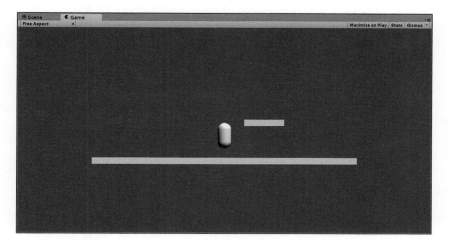

**FIGURE 14.5**
The finished scene.

# Movement

Now that the scene is finished, you want to add the most basic function to your capsule: movement. To move your object, will want to calculate the movement vector and call the Move() method. It is also a good idea (but not required) to store the movement speed you want in a variable so that it is easily changed. Finally, you want to store your movement information is a Vector3. This isn't needed yet, but will be required later when the y axis starts being used:

```
public float speed = 5.0f;
Vector3 movement = Vector3.zero;
void Update () {
    movement.x = Input.GetAxis("Horizontal") * speed;
    controller.Move(movement * Time.deltaTime);
}
```

The preceding code first declares a speed variable that will be used to control how fast the object can move. Next, it declares a Vector3 variable called movement that will be used to store the movement information from frame to frame. Then, inside the Update() method the variable named movement is given a value of the horizontal movement axis (left/right arrows or A/S keys) times the speed. Notice how there is no y or z axis value given. Because this is a 2D controller, there is no z axis movement, and y axis is handled differently. Finally, the Move() method is called, and the movement variable is multiplied by Time.deltaTime. This multiplication is done to make sure that the scene runs exactly the same on any computer regardless of the frame rate.

Run the scene and notice how you can move the capsule back and forth now. You should notice that the capsule is stopped by the platform. You should also notice that the capsule is just floating in the air. There is no gravity applied (yet).

## Gravity

The next thing you want to add to your controller is gravity. There are two ways to handle gravity. You can either use the built-in value for gravity or you can specify your own value. Applying the built-in value for gravity will make everything fall at the same rate. You may, however, want to use your own value if you want a character to fall differently (think of a parachute). You can apply gravity by adding the following code:

```
movement.x = Input.GetAxis("Horizontal") * speed;

if(controller.isGrounded == false)
    movement.y += Physics.gravity.y * Time.deltaTime;

controller.Move(movement * Time.deltaTime);
```

The first and last lines of this code were covered previously. They were left in as a point of reference. Because gravity doesn't always need to be applied, an if statement is used to determine whether the character is not grounded. If it is determined that the character is not currently colliding on the bottom, the y component of the scene's current gravity is applied to the movement vector. This way, when the Move() method is called, the object moves left and right, but it is also affected by gravity.

Run your scene to see this in action. You will notice that the capsule immediately falls and stops when it hits the ground. If you run the capsule off of the side of the platform, you can see it fall out of the scene.

## Jumping

A platformer game wouldn't be much fun if you couldn't jump from platform to platform. Jumping is a little more complex than moving and falling. You need to keep track of how high the character can jump. You also want to make sure that the character can only jump once at a time; otherwise, they would be flying:

```
public float jumpSpeed = 8.0f;

void Update() {
    //movement and gravity code

    if (Input.GetButton("Jump") && controller.isGrounded == true)
        movement.y = jumpSpeed;

    controller.Move(movement * Time.deltaTime);
}
```

Again, more code was given that was already covered. It is placed there simply as a point of reference. The first bit on code declares a new float variable jumpSpeed that dictates how high the character can jump. Then, inside the Update() method, an if statement is used to make sure that the character can jump only if the key is pressed and if the character is currently on the ground.

Run the scene and try it out. See whether you can jump the capsule onto the second platform. Notice how you have control over the capsule while it is in the air. That was a specific design choice and could be changed if need be in future projects.

## Pushing Objects

One final bit of functionality you want to add is the ability to push objects around in your scene. Doing so requires the OnControllerColliderHit() method mentioned earlier. The code for this functionality looks like this:

```
public float pushPower = 2.0f;
void OnControllerColliderHit(ControllerColliderHit hit) {
    Rigidbody body = hit.collider.attachedRigidbody;
    if (body == null || body.isKinematic)
        return;

    if (hit.moveDirection.y < -0.3f)
        return;

    Vector3 pushDir = new Vector3(hit.moveDirection.x, 0f, 0f);
    body.velocity = pushDir * pushPower;
}
```

Be sure to add this code to the class, but outside of any other method. The first line of code creates a variable that determines how hard the controller can push another object. Then, inside the OnControllerColliderHit() method you have your "pushing" code. In the method, you get a reference to the rigidbody of the collided object. If the rigidbody doesn't exist or is kinematic, the method exits. From there, you check the direction of the collision to make sure that you aren't pushing objects below the controller. Once all of that checks out, you calculate the direction of the push and then add the direction, multiplied by the power, to the click object's velocity.

Before trying this out, add a sphere to your scene. Position the sphere at (1.5, 1, –5). Be sure to add a rigidbody component to the sphere as well. Once that is done, run the scene. Notice how the capsule can now move the sphere around. Try pushing the sphere back and forth along the platform.

## Full Code Listing

The full code for the controller script is provided here. Some code has been rearranged from its original listing for the sake of organization:

```
using UnityEngine;
using System.Collections;

public class ControllerScript : MonoBehaviour {

    CharacterController controller;

    Vector3 movement = Vector3.zero;
    public float speed = 5.0f;
    public float jumpSpeed = 8.0f;
    public float pushPower = 2.0f;

    void Start () {
        controller = GetComponent<CharacterController>();
    }

    void Update() {

        movement.x = Input.GetAxis("Horizontal") * speed;

        if(controller.isGrounded == false)
            movement.y += Physics.gravity.y * Time.deltaTime;

        if (Input.GetButton("Jump") && controller.isGrounded == true)
            movement.y = jumpSpeed;

        controller.Move(movement * Time.deltaTime);
    }

    void OnControllerColliderHit(ControllerColliderHit hit) {
        Rigidbody body = hit.collider.attachedRigidbody;
        if (body == null || body.isKinematic)
            return;

        if (hit.moveDirection.y < -0.3f)
            return;
```

```
        Vector3 pushDir = new Vector3(hit.moveDirection.x, 0f, 0f);
        body.velocity = pushDir * pushPower;
    }
}
```

# Summary

In this hour, you learned all about Unity's character controller. You started by examining the basics of the character controller and the component properties. From there, you learned to work with the controller via scripting. You learned about the controller's variables, methods, and collision. Finally, you wrote a custom 2D character controller specifically aimed at a platformer-style game.

# Q&A

**Q. How many character controller types are there?**

**A.** There is only a single character controller component. The number of ways you can use it, however, is nearly limitless. The character controller is made in such a way that it enables you to custom tailor it to any situation.

**Q.** Which is better to use: rigidbodies or character controllers?

**A.** This is an important question. The answer depends on what you hope to achieve. If you are looking to utilize Unity's physics functionality, the rigidbody is the way to go. If you want to custom write more-specific behaviors for your characters, the character controller is paramount.

# Workshop

Take some time to work through the questions here to ensure that you have a firm grasp of the material.

## Quiz

**1.** What shape collider is provided by a character controller?

**2.** Which property determines how far a collider can penetrate a controller before a collision is detected?

**3.** What variable type contains information about the direction collisions are occurring?

**4.** Which method moves a controller while still allowing y axis movement like jumping?

## Answers

1. A capsule collider.

2. The Skin Width property.

3. The CollisionFlags variable type.

4. The Move() method.

# Exercise

This exercise is more of a trial of scripting than anything else. Your challenge is to change the controller script provided for you this hour to contain the following functionality. As always, if you get stuck and need help, you can find the complete project as Hour14_Exercise in the book assets for Hour 14:

▶ Change the controller so that players can change movement direction only while they are grounded. Currently, the player can change direction midair.

▶ Allow players to sprint (move faster) while holding the Shift key.

▶ Allow players to double jump. A double jump is where the player can jump and then jump again (only once) while in the air.

# Game 3: *Captain Blaster*

---

**What You'll Learn in This Hour:**

▶ How to design the game *Captain Blaster*
▶ How to build the *Captain Blaster* world
▶ How to build the *Captain Blaster* entities
▶ How to build the *Captain Blaster* controls
▶ How to further improve *Captain Blaster*

Let's make a game! In this hour, you make a 2D scrolling shooter game titled *Captain Blaster*. You start by designing the various elements of the game. From there, you begin building the scrolling background. Once the idea of motion is established, you begin building the various game entities. After the entities are done, you construct the controls and gamify the project. You finish the chapter by analyzing the game and identifying places for improvement.

---

TIP

**Completed Project**

Be sure to follow along in this hour to build the complete game project. In case you get stuck, you can find a completed copy of the game in the book assets for Hour 15. Take a look at it if you need help or inspiration!

---

# Design

You have already learned what the design elements are in Hour 7, "Game 1: *Amazing Racer*." This time, you get right into them.

# The Concept

As mentioned earlier, *Captain Blaster* is a 2D scrolling shooter style game. The premise is that the player will be flying around a level, destroying meteors and trying to stay alive. The neat thing about 2D scrolling games is that the players themselves don't actually have to move at all. The scrolling background simulates the idea that the player is going forward. This reduces the required player skill and allows you to create more challenges in the form of enemies.

# The Rules

The rules for this game state how to play, but also allude to some of the properties of the objects. The rules for *Captain Blaster* are as follows:

▶ Players play until they are click by a meteor. There is no win condition.

▶ The player can fire bullets to destroy meteors. The player earns 1 point per meteor destroyed.

▶ Players can fire two bullets per second.

▶ The player is bounded by the sides of the screen.

▶ Meteors will come continuously faster until the player loses.

# The Requirements

The requirements for this game are simple, as follows:

▶ A background texture to be outer space.

▶ A ship model and texture.

▶ A meteor model and texture.

▶ A game controller. This will be created in Unity.

▶ A bouncy physics material. This will be created in Unity.

▶ Interactive scripts. These will be written in MonoDevelop.

# The World

Because this game takes place in space, the world will be fairly simple to implement. The idea is that the game will be 2D and tiles will move vertically behind the player to make it seem like the player is moving forward. In actuality, the player will be stationary. Before you get the scrolling in place, though, you need to set your project up. Start with these steps:

1. Create a new project in a folder named **Captain Blaster**. Add a directional light to your scene.

2. Create a **Scenes** folder and save your scene as **Main**.

3. In the Game view, change the aspect ratio to **5:4** (see Figure 15.1).

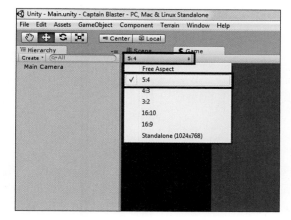

**FIGURE 15.1**
Setting the game aspect ratio.

# The Camera

Now that the scene is set up properly, it is time to work on the camera. In this case, you want an orthographic camera. This camera lacks depth perspective and is great for making 2D games. To set up the Main Camera, follow these steps:

1. Position the camera at (0, 0, –10) with no rotation.

2. Change the Projection property to **Orthographic**.

3. Set the Size property to **6**. (See Figure 15.2 for a list of the camera's properties.)

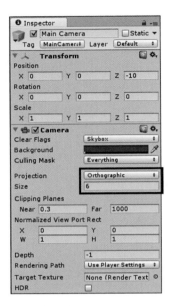

**FIGURE 15.2**
The Main Camera properties.

# The Background

The scrolling background can be a little tricky to get set up correctly. Basically, you have two background objects moving down the screen. As soon as the bottom object goes off screen, you place it above the screen. You keep flipping back and forth between them and the player never knows. To create the scrolling background, follow these steps:

1. Add a cube to the scene. Rename the cube **Background** and place it at (0, 0, 0). Give the cube a scale of (15, 15, .1).

2. Create a new folder named **Textures** in the Project view. Locate the file **Star_Sky.png** in the book assets for Hour 15 and click and drag it into the new Textures folder. From the Project view, drag the **Star_Sky** texture onto the background.

3. Create a new folder named **Scripts** in the Project view. Create a new script in the folder named **BackgroundScript** and drag it onto the background cube. Put the following code in the script:

```
public float speed = -2;

// Use this for initialization
void Start () {
```

```
}

// Update is called once per frame
void Update () {
    transform.Translate(0f, speed * Time.deltaTime, 0f);
    if(transform.position.y <= -15)
    {
        transform.Translate(0f, 30f, 0f);
    }
}
```

4. Duplicate the background cube and place it at (0, 15, 0). Run the scene. You should notice the background seamlessly stream by.

NOTE

**Seamless Scrolling**

You might notice a small line in the previous scrolling background. This is due to the fact that the image used for the background wasn't made specifically to tile together. Generally, this isn't very noticeable, and the actions of the game will more than cover up for it. If you want a more seamless background in the future, however, you want to use an image made to tile together.

# Game Entities

In this game, you need to make three primary entities: the player, the meteor, and the bullet. The interaction between these items is also very simple. The player fires bullets. Bullets destroy meteors. Meteors destroy the player. Because the player can technically fire a large number of bullets, and because a large number of meteors can spawn, you need a way to clean them up. Therefore, you also need to make triggers that destroy bullets and meteors that enter them.

# The Player

Your player will be a spaceship. The models for both the spaceship and the meteors have graciously been provided to you by Duane Mayberry (http://www.duanesmind.co.uk) and can be found in the book assets for Hour 15. To create the player, follow these steps:

1. Create a new folder and call it **Meshes**. In the book assets for Hour 15, locate the folder named **Space Shooter** and drag it into the newly created Meshes folder (to import it).

2. Under the Meshes folder, there should now be a Space Shooter folder. Locate the Space_Shooter.fbx file in there and change the scale factor in the editor to **.09** (see Figure 15.3). Be sure to click **Apply** button at the bottom of the Inspector view.

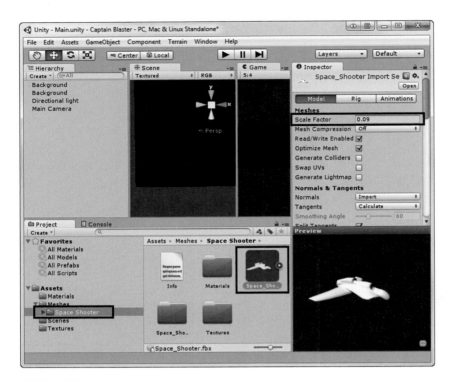

**FIGURE 15.3**
The space shooter model.

3. Click and drag the **Space_Shooter.fbx** from the Project view into the Scene view. Notice that it is facing the wrong way. Give it a position of (0, –4, –5) and a rotation of (270, 0, 0).

4. Locate the Textures folder under the Space Shooter folder and click and drag the **1K_Body-TXTR.jpg** file onto the spaceship model in the Scene view.

5. Add a capsule collider to the spaceship. Put a check in the **Is Trigger** property. Set the radius to **.62**, the height to **1.71**, and the direction to **Z-Axis** (see Figure 15.4).

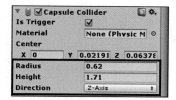

**FIGURE 15.4**
The capsule collider settings.

You should now have a nice, textured, upward-facing spaceship ready to destroy some meteors!

## The Meteors

The steps for the meteors are similar to those of the spaceship. The only difference is that the meteors will end up in a prefab for later use:

1. Locate the folder **Meteor1** and drag it into the Meshes folder you created previously.

2. Locate the Meteor1.fbx file in the new Meteor1 folder and in the Inspector view change the scale factor to **.5**. Be sure to click **Apply** button at the bottom of the Inspector view.

3. Drag the **Meteor1.fbx** file into the Scene view. Position it at (0, 0, –5) and give it a rotation of (0, 0, 0) and a scale of (1, 1, 1). (The mesh is imported with some rotation and scale already applied.)

4. In the Textures folder, locate the file **Meteor1_TXTR.png** and drag it onto the meteor in the scene.

5. Add a rigidbody to the meteor and uncheck the **Use Gravity** property. Add a capsule collider to the meteor as well.

6. Create a new folder named **Prefabs**. Create a new prefab in that folder named **Meteor**. Click and drag the **Meteor1** object from the Hierarchy view onto the newly created prefab. Delete the **Meteor1** object from the scene.

You now have a reusable meteor just waiting to cause havoc.

## The Bullets

Bullets will be simple in this game. Because they will be moving very quickly, they won't need any detail. To create the bullet, follow these steps:

1. Add a capsule to the scene. Position it at (0, 0, 0) with a scale of (.1, .1, .1). Add a rigidbody to the capsule and uncheck the **Use Gravity** property.

2. If you don't already have one, create a Materials folder and create a new material inside named **BulletMaterial**. Give the material a bright green color. Apply the material to the bullet.

3. Create a new prefab named **Bullet**. Click and drag the capsule onto the bullet prefab. Now delete the capsule from the scene.

That's the last of the primary entities. The only thing left to make is the triggers that will prevent the bullets and meteor from traveling forever.

## The Triggers

The triggers are simply two cubes that will sit above and below the screen. Their job is to catch any errant bullets and meteors:

1. Add a cube to the scene and name it **Trigger**. Position it at (0, –9, –5) and give it a scale of (15, 1, 1).

2. In the Inspector view, be sure to put a check in the **Is Trigger** property of the Box Collider component.

3. Duplicate the trigger and place the new one at (0, 9, –5).

Now all of your entities are in place and it is time to begin turning this scene into a game.

# Controls

Various script components need to be assembled to make this game work. The player needs to be able to move the ship and shoot bullets. The bullets and meteors need to be able to move automatically. A meteor spawn object will keep the meteors flowing. The triggers will need to be able to clean up objects, and a control will need to keep track of all the action.

## The Game Control

The game control is basic in this game, so you add that first. Create an empty game object and name it **GameControl**. Create a new script called **GameControlScript** and attach it to the game control object. Overwrite the contents of the script with the following code:

```
using UnityEngine;
using System.Collections;

public class GameControlScript : MonoBehaviour {
```

```
    //is the game still going?
    bool isRunning = true;
    int playerScore = 0;

    void Start () {}
    void Update () {}

    public void AddScore()
    {
        playerScore++;
    }

    public void PlayerDied()
    {
        isRunning = false;
    }

    void OnGUI()
    {
        if(isRunning == true)
        {
            GUI.Label(new Rect(5, 5, 100, 30), "Player Score: " + playerScore);
        }
        else
        {
            GUI.Label(new Rect(Screen.width / 2 - 100, Screen.height / 2 - 50, 200,
➥100), "Game Over. Your score was: " + playerScore);
        }
    }
}
```

In this code, you can see that the control is responsible for drawing the GUI, keeping the score, and knowing when the game is running. The control has two public functions: PlayerDied() and AddScore(). PlayerDied() is called by the player when a meteor hits it. AddScore() is called by a bullet when it kills a meteor. Finally, the GUI is drawn depending on the game state.

# The Meteor Script

Meteors are basically going to fall from the top of the screen and get in the player's way. Create a new script and call it **MeteorScript**. In the Prefabs folder, select the **Meteor** prefab. In the Inspector view, locate the Add Component button (see Figure 15.5). Click **Add Component > Scripts > Meteor Script**.

**FIGURE 15.5**
The Add Component button.

Overwrite the code in the meteor script with the following:

```
using UnityEngine;
using System.Collections;

public class MeteorScript : MonoBehaviour {

    float speed = -5f;

    //random rotation
    float rotation;

    void Start () {
        rotation = Random.Range(-40, 40);
    }

    void Update () {
        transform.Translate(0f, speed * Time.deltaTime, 0f);
        transform.Rotate(0f, rotation * Time.deltaTime, 0f);
    }
}
```

The meteor is very basic. It has variables for both its speed and rotation. The rotation exists just to make each meteor look a little different from each other. In the Start() method, the rotation is randomly determined to be a number between –40 and 40. In the Update() method, the meteor is moved down the screen and then rotated around the y axis based on the rotation variable. Notice that the meteor is not responsible for determining collision.

## The Meteor Spawn

So far, the meteors are just prefabs with no way of getting into the scene. What you need is an object responsible for spawning the meteors at an interval. Create a new empty game object. Rename the game object **MeteorSpawn** and place it at (0, 7, –5). Create a new script named **MeteorSpawnScript** and place it on the meteor spawn object. Overwrite the code in the script with the following:

```
using UnityEngine;
using System.Collections;

public class MeteorSpawnScript : MonoBehaviour {

    //meteor spawning timers
    float spawnThreshold = 100;
    float spawnDecrement = .1f;

    //meteor prefab
    public GameObject meteor;

    void Start () {}

    void Update () {

        //randomly determine if meteor spawns
        if(Random.Range(0, spawnThreshold) <= 1)
        {
            //create a meteor at a random x position
            Vector3 pos = transform.position;
            Instantiate(meteor, new Vector3(pos.x + Random.Range(-6, 6), pos.y,
➥pos.z), Quaternion.identity);

            spawnThreshold -= spawnDecrement;
            if(spawnThreshold < 2)
            {
                spawnThreshold = 2;
            }
        }
    }
}
```

This script is doing a few interesting things. The first thing is that it is creating two variables to manage the meteor timing. It also declares a GameObject variable, which will be the meteor prefab. In the Update() method, the script generates a random number between 0 and the spawn-Threshold variable (100 for starters). If the random number is equal to or less than 1, a meteor is spawned. You can see that the meteor is spawned at the same y and z coordinate as the spawn point, but the x coordinate is offset by a number between –6 and 6. This is to allow the meteors to spawn across the screen and not always in the same spot. Finally, the spawnThreshold is reduced by the spawnDecrement. If the spawnThreshold ever gets below 2, it is set to 2 instead. Effectively, this bit of code makes the meteors spawn faster and faster over time. Because the total range becomes reduced, the likelihood of randomly getting a number that is 1 or below goes up. So, the meteors will spawn more rapidly.

In the Unity editor, click and drag the **Meteor** prefab from the Project view onto the Meteor property of the Meteor Spawn Script component of the meteor spawn object. (Try saying that fast!) Run the scene and you should notice meteors spawning across the screen; they come slowly at first.

## The Trigger Script

Now that you have meteors spawning everywhere, it is a good idea to begin cleaning them up. Create a new script called **TriggerScript** and attach it to both the upper and lower trigger objects you created previously. Add the following code to the script. Ensure that the code is outside of a method but inside of the class:

```
void OnTriggerEnter(Collider other)
{
    Destroy(other.gameObject);
}
```

This basic script simply destroys any object that enters it. Because the player cannot move vertically, you don't need to worry about them getting destroyed. Only bullets and meteors can enter the trigger.

## The Player Script

Right now, meteors are falling down and the player can't get out of the way. You need to create a script to control the player next. Create a new script called **PlayerScript** and attach it to the spaceship. Replace the code in the script with the following:

```
using UnityEngine;
using System.Collections;

public class PlayerScript : MonoBehaviour {

    //player speed
    public float speed = 10f;
```

```
    //bullet prefab
    public GameObject bullet;

    //Control Script
    public GameControlScript control;

    //player can fire a bullet every half second
    public float bulletThreshold = .5f;
    float elapsedTime = 0;

    void Start () {}

    void Update () {
        //keeping track of time for bullet firing
        elapsedTime += Time.deltaTime;

        //move the player sideways
        transform.Translate(Input.GetAxis("Horizontal") * speed * Time.deltaTime,
➥0f, 0f);

        //spacebar fires. The current setup calls this "Jump"
        //this was left to avoid confusion
        if(Input.GetButtonDown("Jump"))
        {
            //see if enough time has passed to fire a new bullet
            if(elapsedTime > bulletThreshold)
            {
                //fire bullet at current position
                //be sure the bullet is created in front of the player
                //so they don't collide
                Instantiate(bullet, new Vector3(transform.position.x, transform.
➥position.y + 1.2f, -5f), Quaternion.identity);

                //reset bullet firing timer
                elapsedTime = 0f;
            }
        }

    }

    //if a meteor hits the player
    void OnTriggerEnter(Collider other)
    {
        Destroy(other.gameObject);
        control.PlayerDied();
        Destroy(this.gameObject);
    }
}
```

A lot of work is done in this script. It starts by creating variables for the speed, the bullet prefabs, the control script, and bullet timing.

In the Update() method, the script starts by getting the current time. This is used to determine whether enough time has passed to fire a bullet. If you remember the rules, the player can only fire a bullet every half second. The player is then moved along the x axis based on input. After that, the script determines if the player is pressing the spacebar. Normally in Unity, the spacebar is considered a jump action. This could be named in the Input Manager, but it was left as it is to avoid any confusion. If it is determined that the player is pressing the spacebar, the script checks the elapsed time against the bulletThreshold (currently half a second). If the time is greater, the script creates a bullet. Notice that the script creates the bullet just a little above the ship. This is to prevent the bullet from colliding with the ship. Finally, the elapsed time is reset to 0 so the count for the next bullet firing can start.

The last part of the script contains the OnTriggerEnter() method. This gets called whenever a meteor hits the player. When that happens, the meteor is destroyed, the control script is informed that the player died, and then the player is destroyed.

Back in the Unity editor, click and drag the bullet prefab onto the Bullet property of the player script. Likewise, click and drag the game control object onto the player script to give it access to the control script (see Figure 15.6). Run the scene and notice how you can now move the player. The player should be able to fire bullets (although they don't move). Also notice that the player can now die and end the game.

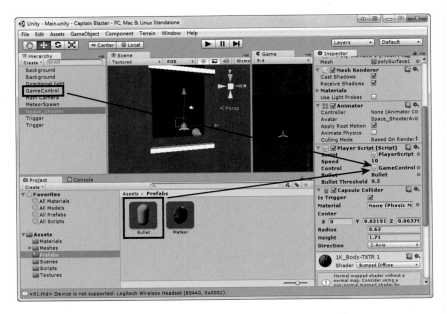

**FIGURE 15.6**
Connecting the player script.

# The Bullet Script

The last bit of interactivity you need is to make the bullets move and collide. Create a new script called **BulletScript** and add it to the bullet prefab. Replace the code in the script with the following:

```
using UnityEngine;
using System.Collections;

public class BulletScript : MonoBehaviour {

    float speed = 10f;

    //Game Control Script
    GameControlScript control;

    void Start () {
        //Because this is instantiated, we must find
        //the game control at run time
        control = GameObject.Find("GameControl").GetComponent<GameControlScript>();
    }

    void Update () {
        //move upward
        transform.Translate(0f, speed * Time.deltaTime, 0f);
    }

    //neither bullet nor meteor is a trigger, so we need
    //to use a different collision method here
    void OnCollisionEnter(Collision other)
    {
        Destroy(other.gameObject);
        control.AddScore();
        Destroy(this.gameObject);
    }
}
```

The major difference between this script and the meteor is that this script needs to account for collision and the player scoring. The script declares a variable to hold the control script, just like the player. Because the bullet isn't actually in the Scene view, however, it needs to get access to the control script a little differently. In the Start() method, the script searches for the GameControl object and then calls the GetComponent() method to find the script attached to it. The control script is then stored in the variable control.

Because neither the bullet nor the meteor has a trigger collider on it, the use of the OnTriggerEnter() method will not work. Instead, the script uses the method OnCollisionEnter(). This method does not read in a Collider variable. Instead, it reads in a Collision variable. The differences between these two methods are irrelevant in this case. The only work being done is destroying both objects and telling the control script that the player scored.

Go ahead and run the game. You notice that the game is now fully playable. Although you cannot win (that is intentional), you certainly can lose. Keep playing and see how high of a score you can get!

# Improvements

It is time to improve the game. Like the previous games, there are several places left intentionally basic. Be sure to play through the game several times and see what you notice. What things are fun? What things are not fun? Are there any obvious ways to break the game? Note that a very easy cheat has been left in the game to allow players to get a high score. Can you find it?

Here are some things you could consider changing:

▶ Try modifying the bullet speeds, firing delay, or bullet flight path.

▶ Try allowing the player to fire two bullets side by side.

▶ Try adding a different type of meteor.

▶ Give the player extra health; maybe even a shield.

▶ Allow the player to move vertically as well as horizontally.

This is a common genre, and there are many ways you can make it unique. Try to see just how custom you can make the game. It is also worth noting that as you learn about particle systems later in this book, this game is a prime candidate for trying them out.

# Summary

In this hour, you made the game *Captain Blaster*. You started by designing the game elements. From there, you built the game world. You constructed and animated a vertically scrolling background. From there, you built the various game entities. You added interactivity through scripting and controls. Finally, you examined the game and looked for improvements.

# Q&A

**Q. Are the meteors supposed to spawn this slow?**

**A.** The game causes meteor spawn rate to grow slowly over time. If they are spawning too slowly for you, feel free to reduce the threshold.

**Q.** **Did Captain Blaster really achieve the military rank of captain or is it just a name?**

**A.** It's hard to say, as it is all mostly speculation. One thing is for certain, they don't just give spaceships to lieutenants!

**Q.** **Why delay bullet firing by half a second?**

**A.** Mostly it is a balance issue. If the player can fire too fast, the game has no challenge.

**Q.** **Why use a capsule collider on the ship?**

**A.** Efficient and accurate collision detection can be difficult. A larger collider would have covered the wings and made for more accurate detection. Such a collider, however, would allow "false positives" when meteors were beside the cockpit. In this way, it is a tradeoff. The best way would be to use multiple colliders to maximum accuracy. This method was avoided to keep things simple.

# Workshop

Take some time to work through the questions here to ensure that you have a firm grasp of the material.

## Quiz

1. What is the win condition for the game?

2. How does the scrolling background work?

3. Which objects had rigidbodies? Which objects had colliders?

4. True or False: The meteor is responsible for detecting collision with the player.

5. What is the simple way for players to cheat the game?

## Answers

1. Trick question. The player cannot win the game. The highest score, however, allows the player to "win" outside of the game.

2. Two cubes with the same texture are stacked on top of each other. They then "leap frog" across the camera to seem endless.

3. The bullets and meteors had rigidbodies. The bullets, meteors, player, and triggers had colliders.

4. False.

5. That is still up to you to find out. This is just here to remind you to look if you haven't already.

# Exercise

This exercise will be a little strange compared to the ones you have done so far. A common part of the game refinement process is to have the game play tested by people who aren't involved with the development process. This allows people who are completely unfamiliar with the game to give honest, first-experience feedback. This is incredibly useful. The exercise is to have other people play the game. Try to get a good diverse group of people. Try to get some avid gamers and some people who don't play games. Try to get some people who are fans of this genre and some people who aren't. Compile their feedback into groupings of good features, bad features, and things that can be improved. In addition, try to see whether there are any commonly requested features that currently aren't in the game. As a last part, see if you can implement or improve your game based on the feedback received.

# Particle Systems

▶ The basics of particle systems

▶ How to work with modules

▶ How to use the curve editor

In this hour, you learn how to use Unity's particle system. You start by learning all about particle systems in general and how they work. You focus on Unity's new Shuriken particle system. From there, you experiment with the many different particle system modules. You wrap the hour up by experimenting with the Unity curve editor.

# Particle Systems

A particle system is basically an object or component that emits other objects, commonly referred to as *particles*. These particles can be fast, slow, flat, shaped, small, or large. The definition is very generic because these systems can achieve a great variety of effects with the proper settings. They can make jets of fire, plumes of billowing smoke, fireflies, rain, fog, or anything else you can think of. These effects are commonly referred to as *particle effects*.

## Particles

A particle is a single entity that is emitted by a particle system. Because many particles are generally emitted quickly, it is important for particles to be as efficient as possible. This is the reason that most particles are 2D billboards. Remember that a billboard is a flat image that always faces the camera. This gives them the effect that they are three dimensional.

## Unity Particle Systems

As of update 3.5, Unity uses a new particle engine called the *Shuriken* particle system. Any systems you create will be using this new particle engine; however, particle systems created before update 3.5 will still work. Later this hour, you actually get a chance to try out some of the legacy particle systems that come as part of Unity.

To create a particle system in a scene, you can either add a particle system object or add a particle system component to an existing object. To add a particle system object, click **GameObject > Create Other > Particle System**. To add a particle system component to an existing object, select the object and click **Component > Effects > Particle System**.

▼ TRY IT YOURSELF

## Creating a Particle System

In this exercise, you create a particle system object in your scene:

1. Create a new project or scene.

2. Add a particle system by clicking **GameObject > Create Other > Particle System**.

3. Notice how the particle system is emitting white particles in the Scene view (see Figure 16.1). This is the basic particle system. Try rotating and scaling the particle system to see how it reacts.

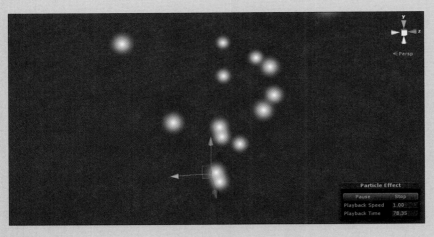

**FIGURE 16.1**
The basic particle system.

NOTE

## Custom Particles

By default, the particles in Unity are small white spheres that fade into transparency. This is a really useful generic particle, but it can only take you so far. Sometimes, you want something more specific though (to make fire, for example). If you want, you can make your own particles out of any 2D image to make effects to exactly suit your needs.

## Particle System Controls

You might have noticed that when you added a particle system to your scene it began emitting particles in the Scene view. You may have also noticed the particle effect controls that appeared (see Figure 16.2). These controls allow you to pause, stop, and restart the particle animation in a scene. This can be very helpful when tweaking the behavioral components of a particle system.

**FIGURE 16.2**
The particle effects control.

The control also allows you to speed up the play back and also tells you how long the effect has been playing. This can prove very useful when testing duration effects.

NOTE

### Particle Effects

To create complex and visually appealing effects, you want several particle systems to work together (a smoke and a fire system, for example). When multiple particle systems are working together, it is called a *particle effect*. In Unity, creating a particle effect is achieved by nesting particle systems together. One particle system can be the child of another, or they can both be children of a different object. The result of a particle effect in Unity is that they are treated as one system and that the particle effect controls will control the entire effect as one unit.

# Particle System Modules

At its root, a particle system is just a point in space that emits particle objects. How the particles look, behave, and the effects they cause are all determined by modules. Modules are various properties that define some form of behavior. In Unity's new Shuriken system, modules are an integrated and essential component. This section is going to list each module and explain briefly what it does. Note that with the exception of the default module (covered first) all modules can be turned on and off. To turn modules on or off, put a check mark by the module's name. To hide or show modules, click the plus sign (+) next to the Particle System modules (see Figure 16.3). By default, all modules are visible and only the Emission, Shape, and Renderer modules are enabled. To expand a module, simply click its title.

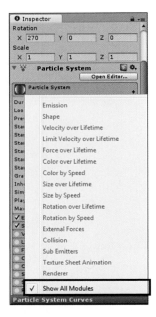

**FIGURE 16.3**
Showing all modules.

NOTE

## Brief Overview

Several modules have properties that are either self-explanatory (like the length and width property of a rectangle) or have been covered previously. For the sake of simplicity (and to prevent this hour from being 30 pages) these will be omitted. If you see more properties on your screen than are covered in this text, don't worry. That is intentional.

NOTE

## Constant, Curve, Random

The new Shuriken system has introduced the concept of value curves. A curve allows you to change the value of a property over the lifetime of a particle system. You know which properties can use curves by the downward-facing arrow next to the value. The options you are given are Constant, Curve, Random Between Two Constants, and Random Between Two Curves. For the sake of this section, all values are treated as constant. Later this hour, you get a chance to explore the curve editor in detail.

# Default Module

The default module is simply labeled Particle System. This module contains all the specific information that every particle system requires. Table 16.1 describes the properties of the default module.

**TABLE 16.1**   Default Module Properties

| Property | Description |
|---|---|
| Duration | How long, in seconds, the particle system runs. |
| Looping | Determines if the particle system starts over once the duration has been reached. |
| Prewarm | If this is selected, the particle system starts as if it had already emitted particles from a previous cycle. |
| Start Delay | How long, in seconds, the system will wait before emitting particles. |
| Start Lifetime | How long, in seconds, each particle will live. |
| Start Speed | The initial speed of particles. |
| Start Rotation | The initial rotation of particles. |
| Start Color | The color of emitted particles. |
| Gravity Modifier | How much of the world's gravity is applied to the particles. |
| Inherit Velocity | How much of the system's velocity (if any) is imparted on the particles. |
| Simulation Space | Determines if the particles are simulated in local or world space. |
| Play On Wake | Determines whether the particle system begins emitting particles immediately when created. |
| Max Particles | The total number of particles that can exist for a system at a time. If this number is reached, the system ceases emitting until some particles die. |

# Emission Module

The Emission module is used to determine the rate in which particles are emitted. Using this module, you can dictate whether particles stream at a constant rate, in bursts, or somewhere in between. Table 16.2 describes the Emission module properties.

**TABLE 16.2**   Emission Module Properties

| Property | Description |
|---|---|
| Rate | Number of particles emitted over time or distance. |
| Bursts | If the time option for rate is chosen, this is used to dictate the number of bursts. Create a burst by clicking the plus sign (+) and remove a burst by clicking the minus sign (−) (see Figure 16.4). |

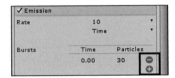

**FIGURE 16.4**
The Emission module.

# Shape Module

Just as its name would imply, the Shape module determines the shape formed by the emitted particles. The shape options are Sphere, Hemisphere, Cone, Box, and Mesh. In addition, each shape has a set of properties used to define it. These properties are things like radius for cones and spheres. There are fairly self-explanatory and are not covered here.

# Velocity over Lifetime Module

The Velocity over Lifetime module directly animates each particle by applying an x, y, and z axis velocity to it. Note that this is a velocity change of each particle over the lifetime of the particle, not over the lifetime of the particle system. Table 16.3 describes the properties of the Velocity over Lifetime module.

**TABLE 16.3**   Velocity over Lifetime Module Properties

| Property | Description |
|---|---|
| XYZ | The velocity applied to each particle. This can be a constant, curve, or random number between a constant or curve. |
| Space | Dictates whether the velocity is added based on local or world space. |

# Limit Velocity over Lifetime Module

This long-named module can be used to dampen or clamp the velocity of a particle. Basically, it prevents, or slows down, particles that exceed a threshold speed on one or all of the axes. Table 16.4 describes the properties for the Limit Velocity over Lifetime module.

**TABLE 16.4**  Limit Velocity over Lifetime Module Properties

| Property | Description |
| --- | --- |
| Separate Axis | If unchecked, this property uses the same value for each axis. If checked, speed properties for each axis appear as well as a property for local or world space. |
| Speed | The threshold speed for each or all axes. |
| Dampen | The value, between 0 and 1, that a particle will be slowed by if it exceeds the threshold determined by the speed property. A value of 0 will not slow a particle at all, but a value of 1 will slow the particle 100%. |

# Force over Lifetime Module

The Force over Lifetime module is similar to the Velocity over Lifetime module. The difference is that this module applies a force, not a velocity, to each particle. This module also allows you to randomize the force each frame, as opposed to all upfront.

# Color over Lifetime Module

The Color over Lifetime module allows you to change the color of the particle as time passes. This is useful for creating effects like sparks, which start our bright orange and end a dark red before disappearing. To use this module you must specify a gradient of color. You can also specify two gradients and have Unity randomly pick a color between them. Gradients can be edited using Unity's gradient editor (see Figure 16.5).

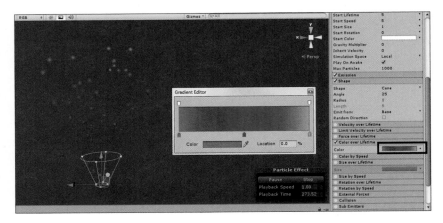

**FIGURE 16.5**
The gradient editor.

Note that the color of the gradient will be multiplied by the Start Color property of the default module. This means that if your start color is black, this module will have no effect.

## Color by Speed Module

The Color by Speed module allows you to change the color of a particle based on its speed. Table 16.5 describes the properties of the Color by Speed module.

**TABLE 16.5  Color by Speed Module Properties**

| Property | Description |
| --- | --- |
| Color | A gradient (or two gradients for random colors) that is used to dictate the color of the particle. |
| Speed Range | The minimum and maximum speed values that are mapped to the color gradient. Particles going the min speed are mapped to the left side of the gradient, and colors at the max speed (or beyond) are mapped to the right side of the gradient. |

## Size over Lifetime Module

The Size over Lifetime module allows you to specify a change in the size of a particle. The size value must be a curve and will dictate whether the particle grows or shrinks as time elapses.

# Size by Speed Module

Much like the Color by Speed module, the Size by Speed module changes the size of a particle based on its speed between a minimum and maximum value.

# Rotation over Lifetime Module

The Rotation over Lifetime module allows you to specify a rotation over the life of a particle. Note that the rotation is of the particle itself, and not a curve in the world coordinate system. What this means is that if your particle is a plain circle, you will not be able to see the rotation. If the particle has some detail, however, you will notice it spin. The values for the rotation can be given as a constant, curve, or random number.

# Rotation by Speed Module

The Rotation by Speed module is the same as the Rotation Over Lifetime module except that it changes values based on the speed of the particle. Rotation will change based on a min and max speed value.

# External Forces Module

The External Forces module allows you to apply a multiplier to any forces that exist outside of the particle system. A good example of this is any wind forces that may exist in a scene. The Multiplier property scales the forces either up or down depending on its value.

# Collision Module

The Collision module allows you to set up collisions for particles. This is useful for all sorts of collision effects, like fire rolling off a wall or rain hitting the ground. You can set the collision to work with predetermined planes (Plane mode: most efficient), or with objects in the scene (World mode: slows performance). The Collision module has some common properties and some unique properties depending on the collision type chosen. Table 16.6 describes the common properties of the Collision module. Tables 16.7 and 16.8 describes the properties that belong to Planes mode and World mode, respectively:

**TABLE 16.6    Common Collision Module Properties**

| Property | Description |
| --- | --- |
| Planes / World | Dictates the type of collision used. Planes mode will collide off of predetermined planes. World mode will collide off of any object in a scene. |
| Dampen | Determines the amount a particle is slowed when it collides. Values range from 0 to 1. |

| Property | Description |
| --- | --- |
| Bounce | Determines what fraction of the component of velocity is kept. Unlike dampen, this only affects the axes the particle bounces on. Values range between 0 and 1. |
| Lifetime Loss | Determines how much life of a particle is lost on collision. Values range from 0 to 1. |
| Min Kill Speed | The minimum speed of a particle before it is killed by collision. |
| Send Collision Messages | Determines whether collision messages are sent to objects that collider with particles. |

**TABLE 16.7**  Plane Mode Properties

| Property | Description |
| --- | --- |
| Planes | A collection of transforms used to determine where the particles can collide. The y axis of the transforms provided determines the rotation of the plane. |
| Visualization | Used to determine how the planes are drawn in the Scene view. They can either be solid or grid. |
| Scale Plane | Resizes the visualization of the planes. |
| Particle Radius | Can be used to make the particles seem bigger or smaller for collision purposes. |

**TABLE 16.8**  World Mode Properties

| Property | Description |
| --- | --- |
| Collides With | Determines which layers the particles collide with. This is set to Everything by default. |
| Collision Quality | The quality of the world collision. The values are High, Medium, and Low. Obviously, High is the most CPU intensive and most accurate, and Low is the least. |
| Voxel Size | This property is more advanced and is used to determine the density of the Voxels used in medium and low-quality settings. Basically, leave this value as is unless you know what you are doing. |

## Making Particles Collide

In this exercise, you set up collision with a particle system. This exercise uses both Planes and World collision modes:

1. Create a new project or scene. Add a particle system to the scene and place it at (0, 0, 0).

2. In the Inspector, enable the Collision module by clicking the circle next to its name. Click the small plus sign (+) next to the Planes property and a plane should appear (see Figure 16.6). You might need to change your visualization to **Grid** to make it match the one in Figure 16.6. Notice how the particles are already bouncing off of the plane. Move and rotate the plane around and see how it affects the particles.

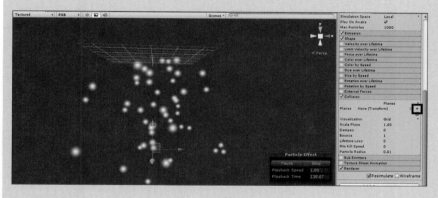

**FIGURE 16.6**
Adding a plane transform.

3. Add a cube to the scene. Position the cube at (0, 4, 0) and give it a scale of (5, 1, 5).

4. Notice how the particles move right through the cube. Set the Collision module to World mode (see Figure 16.7) and notice how the particles now begin to bounce off of the cube. Continue experimenting with the different properties of the module and see how they affect the particles.

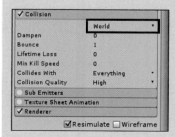

**FIGURE 16.7**
Changing collision type to World mode.

# Sub Emitter Module

The Sub Emitter module is an incredibly powerful module that enables you to spawn a new particle system at certain events for each particle of the current system. You can create a new particle system every time a particle is created, dies, or collides. This can be used to generate complex and intricate effects (like fireworks). This module has three properties: Birth, Death, and Collision. Each of these properties holds zero or more particle systems to be created on the respective events.

# Texture Sheet Module

The Texture Sheet module allows you to change the texture coordinates used for a particle over the life of the particle. In essence, this means that you can put several textures for a particle in a single image and then switch between them during the life of a particle. Table 16.9 describes the properties of the Texture Sheet module.

**TABLE 16.9**  Texture Module Properties

| Property | Description |
| --- | --- |
| Tiles | Determines the tiling of the texture. |
| Animation | Determines if the whole image contains textures for the particle or if only a single row does. |
| Cycles | Specifies the speed of the animation. |

# Renderer Module

The Renderer module dictates how the particles are actually drawn. It is here that you can specify the texture used for the particles and their other drawing properties. Table 16.10 describes the properties of the Renderer module.

**TABLE 16.10**  Renderer Module Properties

| Property | Description |
| --- | --- |
| Render Mode | Determines how the particles are actually drawn. The modes are Billboard, Stretched Billboard, Horizontal Billboard, Vertical Billboard, or Mesh. All the billboard modes cause the particles to align with either the camera or two out of three axes. The mesh mode causes the particles to be drawn in 3D as determined by a mesh. |
| Normal Direction | Dictates how much the particle faces the camera. A value of 1 causes the particles to look directly at the camera. |

| Property | Description |
|----------|-------------|
| Material | The material used to draw the particle. |
| Sort Order | The order that particles are drawn. Can be None, By Distance, Youngest First, or Oldest First. |
| Sorting Fudge | Determines the order that the particle system is drawn. The lower the value, the more likely the system is to be drawn on top of other objects and particles. |
| Cast Shadows | Determines if particles cast shadows. |
| Receive Shadows | Determines if particles receive shadows. |
| Max Particle Size | Set max relative size. Values range between 0 and 1. |

# The Curve Editor

Several values in the various modules listed previously had the option to be set as Constant or Curve. The Constant option is fairly self-explanatory. You give it a value, and it is that value. What if you want that value to change over a period of time, though? That is where the new curve system comes in very handy. Using this feature, you have a very fine level of control over how a value behaves. You can see the curve editor at the bottom of the Inspector view (see Figure 16.8).

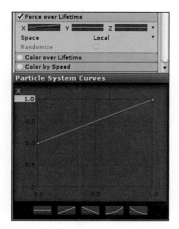

**FIGURE 16.8**
The curve editor.

The title of the curve is whatever value you are determining. In Figure 16.8, the value is for the force applied along the x axis in the Force over Lifetime module. The range dictates the minimum and maximum values available. This can be changed to allow for a greater (or lesser) range. The curve is the values themselves over a given course of time and the presets are generic shapes that you can give to the curve.

The curve is moveable at any of the key points. These key points are show as visible points along the curve. By default, there are only two key points: one at the beginning and one at the end. You can add a new key point anywhere on the curve by right-clicking it and choosing **Add Key Point**.

▼ TRY IT YOURSELF

### Using the Curve Editor

Let's get familiar with the curve editor. In this exercise, you change the size of the particles emitted over the duration of one cycle of the particle system:

1.  Create a new project or scene. Add a particle system and position it at (0, 0, 0).

2.  Click the drop-down arrow next to the Start Size property and chose **Curve**.

3.  Change the range of the curve from 1 to **2**. Right-click the curve at about the midpoint and add a key. Do the same for the end of the curve. Now drag the midpoint to the top of the curve editor, which will give it a value of 2 (see Figure 16.9). Notice how the particles emitted change in size over the 5-second cycle of the particle system.

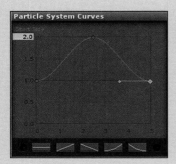

**FIGURE 16.9**
Start Size curve settings.

# Summary

In this hour, you were introduced to particle systems in Unity. You learned the basics of particles and particle systems. You then went on a lengthy review of the many modules that make up the Unity particle system. You wrapped the hour up by looking at the functionality of the curve editor.

# Q&A

**Q. Are particle systems inefficient?**

**A.** They can be. It depends on the settings you give them. A good rule of thumb is to only use a particle system if it provides some value to you. They can be great visually, but don't overdo it.

# Workshop

Take some time to work through the questions here to ensure that you have a firm grasp of the material.

## Quiz

1. What is the term for a 2D image that always faces the camera?

2. What is the name of Unity's new particle system?

3. Which module controls how a particle is drawn?

4. True or False: The curve editor is used for creating curves that change values over time.

## Answers

1. A billboard.

2. The Shuriken particle system.

3. The Renderer module.

4. True.

# Exercise

In this exercise, you experiment with some existing particle effects and attempt to create your own. First, note that the particle effects that are included with Unity were made using the older system. This means that they will not have the same modules or settings. This is completely fine and is useful for comparing how the old system works in relation to the new system. Because this exercise is both a chance to play around with existing effects and to create your own, there is no correct "solution" for you to look at. Just follow the steps here and use your imagination:

1. Import the particle effects package by clicking **Assets > Import Package > Particles**. Be sure to leave all assets checked and click **Import**.

2. Locate the Fire folder, which is located under the newly created Standard Assets and Particles folders. Click and drag the Fire and Flame prefabs into the scene. Experiment with positioning and settings of these effects.

3. Continue experimenting with the rest of the provided particle effects. (Be sure to check out the Dust and Water effects.)

4. Now that you have seen what it possible, see what you can create yourself. Try out the various modules and try to come up with your own custom effects.

# HOUR 17
# Animations

**What You'll Learn in This Hour:**

▶ The requirements for animation
▶ How to prepare a model for animation
▶ How to apply animations
▶ How to trigger animations via scripts

In this hour, you learn about animations in Unity. You start by learning exactly what animations are and what is required for them to work. After that, you look at an actual model and see how to get it ready for animations. From there, you learn about the anatomy of an animation and apply it to a model. You wrap the hour up by learning to trigger animations through scripts.

NOTE

## Animation Systems

In Unity, two systems can be used for animation. In this hour, you review the legacy animation system. You will be controlling your characters on a very granular level. Don't worry, though; in the next hour, you will be looking at the new Mecanim animation system and get to play with the new and powerful Animator controller.

# Animation Basics

Animations are premade sets of visual motions. In a 2D game, this involves having several sequential images that can be flipped through very quickly. The result is that the object appears to be moving. This effect is similar to an old-fashioned flip book. Animation in a 3D world is much different. In 3D games, you use models to represent your game entities. You cannot simply switch between models to give the illusion of motion. Instead, you have to actually move the parts of the model. Doing so requires both a rig and an animation.

## The Rig

Animating a model without a rig is impossible (or impossibly difficult). The reason is that without a rig, the computer has no way of knowing which parts of a model are supposed to move and how they are supposed to move. So, what exactly is a rig? Much like a human skeleton (see Figure 17.1), the rig dictates the parts of a model that are rigid, which are often called *bones*. It also dictates which parts can bend. These bendable parts are called *joints*.

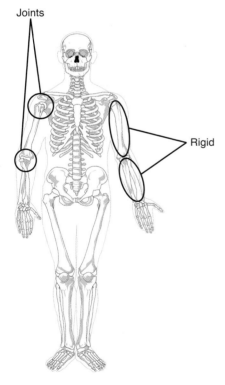

**FIGURE 17.1**
The skeleton as a rig.

The bones and joints work together to define a physical structure for a model. It is this structure that will be used to actually animate the model.

## The Animation

Once a model has a rig, it can be given an animation. On the technical level, an animation is just a series of instructions for the rig. (Put the right hand in, pull the right hand out, now put the right hand in and shake it all about....) These instructions can be played just like a movie. They can even be paused, stepped through, or reversed. Furthermore, with a proper rig, changing the action of a model is as simple as changing the animation. Sometimes these animations can event come with instructions that move the entire model in 3D space. The best part of all is that if you have two completely different models that have the same rigging you can apply the same animations to each of them identically. Thus, an orc, a human, a giant, and a werewolf can all perform the exact same dance animation.

---

NOTE
_____

### 3D Artists Wanted

The truth about animation is that most of the work is done outside of programs like Unity. Generally speaking, the modeling, texturing, rigging, and animations are all created by professionals known as 3D artists in programs such as Blender, Maya, 3D Studio Max, or any other 3D creation software. Creating these assets requires a significant amount of skill and practice. Therefore, their creation is not covered in this text. Instead, this book shows you how to take already made assets and put them together in Unity to build interactive experiences. Remember that there is more to making a game than simply putting pieces together. You may make a game work, but artists make it look good!

_____

# Preparing a Model for Animation

There isn't much that needs to be done to properly prepare a model for animation. Hopefully, the process of rigging the model has already been completed. If it hasn't, it will need to be done before importing into Unity. In this section, you begin working with a model that has already been rigged, and you acquire animations specifically made for the model. In a real production environment, either you or some other 3D artist has to develop these items before they can be used in Unity.

In this section, you acquire a model from the Unity Asset Store. This model comes with a lot of different items, and you will go through each piece to ensure that it is configured properly. To access the Unity Asset Store, click **Window > Asset Store**. You may be asked to log in. If so, just use the login that you created in Hour 1, "Introduction to Unity." Once the Asset Store is loaded, locate the search window and search for Warrior (see Figure 17.2).

**FIGURE 17.2**
The Asset Store search bar.

Locate the free model 3dsmax Bip Warrior Anim Free and click **Import** (see Figure 17.3). When the Import Package dialog appears, ensure that everything is selected and click **Import**.

**FIGURE 17.3**
The required model.

You should now notice a new folder on your Project view named 3dsmax Bip Warrior Anim Free. Take a moment to familiarize yourself with the contents of that folder; you will be using them for the rest of this hour.

NOTE

**Demo**

The soldier model comes with a demo scene. You can find this demo in the Scenes folder under the folder 3dsmax Bip Warrior Anim Free. Opening this scene will allow you to test out the model with the various animations applied.

## The Model

You can locate the model that you will be using in the Models folder under the newly created 3dsmax Bip Warrior Anim Free folder. The model is named Soldier_f_0. Locate the model and select it. In the Inspector view, you should see three primary tabs: Model, Rig, and Animations (see Figure 17.4).

**FIGURE 17.4**
The model Inspector view.

The Model tab is responsible for all of the settings that dictate how the model itself is imported into Unity. These items can be safely ignored for the purposes of this hour. The two tabs you are concerned with are the Rig and Animations tabs. Under the Rig tab, ensure that the Animation Type property is set to **Legacy** and that the Generation property is set to **Store in Root (New)**. Figure 17.5 shows the proper settings.

**FIGURE 17.5**
The rig settings.

Next is the Animations tab. Animations often come as a part of the models. This is nice because you don't have to manage multiple files and can instead keep everything packaged together. The Animations tab contains all the properties and control required to manage built-in animation. For the purposes of this text and for learning, however, you need to disable these. Under the Animations tab, uncheck the **Import Animation** check box, and then click **Apply**. Your screen should now match Figure 17.6.

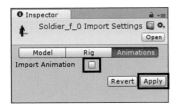

**FIGURE 17.6**
The animation settings.

TIP

### Is the Model Rigged?

You might be wondering how to know whether a model is rigged. The easiest way to know is to ask whoever made the model. If that isn't possible, you can always look at the model in the Hierarchy view. Generally, a rigged model will contain several child game objects. These objects will correspond with the various rigging joints. Figure 17.7 illustrates some of the child objects that you can use to determine whether the model is rigged.

**FIGURE 17.7**
The soldier child objects.

# Animation Assets

The next thing you want to do is look through the animation assets and ensure that they are set up the way you want. Locate the Animations folder under the 3dsmax Bip Warrior Anim Free folder. This folder contains four available animations: death, idle0, idle1, and idle2. Selecting any of these animation assets will allow you to modify their Wrap Mode property and preview them. Before previewing an animation, however, you need to provide a model. Figure 17.8 illustrates what the Preview window looks like before a model is provided.

**FIGURE 17.8**
The Preview window with no available model.

To remedy this, just click and drag the **Soldier_f_0** model from the Models folder into the Preview window for the animation (see Figure 17.9).

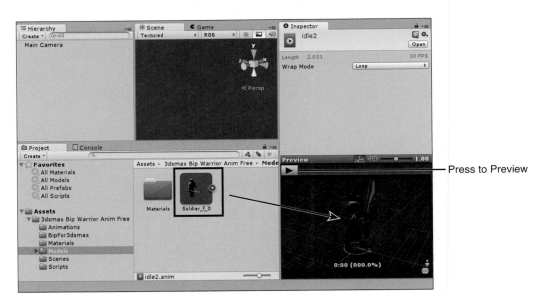

**FIGURE 17.9**
Adding a model to the preview window.

Once that is done, simply click the **Play** button to preview the animation on that model. Take a moment to preview each of the four animations. Don't worry about the Wrap Mode property for now. That is covered in greater detail later this hour.

## Adding the Soldier to a Scene

Let's add the soldier model to a scene and try it out. The scene created in this exercise will be used later, so be sure to save it:

1. Create a new project or scene. Add a directional light to the scene.

2. Locate the Soldier_f_0 model asset and drag it into the Scene view. Position the newly created soldier at (0, 0, −5) with a rotation of (0, 180, 0). Ensure that the soldier in the scene has an Animation component in the Inspector view. Any other component, such as Animator, means that you completed a previous step incorrectly.

3. Run the scene. Notice how the soldier model is there, but is not moving. That is what you want, because no animations have actually been applied yet. Be sure to save this scene for later use.

# Applying Animations

As you saw in the previous section, the soldier model has an Animation component attached to it. This component works as a collection of different animations that can be applied to the model at runtime. Table 17.1 describes the Animation component's properties.

**TABLE 17.1   Animation Component Properties**

| Property | Description |
| --- | --- |
| Animation | This is the default animation for the model. If no animation is placed here, the model won't be animated. |
| Animations | This is a list of all of the animations that can be applied to this model. You can add animations by dragging them onto this property. |
| Play Automatically | If enabled, this property causes the model to begin running the default animation when it is created. |
| Animate Physics | This determines whether the animation interacts with physics. |
| Culling Type | This determines when the animations will play. The options are Always Animate, Based on Renderer, Based on Clip Bounds, and Based on User Bounds. Generally speaking, leave this at its default setting unless you are trying to achieve a specific functionality. |

## Adding Animations

As mentioned previously, animations can be applied to a model by dragging them onto the Animations property of the Animation component (see Figure 17.10).

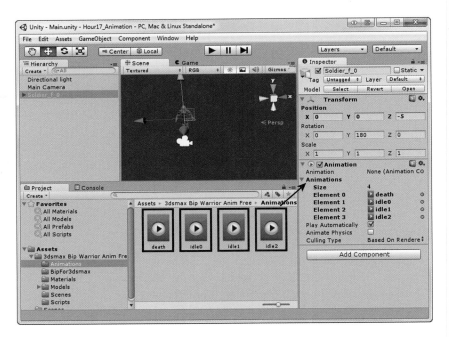

**FIGURE 17.10**
Adding animations to the model.

Doing this simply makes the animations available to the model. It doesn't actually animate the model, yet. Switching through the various animations is done via scripting and is covered in the next section. By now, you are probably pretty anxious to actually see an animation work. To see an animation run on your model, drag the animation you want onto the Animation property of the Animation component. This will set the default animation for the model. Ensure that the **Play Automatically** option is also set. Now when you run your scene you will see the model actually move!

**TRY IT YOURSELF** ▼

## Animating a Model

This exercise uses the scene you created previously. If you have not done so already, go back and complete the previous exercise "Adding the Soldier to a Scene." In this exercise, you animate the soldier. Be sure to save this scene when finished because you'll use it for a later exercise:

1. Open the previously created scene.

2. Drag each of the animations onto the Animations property of the Animation component. Drag the Idle0 animation onto the Animation property of the Animation component.

3. Play the scene. Notice how the Idle0 animation begins playing on the soldier. Stop the scene and go back to the editor and try out each of the animations on the model. See how each of them behaves. Also notice that the death animation doesn't loop and instead stops after completing.

# Wrap Modes

Previously, you looked at the animation assets in the Inspector view. You might have noticed that there was a property called Wrap Mode that you skipped over. Essentially, the wrap mode determines what an animation does once it is done running. Table 17.2 describes the five different modes.

**TABLE 17.2**   Wrap Modes

| Property | Description |
|---|---|
| Default | This option allows the animation to do whatever is defaulted for it. Usually the default is to play only once. |
| Once | The animation plays one time and then stops. |
| Loop | The animation starts over when the end is reached. |
| Ping Pong | The animation runs again when the end is reached. The difference, however, is that the animation runs backward. The animation continues to loop forward and then backward, over and over. |
| Clamp Forever | The animation runs one time. When the animation reaches the end, it continues to play the last frame over and over again. This differs from Once property because Once plays a single time and then reverts to the first frame. |

▼ TRY IT YOURSELF

### Using Wrap Modes

This exercise uses the scene you created previously. If you have not done so already, go back and complete the previous exercise "Animating a Model." In this exercise, you work with different wrap modes:

1. Open the previously created scene.

2. Ensure that the Idle0 animation is set as the default animation for the soldier model. Play the scene and notice how the soldier moves.

3. In the Project view, locate the Idle0 animation asset. Change the Wrap Mode property to **Ping Pong**. Run the scene again and notice how the model moves differently.

4. Continue experimenting with the different animations and wrap modes.

# Scripting Animations

Although it is nice to have a model running a looping idle animation, it can get a bit boring. More than likely, you need your models to do something other than just loop the same animation. As you saw previously, you can add a bunch of animations to the Animations property of an Animation component. What you haven't seen, though, is how to switch between them while the scene is running. A lot of complex functionality can be achieved through scripting, but you are going to focus primarily on just playing animations in this section. The next hour covers more advanced animation scripting.

To play an animation on a model, you need to use the transform.animation.Play() method. For instance, to play an animation called walk, you write the following:

```
transform.animation.Play("walk");
```

Animations can be changed at any time simply by playing another animation. If an animation is set to loop, it will do so automatically.

▼ TRY IT YOURSELF

### Changing Animations

In this exercise, you change model animations while the scene is running via scripting. You change the animation of this model in the Start() method. This exercise uses the scene created in the previous exercise "Adding the Soldier to a Scene":

1. Open the previously created scene. Ensure that idle0 is the default animation of the soldier. Ensure that the Animations property of the Animation component has been filled with the four animations you have been using.

2. Create a new script called **SoldierScript** and attach it to the soldier model currently in the scene. Add the following code to the Start() method of the script:

```
void Start() {
    transform.animation.Play("idle1");
}
```

3. Run the scene and notice that the character is looping the idle1 animation. Stop the scene and go back into the script. Change the animation from idle1 to **idle2** and rerun the scene. Do the same for the death animation. Test out the various animations and see how they behave.

# Summary

In this hour, you were introduced to animations in Unity. You started by looking at the basics of animations. You learned about animations and rigging. From there, you imported a rigged model and animations from the Asset Store. After that, you applied animations to the model and saw them in a running scene. You finished the hour by learning how to change animations via scripting.

TIP

## Animations Not Working

After completing this hour, you may try to animate some of your own models (or others in the Asset Store). Just remember that if you apply the animations correctly and the model still doesn't move, the problem is likely that the model is rigged differently than the animation. This tip is just a reminder that the model and animation have to be rigged the same. Otherwise, you are likely to bang your head against the wall in frustration.

# Q&A

**Q. Can animations be blended together?**

**A.** Yes, they can. This is covered next hour with the new Unity Mecanim system.

Q. **Can any animation be applied to any model?**

A. Only if they are rigged exactly the same. Otherwise, the animations may behave very strangely or just do not work at all.

Q. **Can a model be re-rigged in Unity?**

A. Yes, and you see how in the next hour.

# Workshop

Take some time to work through the questions here to ensure that you have a firm grasp of the material.

## Quiz

1. The "skeleton" of a model is known as what?

2. Which wrap mode plays an animation forward and then backward while looping?

3. True or False: The Animation property of the Animation component contains all the available animations for a model.

4. True or False: Animations are played using the transform.animation.Play() method.

## Answers

1. The rig or rigging.

2. Ping Pong mode.

3. False. The Animation property is the default animation, whereas the Animations property is the collection.

4. True.

# Exercise

In this exercise, you create a script to change animations on-the-fly using the number keys. You can find the completed solution for this exercise as Hour17_Exercise in the book assets for Hour 17. This exercise uses the scene created in the previous exercise "Adding the Soldier to a Scene."

1. Open the previously created scene. Ensure that idle0 is the default animation of the soldier. Ensure that the Animations property of the Animation component has been filled with the four animations you have been using.

2. Create a new script called **SoldierScript** and attach it to the soldier model currently in the scene. Add the following code to the Start() method of the script:

```
void Start() {
    if(Input.GetKeyDown(KeyCode.Alpha1))
        transform.animation.Play("idle0");
    else if(Input.GetKeyDown(KeyCode.Alpha2))
        transform.animation.Play("idle1");
    else if(Input.GetKeyDown(KeyCode.Alpha3))
        transform.animation.Play("idle2");
    else if(Input.GetKeyDown(KeyCode.Alpha4))
        transform.animation.Play("death");
}
```

3. Run the scene and notice that the character is looping the idle0 animation. Press the **2** key and notice that the animation changed. Experiment with the keys 1 to 4 and see how they change the animation. Note that this does not work with the numpad keys because it is specifically programmed to work with the numbers keys above the letter rows.

# HOUR 18
# Animators

## What You'll Learn in This Hour:

▶ The basics of animators
▶ How to create the animators
▶ How to manage an animator with scripts

In this hour, you take what you learned about animations previously and put it to use with Unity's new Mecanim animation system and animators. You start by learning about animators and how they work. From there, you look at how to rig, or change the rigging, of models in Unity. After that, you create an animator and configure it. You finish the hour by manipulating your animator through scripts to build an interactive demo.

NOTE

### Try It Yourself

Because of the complexity of animators, this hour will function like a big Try It Yourself. This means that you should be following along and completing all the steps in the text as they are covered. By doing so, you are sure to have a project ready to go when things start coming together. There are several hours in this book where you can idly read along. This isn't one of them.

# Animator Basics

In the preceding hour, you learned to manually control individual animations. Using that system, you can now perform advanced processes like transitions and blending. Doing so, however, is cumbersome and tedious. In this hour, you get to work with Unity's new animation system, which is called *Mecanim*. This system utilizes an asset called an *animator*, which has several animations and transitions applied to it. The animator is then applied to a model to make it move. The nice thing about this system is that you can create a single animator and apply it to several different models and have them all animate in a similar fashion. Before you can build an animator, though, you need to ensure that your models are properly rigged and your animations are properly set up.

## Rigging Models

If you recall from the preceding hour, models and animations have to be rigged exactly the same way to function. This means that getting animations made for one model to work on a different model is very difficult. With the new Mecanim system, models can have their rigging remapped in the editor without using any 3D modeling tools. The result is that any animation made for a Mecanim model can work with any model that has its rigging remapped in Unity. Now animators can produce large libraries of animations that can be applied to a large range of models using many different rigs.

The rigging for models is completed in the Inspector view. For this section, you use a model called Jack, which was made by the talented Matt Muzzy (http://www.mattmuzzy.com/). You can find this model in the folder named Jack, which is located in the book assets for Hour 18. The Jack model comes with a rigging already, and it will need to be configured in Unity to work with an animator. To import and configure the model, follow these steps:

1. In Unity, create a folder named **Models** and drag the Jack folder from the book assets into it.

2. Look in the Jack folder for the model named **Jack1** and select it. In the Inspector, click the **Animations** tab and unselect the **Import Animation** property. Click **Apply**.

3. On the Rig tab, change the animation type to **Humanoid**. This will cause the Avatar Definition property to appear. This is where the rig mapping is done. Look at Figure 18.1 to ensure that your properties match, and then click **Apply**.

**FIGURE 18.1**
The rig settings.

**4.** Click the **Configure** button to open of the rig editor. If you are prompted to save the scene, go ahead and do so. In the rig editor, you see the model standing in what is called the T-Pose (see Figure 18.2).

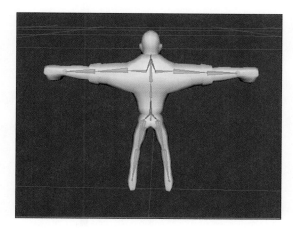

**FIGURE 18.2**
Jack in a T-Pose.

**5.** Ensure that all the joints are green (see Figure 18.3) and click **Done**. If they aren't all green, see the following section, "Red Rig of Death."

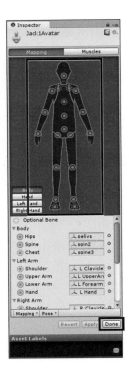

**FIGURE 18.3**
A successful rigged model.

The model Jack is now ready to go.

## Red Rig of Death

Hopefully, the previous steps worked exactly as planned and everything appeared green right away. That is not always the case, though. Unity sometimes needs some assistance with guessing how a model is rigged. Figure 18.4 illustrates a model that was incorrectly rigged. In this instance, the spine joint was incorrectly matched. To fix this, you click **Mapping > Automap**. Doing so causes Unity to correctly analyze the model and fix the issue. If automapping isn't working for your particular model, you may need to find and map the joints manually.

Sometimes, the model's rig will be mapped correctly, but with some of the joints appearing red (see Figure 18.5). This is the result of pose restrictions and can be solved by clicking **Pose > Enforce T-Pose**.

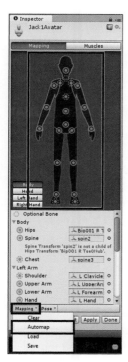

**FIGURE 18.4**
An incorrectly mapped model.

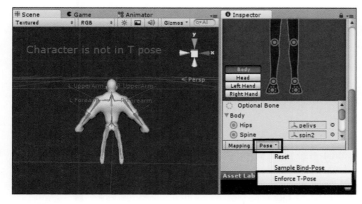

**FIGURE 18.5**
Enforcing a T-Pose.

These simple methods will fix most if not all of your model rigging issues.

# Animation Preparation

For this hour, you will be using a set of Mecanim animations. These animations were provided by Unity in their Mecanim demo. For the sake of time savings, however, you can find the animation files in the folder named Animations located in the book assets for Hour 18. If you look in that folder, you will see that the animations are actually .fbx files. This is because the animations themselves are located inside their default models. Don't worry, though; we will be able to modify and extract them inside Unity.

Each animation must be specifically configured the way you want it. For example, you need to ensure that the walking animation loops appropriately so that transitions don't have any obvious seams. In this section, you go through each animation and prepare it. Start by dragging the Animations folder from the book assets into the Unity editor. There are three animations that you will be working with: Idles, WalkForward, and WalkForwardTurns. Also, each of these three animations need to be set up uniquely.

## Idle Animation

To set up the idle animation, follow these steps:

1. Select the **Idles.fbx** file in the Animations folder. In the Inspector, select the **Rig** tab. Change the animation type to **Humanoid** and configure the rig exactly as you did for the Jack model previously. You might need to go back and reference that section and repeat the steps.

2. Once the rig is configured, click the **Animations** tab in the Inspector. The only thing you need to do here is check the **Loop Pose** property. Ensure that your settings match the ones in Figure 18.6.

3. The animation itself should now be properly configured. You can find it by expanding the Idles.fbx file (see Figure 18.7). Be sure to remember how to access that animation. The model itself is irrelevant. It's the animation you want.

NOTE

## Red Light, Green Light

You might have noticed the green circles present in the animation settings (as in Figure 18.6). Those are nifty little tools that are used to designate whether your animations are lined up. The fact that the circles are green means that they will loop seamlessly. If any circles had been yellow, it would have indicated that the animation came close to looping seamlessly but there was a minor difference. A red circle indicates that the beginning and end of the animation don't line up at all and a seam would be very apparent. If you have an animation that doesn't line up, you can change the Start and End properties to find a segment of the animation that does.

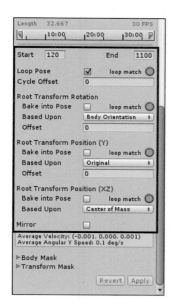

**FIGURE 18.6**
The idle animation properties.

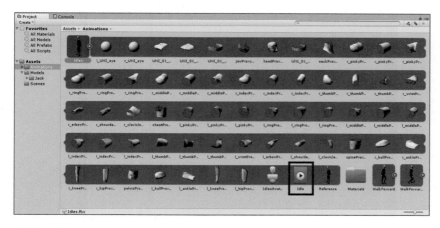

**FIGURE 18.7**
Finding the animation in the model.

## Walk Animation

To set up the walking animation, follow these steps:

1. Select the **WalkForward.fbx** file in the Animations folder and complete the rigging the same way you did for the idle animation.

2. Under the Animations tab, you should have the settings demonstrated in Figure 18.8. You should note two things. First, the Root Transform Position (XZ) has a red circle next to it. This is good. What this means is that at the end of the animation the model is in a different x and z axis position. Because this is a walking animation, that is the behavior that you want. The other thing you should notice is the Average Velocity indicator. You should notice an x axis velocity of –0.034 and a z axis velocity of 1.534. The z axis velocity is good because you want the model moving forward, but the x axis velocity is a problem because it will cause the model to drift sideways while walking. You need to adjust this setting.

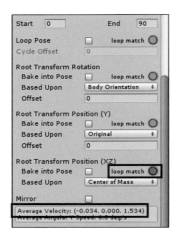

**FIGURE 18.8**
The walk animation settings.

3. To adjust the x axis velocity, you need to check the **Bake into Pose** properties for both the Root Transform Rotation and Root Transform Position (Y) properties. You also need to set the Root Transform Position offset to **–2.26**. Finally, you want to check the **Loop Pose** property. Figure 18.9 contains the fixed settings. When done, click the **Apply** button.

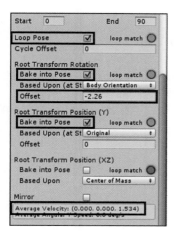

**FIGURE 18.9**
The fixed walk animation settings.

## Walk Turn Animation

The walk turn animation allows the model to smoothly change direction while walking forward. This one differs a little from the other two because you need to make two animations out of a single animation recording. This sounds trickier than it really is. The steps to complete this are as follows:

1. Select the **WalkForwardTurns.fbx** file in the Animations folder and complete the rigging the same way you did for the idle animation.

2. By default, there will be a long animation with the name _7_a_U1_M_P_ WalkForwardTurnRight. You could modify that, but it will be easier to just delete it and start over. Type **WalkForwardTurnRight** into the Clip Name text field, and then click the plus sign (+) to create a new clip (see Figure 18.10).

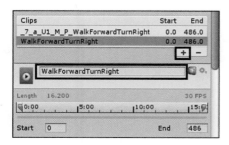

**FIGURE 18.10**
Adding an animation clip.

3. Now you can remove the old animation clip. Select **_7_a_U1_M_P_ WalkForwardTurnRight** and click the minus sign (–) to remove it.

4. With the WalkForwardTurnRight clip selected, set the properties to match Figure 18.11. This will cut the clip down and ensure that it only contains the model moving is a rightward circle. (Be sure to preview it to see what it looks like.) After you have done this, click **Apply**.

**FIGURE 18.11**
The right turn settings.

5. Create a **WalkForwardTurnLeft** animation clip the same way you made the right turning clip in step 2. The properties for the WalkForwardTurnLeft clip will be exactly the same as the WalkForwardTurnRight clip except that you need to put a check in the **Mirror** property (see Figure 18.12).

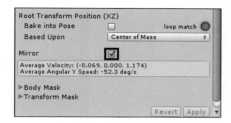

**FIGURE 18.12**
Mirroring the animation.

At this point, all the animations are set up and ready to go. Now all that's left to do is build the animator.

# Creating an Animator

Animators in Unity are assets. This means that they are a part of a project and exist outside of any one scene. This is nice because it allows easy reuse over and over again. To add an animator to your project, in Project view right-click a folder and select **Create > Animator Controller**.

---

TRY IT YOURSELF ▼

### Setting Up the Scene

In this exercise, you set up a scene and prepare for the rest of the materials for the hour. Be sure to save the scene created here, because you'll need it later:

1. If you have not done so already, create a new project and complete the model and animation preparation steps in the previous section.

2. Drag the Jack1 model into your scene and give it a position of (0, 0, −5). Add a directional light to the scene.

3. Select the Jack1 model in the scene. Locate the Jack Diffuse1.psd texture in the Jack folder and drag it onto the Jack1 model in the scene. Nest the Main Camera under the Jack1 model (in the Hierarchy view, drag the Main Camera onto the model) and position the camera at (0, 1.5, −1.5) with a rotation of (20, 0, 0).

4. Create a new folder named **Animators**. Right-click the new folder and select **Create > Animator Controller**. Name the animator **PlayerAnimator**. With Jack1 selected in the scene, drag the animator onto the Controller property of the Animator component in the Inspector (see Figure 18.13).

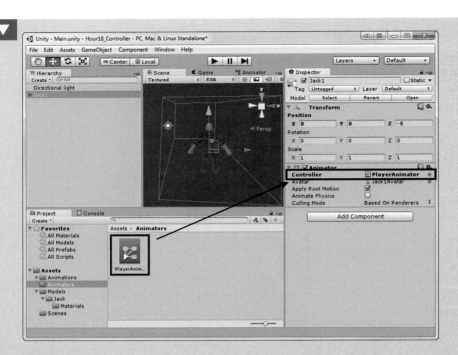

**FIGURE 18.13**
Adding the animator to the model.

5. Add a plane to your scene. Position the plane at (0, 0, –5) with a scale of (50, 1, 50). Locate the file Checker.tga in the book assets for Hour 18 and import it into your project. Apply the texture to the plane.

6. Run the scene and make sure that everything looks correct. Note that at this point nothing is animated.

## The Animator View

Double-clicking an animator brings up the Animator view. This view functions like a flow graph, allowing you to visually create animation paths and blending. This is the real power of the Mecanim system. Figure 18.14 shows the basic Animator view. For a new animator, this is very plain. There is only a base layer, no parameters, and an Any State. These will soon be discussed more fully.

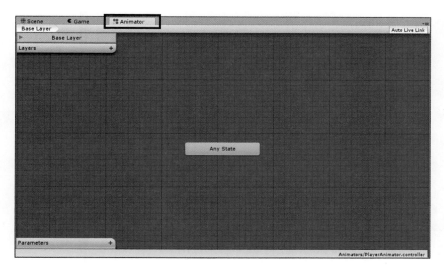

**FIGURE 18.14**
The Animator view.

## The Idle Animation

The first animation you want to apply to Jack is the idle animation. Now that the entire long set up process is complete, adding this animation is simple. You need to locate the Idle animation clip, which is stored inside the Idles.fbx file (see Figure 18.7), and drag it onto the animator in the Animator view (see Figure 18.15).

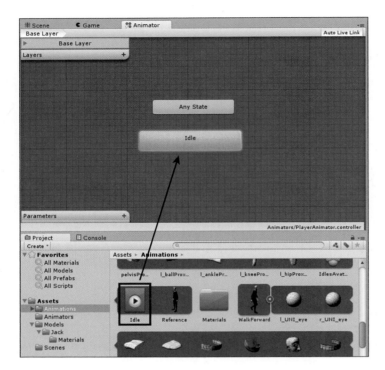

**FIGURE 18.15**
Applying the idle animation.

You should now be able to run your scene and see the Jack model looping through the idle animation.

## Parameters

Parameters are like variables for the animator. You set them up in the animator view and then manipulate them with scripts. These parameters control when animations are transitioned and blended. To create a parameter, simply click the plus sign (+) in the Parameters box in the Animator view.

▼ TRY IT YOURSELF

### Adding Parameters

In this exercise, you add two parameters. This exercise builds off of the project and scene you have been working on thus far this hour:

1. Make sure that you've completed all of the steps up to this point.

2.  In the Animator view, click the plus sign (+) to create a new parameter. Choose a **Float** parameter and name it **Speed** (see Figure 18.16).

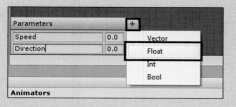

**FIGURE 18.16**
Adding parameters.

3.  Repeat step 2 to create a parameter named **Direction**.

## States and Blend Trees

Your next step is to create a new state. States are essentially statuses that the model is currently in that define what animation is playing. The model Jack will have two states: Idle and Walking. Idle is already in place. Because the walking state can be any of three animations, you want to create a state that uses a blend tree. A blend tree will seamlessly blend one or more animations together based on some parameter. To create a new state, follow these steps:

1.  Right-click a blank spot in the Animator view and select **Create State > from New Blend Tree**. In the Inspector view, name the new state **Walking** (see Figure 18.17).

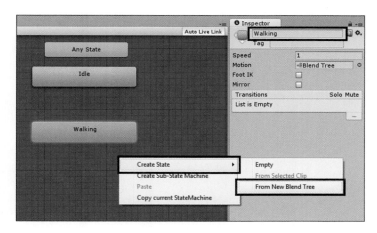

**FIGURE 18.17**
Creating and naming a new state.

**2.** Double-click the new state to expand it. In the Inspector, change the Parameter property to **Direction** and add three motions by clicking the plus sign (+) under motions and selecting **Add Motion Field** (see Figure 18.18).

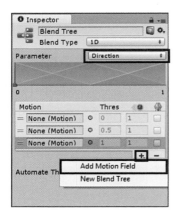

**FIGURE 18.18**
Adding motion fields.

**3.** Change the minimum value to –1 (see Figure 18.19) and drag each of the three walking animations into the three motion fields. (Remember that the turning animation clips are located under WalkForwardTurns.fbx.) Make sure that they are in the order: Turn Left, Straight, Turn Right. Note that the walk straight animation will have a strange name because you never renamed it. You know which one it is because it should be the only animation clip in the WalkForward.fbx file.

Your walking animation is now ready to blend based on the direction parameter. You can get out of the expanded view by clicking the Base Layer breadcrumb at the top of the animator view (see Figure 18.20).

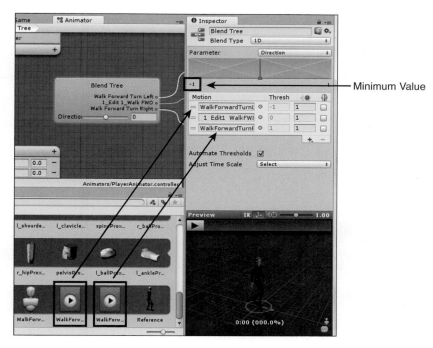

**FIGURE 18.19**
Changing minimum values and adding animations to a blend tree.

**FIGURE 18.20**
Navigating the Animator view.

# Transitions

The last thing you need to do to ensure that your animator is finished is to tell the animator how to transition between the idle and walking animations. You need to set up two transitions. One transitions the animator from idle to walking, and the other transitions back. To create a transition, follow these steps:

1. Right-click the **Idle** state and select **Make Transition**. This will create a white line that follows your mouse. Click the **Walking** state to connect the two.

2. Repeat step 1, except this time connecting the Walking state to the Idle state.

**3.** Edit the Idle to Walking transition by clicking the white arrow on it. Set the Conditions to
be **Speed Greater** than the value **0.1** (see Figure 18.21). Do the same for the Walking to
Idle transition, except set the condition to **Speed Less Than** the value **0.1**.

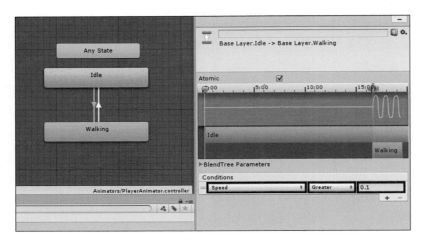

**FIGURE 18.21**
Modifying transitions.

The animator is finished. You might notice that when you run the scene there aren't any
working movement animations. This is because the speed and direction parameters are never
changed. In the next section, you learn how to change these through scripting.

# Scripting Animators

Now that everything has been set up with the model, the rigging, the animations, the animator,
the transitions, and the blend tree, it is finally time to make the whole thing interactive. Luckily,
the actual scripting components are simple. Most of the hard work was already done in the editor. At this point, all you need to do is manipulate the parameters you created in the animator
to get Jack up and running. Because the parameters you set up were of type float, you need to
call the animator method:

```
SetFloat(<name> , <value>);
```

TRY IT YOURSELF ▼

## The Final Touches

This exercise takes the project you have been working on during this hour and adds the scripted component to make it all work:

1. Create a new folder called **Scripts** and add a new script to it. Name the script **AnimationControlScript**. Attach the script to the Jack1 model in the scene.

2. Add the following code to the script:

```
Animator anim;

void Start () {
    //Get a reference to the animator
    anim = GetComponent<Animator>();
}

void Update () {
    anim.SetFloat("Speed", Input.GetAxis("Vertical"));
    anim.SetFloat("Direction", Input.GetAxis("Horizontal"));
}
```

3. Run the scene and notice that the animations are controlled with the vertical and horizontal axes.

That's it! If you run your scene after adding this script, you might notice something strange. Not only does Jack animate through idle, walking, and turning, but the model also moves. This is due to two factors. The first is that the animations chosen have a built-in movement to them. This was done by the animators outside of Unity. If this hadn't been done, you would have to program the movement yourself. The second factor is that by default the animator allows the animation to move the model. This can be changed in the Apply Root Motion property of the Animator component (see Figure 18.22).

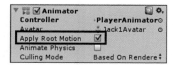

**FIGURE 18.22**
Root motion animator property.

# Summary

In this hour, you worked through creating an animator in Unity. You started by learning about animators. From there, you went through the steps of preparing a rigging and animations for use with the Mecanim system. Once that was done, you created an animator. You added parameters, states, a blend tree, and animations to it. You finished by learning how to manipulate the parameters via a script to control the animator.

# Q&A

**Q.** **There are a lot of steps here, is the Mecanim system really better than the legacy system?**

**A.** The amount of work this hour might be daunting. Be aware, though, that with a little familiarity, these steps become very simple. Furthermore, remember that without the Mecanim system, animations had to be made for specific rigging. In the legacy system, you couldn't remap the rigging like you can now.

# Workshop

Take some time to work through the questions here to ensure that you have a firm grasp of the material.

## Quiz

1. What pose must a model be in to correctly map in the rigging editor?

2. Variables that exist inside an animator are called what?

3. What method is used to set float parameters in a script?

## Answers

1. The T-Pose.

2. Parameters.

3. SetParam(<name>, <value>).

# Exercise

There is a lot of information required to produce a robust and high-quality animation system. In this hour, you got to see one way and one group of settings to achieve this. Plenty of other assets are available, however, and learning is paramount to success. Your exercise for this hour is to continue studying the Mecanim system. Be sure to start by browsing Unity's documentation on the system. You can find this on Unity's website at http://docs.unity3d.com/Documentation/Manual/MecanimAnimationSystem.html. In case you want spend some more time learning about the system, Unity has provided a great demo on the system at http://video.unity3d.com/video/7362044/unity-40-mecanim-animation-tutorial.

HOUR 19

# Game 4: *Gauntlet Runner*

---

**What You'll Learn in This Hour:**

▶ How to design the game *Gauntlet Runner*

▶ How to build the *Gauntlet Runner* world

▶ How to build the *Gauntlet Runner* entities

▶ How to build the *Gauntlet Runner* controls

▶ How to further improve *Gauntlet Runner*

Let's make a game! In this hour, you make a 3D gauntlet running game appropriately titled *Gauntlet Runner*. You start the hour off with the design of the game. From there, you focus on building the world. Once done, you build the entities and controls. You wrap the hour up by playing the game and seeing where improvements can be found.

---

TIP

**Completed Project**

Be sure to follow along in this hour to build the complete game project. If you get stuck, you can find a complete copy of the game in the book assets for Hour 19. Take a look at it if you need help or inspiration.

---

# Design

You have already learned what the design elements are in Hour 7, "Game 1: *Amazing Racer*." This time you get right into them.

## The Concept

In this game, you will be playing as a robot running through a gauntlet tunnel, attempting to grab power ups to extend your game time. You need to avoid obstacles that will slow you down. The game ends when you run out of time.

## The Rules

The rules for this game state how to play, but also allude to some of the properties of the objects. The rules for *Gauntlet Runner* are as follows:

▶ Players can move left or right and jump. They run at a fixed pace and cannot move in any other manner.

▶ If players hit an obstacle, they will be slowed by 50% for 1 second.

▶ If players grab a power up, their time is extended by 1.5 seconds.

▶ Players are bounded by the sides of the screen.

▶ The loss condition for the game is running out of time. There is no win condition.

## The Requirements

The requirements for this game are simple, as follows:

▶ A gauntlet texture.

▶ A player model.

▶ A power up and obstacle. These will be created in Unity.

▶ A game controller. This will be created in Unity.

▶ A power up particle effect. This will be created in Unity.

▶ Interactive scripts. These will be written in MonoDevelop.

# The World

The world for this game will simply be three cubes configured to look like a gauntlet. The entire setup is fairly basic; it's the other components of the game that add challenge and fun.

## The Scene

Before setting up the ground with its functionality, get your scene set up and ready to go. To prepare the scene, do the following:

**1.** Create a new project called **Gauntlet Runner**. Create a new folder called **Scenes** and save your scene as **Main** in that folder.

**2.** Add a directional light to your scene.

**3.** Position the Main Camera at (0, 3, –10.7) with a rotation of (33, 0, 0). Save your scene.

The camera for this game will be in a fixed position hovering over the gameplay. The rest of the world will pass underneath it.

## The Ground

The ground in this game will be scrolling in nature; however, unlike the scrolling background used in *Captain Blaster*, you will not actually be scrolling anything. This is explained more in the next section, but for now just understand that you need to create only one ground object to make the scrolling work. The ground itself will consist of three basic cubes and a simple texture. To create the ground, follow these steps:

1. Add a cube to the scene. Name it **Ground** and position it at (0, 0, 15.5) with a scale of (10, .5, 50). Add another cube to the scene named **Wall** and position it at (–5.5, .7, 15.5) with a scale of (1, 1, 50). Duplicate the wall piece and position the new wall items at (5.5, .7, 15.5).

2. Create two new folders: **Textures** and **Materials**. In the book assets for Hour 19, locate the Checker.tga file and drag it into the Textures folder. In the Materials folder, create a new material named **GroundMaterial**.

3. Set the texture of GroundMaterial to be the Checker file that you just imported. Modify the Main Color property of the material to give it a slight reddish color. Apply the material to the ground and walls.

That's it! The ground is fairly basic.

## Scrolling the Ground

You have seen before that you can scroll a background by creating two instances of that background and moving them in a "leap frog" manner. In this game, you are going to use a more clever solution. Each material has a set of texture offsets. These can be seen in the Inspector when a material is selected. What you want to do it modify those offsets at runtime via a script. If the texture is set to repeat (which it is by default), the texture will loop around seamlessly. The result, if done correctly, is a seemingly scrolling object without any actual movement. To create this effect, follow these steps:

1. Create a new folder named **Scripts**. Create a new script called **GroundScript**. Attach the script to both the ground and the walls.

2. Add the following code to the script (replacing the Update() method that is already there):

```
float speed = .5f;
void Update () {
    float offset = Time.time * speed;
    renderer.material.mainTextureOffset = new Vector2(0, -offset);
```

```
    }

    public void SlowDown()
    {
        speed = speed / 2;
    }

    public void SpeedUp()
    {
        speed = speed * 2;
    }
```

3. Run the scene and notice your gauntlet scrolling. This is an easy and efficient way to create a scrolling 3D object.

You might have noticed the two additional methods in the previous scrip: SlowDown and SpeedUp. These aren't used now, but they will be necessary later when the player hits an obstacle. Figure 19.1 illustrates the running scene set up as described previously.

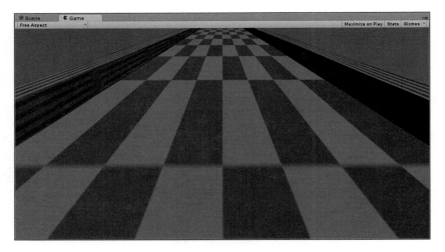

**FIGURE 19.1**
The running gauntlet.

# The Entities

Now that you have a scrolling world, it is time to set up the entities. There are four primary entities to be aware of: the player, the power ups, the obstacles, and a trigger zone. The trigger zone will be used to clean up any items that make it past the player. You do not need to create a spawn point for this game. Instead, you are going to explore a different way of handling it, by letting the game control create the power ups and obstacles.

## The Power Ups

The power ups in this game are going to be simple spheres with some effects added to it. You will be creating the sphere, positioning it, and then making a prefab out of it. To create the power up, follow these steps:

1. Add a sphere to the scene. Position the sphere at (0, 1, 42). Add a rigidbody to the sphere and uncheck **Use Gravity**.

2. Create a new material named **PowerupMaterial** and give it a yellow color. Apply the material to the sphere.

3. Add a point light to the sphere (click **Component > Rendering > Light**). Give the light a yellow color. Add a particle system to the sphere (click **Component > Effects > Particle System**). Give the particles a start color of yellow and a start lifetime of **2.5**.

4. Create a new folder called **Prefabs**. Create a new prefab in the folder and name it **Powerup**. Click and drag the sphere from the Hierarchy view onto the prefab. Delete the sphere from the scene.

Note that by setting the position of the object before putting it into the prefab you can simply instantiate the prefab and it will appear at that spot. The result is that you will not need a spawn point. Figure 19.2 illustrates the finished power up.

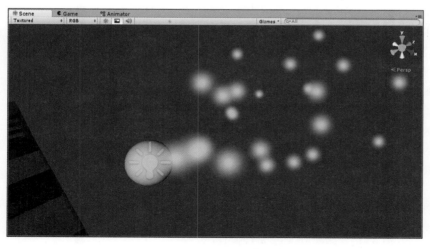

**FIGURE 19.2**
The power up.

# The Obstacles

For this game, the obstacles are represented by small black cubes. The player has the option of either avoiding them or jumping over them. To create the obstacles, follow these steps:

1. Add a cube to the scene. Position it at (0, .4, 42) with a scale of (1, .2, 1). Add a rigidbody to the cube and uncheck **Use Gravity**.

2. Create a new material called **ObstacleMaterial**. Make the color of the material black and apply it to the cube.

3. Create a new prefab named **Obstacle**. Drag the cube from the hierarchy onto the prefab and then delete the cube.

# The Trigger Zone

Just like in previous games, the trigger zone exists to clean up any game objects that make it past the player. To create the trigger zone, follow these steps:

1. Add a cube to the scene. Rename the cube **TriggerZone** and position it at (0, 1, −20) with a scale of (10, 1, 1).

2. On the Box Collider component of the trigger zone, put a check mark in the **Is Trigger** property.

# The Player

The player is where a large portion of the work for this game will go. The player will be using two new animations that you haven't worked with yet: run and jump. You'll start by getting the player ready for Mecanim animations:

1. Locate the folder named Robot Kyle in the book assets for Hour 19. This is a model provided free for use by Unity. To save the time of finding it on the Asset Store, though, it has been provided here. Drag that folder into the Project view in Unity to import it.

2. Locate and select the Robot Kyle.fbx file in the Model folder under the Robot Kyle folder. In the Inspector, select the **Animations** tab and deselect **Import Animation**. Click **Apply**.

3. Under the Rig tab, change the animation type to **Humanoid**. Click **Apply**.

You should now see a check mark next to the Configure button (see Figure 19.3). If you don't, you need to click **Configure** and configure the rig. You can find instructions for doing so in Hour 18, "Animators" (although it shouldn't be necessary).

**FIGURE 19.3**
The rig settings.

You now need to get the animations ready to be placed in an animator, as follows:

1. Locate the Animations folder in the book assets for Hour 19. Drag the folder into the Project view in Unity to import it.

2. In the newly imported Animations folder, locate the **Jump.fbx** file and select it. In the Inspector, click the **Rig** tab and change the animation type to **Humanoid**. Click **Apply**.

3. Under the Animations tab, change the properties of the jump animation to match Figure 19.4. Note that the Offset property under the Root Transform Rotation property might need to be different from the one in the image. What is important is that the Average Velocity property has a value of 0 for the x axis. Click **Apply**.

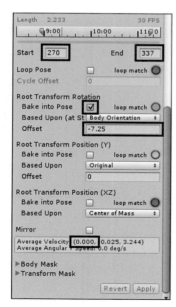

**FIGURE 19.4**
Properties for the jump animation.

**4.** Select the **Runs.fbx** file in the Animations folder. Complete step 2 again to correct the rig for this model. Under the Animations tab, notice that there are three clips: RunRight, Run, and RunLeft. Select **Run** and ensure that the properties match Figure 19.5. Again, the important part is that the x axis value for the Average Velocity property is 0. Click **Apply**.

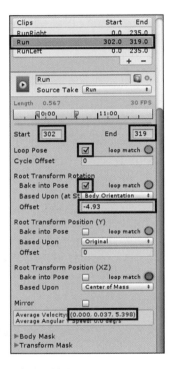

**FIGURE 19.5**
The run animation properties.

Now that the animations are prepared, you can begin making the animator. This will be a simple two-state animator without the need for any blending trees. To prepare the animator, follow these steps:

**1.** Create a new folder called **Animators**. Create a new animator in the folder (right-click and select **Create > Animator Controller**). Name it **PlayerAnimator**.

**2.** Double-click the animator to open the Animator view. In the Animations folder, locate the Runs.fbx file by clicking the arrow to the right of it. In the expanded model, locate the Run animation clip and drag it onto the Animator view (see Figure 19.6). Click the newly created **Run** state, and in the Inspector put a check mark in the **Foot IK** property.

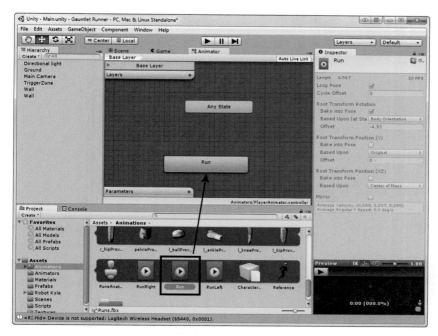

**FIGURE 19.6**
Adding the Run animation clip.

**3.** Locate the Jump.fbx file in the Animations folder. Expand the file and locate the Jump animation clip. Drag the clip onto the Animator view. Click the newly created **Jump** state, and in the Inspector put a check mark in the **Foot IK** property and change the Speed property to **1.25**.

**4.** Add a new parameter to the animator by clicking the plus sign (+) in the Parameters box in the Animator view. The parameter should be a Bool named Jumping (see Figure 19.7).

**FIGURE 19.7**
Adding the Jumping parameter.

**5.** Right-click the **Run** state in the animator and select **Make Transition**. Click the **Jump** state to link them together. Right-click the **Jump** state and select **Make Transition**. Link it back to the Run state.

**6.** Click the white arrow that transitions from Run to Jump. In the Inspector, change the Conditions to be when **Jumping** is **True** (see Figure 19.8).

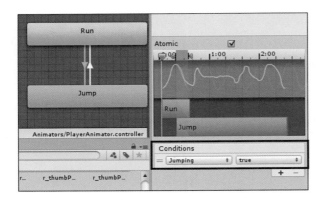

**FIGURE 19.8**
The Run transition properties.

**7.** Click the white arrow that transitions from Jump to Run. Ensure that the properties in the Inspector match Figure 19.9.

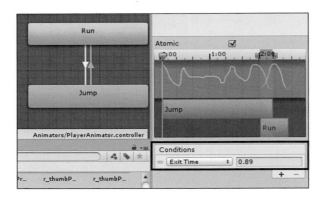

**FIGURE 19.9**
The Jump transition properties.

Now that the player model is ready for animations, you need to place it in the scene, as follows:

**1.** Locate the Robot Kyle.fbx file and drag it into your scene. Position the robot at (0, .25, −8.5).

**2.** Add a capsule collider to the model (click **Component > Physics > Capsule Collider**). Set the Y value of the collider to **.95** and the height of the collider to **1.72**.

**3.** Drag the PlayerAnimator onto the Controller property of the Animator component. Also ensure that the **Apply Root Motion** check box is unchecked.

The player entity should now be set up and ready to go. If you run the scene, you should notice the robot running with the gauntlet moving underneath it. The effect is that the robot looks like it is running forward.

# The Controls

It's now time to add the controls and interactivity to get this game going. Because the positions for the power ups and obstacles are in the prefabs already, there is no need to create a spawn point. Therefore, most all of the control will be placed on a game control object.

## Trigger Zone Script

The first script you want to make is the one for the trigger zone. Remember that the trigger zone simply destroys any objects that make their way past the player. To create this, simply create a new script named **TriggerZoneScript** and attach it to the trigger zone game object. Place the following code in the script:

```
void OnTriggerEnter(Collider other)
{
    Destroy (other.gameObject);
}
```

The trigger script is very basic and just destroys any object that enters it.

## The Game Control Script

This script is where a majority of the work takes place. To start, create an empty game object in the scene and name it **GameControl**. This will simply be a place holder for your scripts. Create a new script named **GameControlScript** and attach it to the game control object you just created. Following is the code for the game control script. There is some complexity here, so be sure to read each line carefully to see what it is doing. Add the following code to the script:

```
public float objectSpeed = -.3f;
float minSpeed = -.15f;
float maxSpeed = -.3f;

public GroundScript ground;
public GroundScript wall1;
public GroundScript wall2;

float timeRemaining = 10;
float timeExtension = 1.5f;
float totalTimeElapsed = 0;
```

```
bool isGameOver = false;

void Update () {

    if(isGameOver)
        return;


    totalTimeElapsed += Time.deltaTime;
    timeRemaining -= Time.deltaTime;
    if(timeRemaining <= 0)
    isGameOver = true;
}

public void SlowWorldDown()
{
    CancelInvoke("SpeedWorldUp");

    objectSpeed = minSpeed;
    ground.SlowDown();
    wall1.SlowDown();
    wall2.SlowDown();

    Invoke ("SpeedWorldUp", 1);
}

void SpeedWorldUp()
{
    objectSpeed = maxSpeed;
    ground.SpeedUp();
    wall1.SpeedUp();
    wall2.SpeedUp();
}

public void PowerupCollected()
{
    timeRemaining += timeExtension;
}

void OnGUI()
{
    if(!isGameOver)
    {
        GUI.Box(new Rect(Screen.width / 2 - 50, Screen.height - 100, 100, 50),
                "Time Remaining");
        GUI.Label(new Rect(Screen.width / 2 - 10, Screen.height - 80, 20, 40),
                ((int)timeRemaining).ToString());
    }
```

```
    else
    {
        GUI.Box(new Rect(Screen.width / 2 - 60, Screen.height / 2 - 100, 120, 50),
                "Game Over");
        GUI.Label(new Rect(Screen.width / 2 - 55, Screen.height / 2 - 80, 90, 40),
                "Total Time: " + (int)totalTimeElapsed);
    }
}
```

Remember that one of the premises of this game is that everything slows down when the player hits an obstacle. Therefore, objects will need to get their speeds from the game control. The first three variables are the current, minimum, and maximum object speeds. You also keep track of the ground and walls so that you can slow them down if needed. The remaining variables maintain the game timing and state.

The Update() method keeps track of time. It adds the time since the last frame (Time.deltaTime) to the totalTimeElapsed variable. It also checks to see whether the game is over, which happens when the time remaining reaches 0. If the game is over, it sets the isGameOver flag.

The SlowWorldDown() and SpeedWorldUp() methods work in conjunction. Whenever a player hits an obstacle, the SlowWorldDown() method is called. This method basically slows down all of the objects in the scene. It then calls the Invoke() method. This method basically says, "Call the method written here in x seconds," where the method called is the one named in the quotes and the number of seconds is the second value. You might have noticed the call to CancelInvoke() at the beginning of the SlowWorldDown() method. This basically cancels any SpeedWorldUp() methods waiting to be called because the player hit another obstacle. In the previous code, after 1 second, the SpeedWorldUp() method is called. This method speeds everything back up so that play can resume like normal.

The PowerupCollected() method is called by the player and adds the extension time to the time remaining.

Finally, the OnGUI method draws the remaining time to the scene while the game is running and the total time the game lasted once it has ended.

## The Player Script

This script has two responsibilities: manage the player movement and collision controls, and manage the animator. Create a new script called **PlayerScript** and attach it to the robot model in the scene. Add the following code to the script:

```
public GameControlScript control;
Animator anim;

float strafeSpeed = 2;
bool jumping = false;
```

```
void Start () {
    anim = GetComponent<Animator>();
}

void Update () {
    transform.Translate(Input.GetAxis("Horizontal") * Time.deltaTime * strafeSpeed,
➥0f, 0f);

    if(transform.position.x > 3)
        transform.position = new Vector3(3, transform.position.y, transform.
➥position.z);
    else if(transform.position.x < -3)
        transform.position = new Vector3(-3, transform.position.y, transform.
➥position.z);

    if (anim.GetCurrentAnimatorStateInfo(0).IsName("Base Layer.Jump"))
    {
        anim.SetBool("Jumping", false);
        jumping = true;
    }
    else
    {
        jumping = false;
        if(Input.GetButtonDown("Jump"))
            anim.SetBool("Jumping", true);
    }
}

void OnTriggerEnter(Collider other)
{
    if(other.gameObject.name == "Powerup(Clone)")
    {
        control.PowerupCollected();
    }
    else if(other.gameObject.name == "Obstacle(Clone)" && jumping == false)
    {
        control.SlowWorldDown();
    }

    Destroy(other.gameObject);
}
```

The first two variables hold the game control and animator references. The second two variables contain the movement-related information. The value for the anim variable is set in the Start() method.

The Update() method starts by moving the player based on input. It then checks to make sure that the player isn't farther than –3 or 3 on the x axis. If the player is, the player is set back to –3 or 3. This keeps the player in the gauntlet. The Update() method then checks to see whether the player is currently in the jumping animation. If he is, the local jumping flag is set to true (so that the player doesn't collide with obstacles), and the animator jumping parameter is set to false (so the jump animation doesn't loop). If the player isn't currently jumping, the animator sets the appropriate flag and checks to see whether the player presses the Jump button (spacebar by default).

In the OnTriggerEnter() method, the script checks to see what the player collided with. If a player collides with a power up, the appropriate method is called. To collide with an obstacle, the player must also not be jumping. If this is the case, the SlowWorldDown() method is called.

## The Power Up and Obstacle Scripts

The power up and obstacle scripts are completely identical. In fact, they could have been made as a single script. They have been kept separate to make it easy to make differential changes in the future. Create two scripts named **PowerupScript** and **ObstacleScript**. Add the power up script to the power up prefab by selecting the prefab and in the Inspector clicking **Add Component > Scripts > Powerup Script**. Do the same for the obstacle prefab and the obstacle script. Add the following to each script:

```
public GameControlScript control;
void Update () {
    transform.Translate(0, 0, control.objectSpeed);
}
```

This script is simple. There is a placeholder for the game control script. Then, at each Update() method call, the object is moved by the control's current speed. In this way, the control can change the speed of every object in the scene.

## The Spawn Script

The spawn script is responsible for creating the objects in this scene. Because position data is in the prefabs, this script will be placed on the game control object. Create a new script called **SpawnScript** and attach it to the GameControl object. Add the following code to the script:

```
GameControlScript control;

public GameObject obstacle;
public GameObject powerup;

float timeElapsed = 0;
float spawnCycle = .5f;
bool spawnPowerup = true;
```

```
void Start () {
    control = GetComponent<GameControlScript>();
}

void Update () {
    timeElapsed += Time.deltaTime;
    if(timeElapsed > spawnCycle)
    {
        GameObject temp;
        if(spawnPowerup)
        {
            temp = (GameObject)Instantiate(powerup);
            temp.GetComponent<PowerupScript>().control = control;
            Vector3 pos = temp.transform.position;
            temp.transform.position = new Vector3(Random.Range(-3, 4), pos.y,
➥pos.z);
        }
        else
        {
            temp = (GameObject)Instantiate(obstacle);
            temp.GetComponent<ObstacleScript>().control = control;
            Vector3 pos = temp.transform.position;
            temp.transform.position = new Vector3(Random.Range(-3, 4), pos.y,
➥pos.z);
        }

        timeElapsed -= spawnCycle;
        spawnPowerup = !spawnPowerup;
    }
}
```

The script starts with a reference to the game control script. It also contains a reference to the power up and obstacle game objects. The next variables control the timing and order of the object spawns. The power ups and obstacles will take turns spawning, and therefore there is a flag to keep track of which one is going.

In the Update() method, the elapsed time is incremented and then checked to see if it is time to spawn a new object. If it is time, the script then checks to see which object it should spawn. It then spawns either a power up or an obstacle. It then passes the reference to the game control script into the new object's script. This is how the power ups and obstacles know where to find the game control script. The created object is then moved left or right randomly. Finally, the Update() method decreases the elapsed time and flips the power up flag so that the opposite object will be spawned next time.

# Putting It All Together

This is the last part of the game. You need to link the scripts and objects together. Start by select-ing the GameControl object in the Hierarchy view. Drag the Ground and both Wall objects to their corresponding properties in the Game Control Script component (see Figure 19.10). Drag the Powerup and Obstacle prefabs onto their corresponding properties in the Spawn Script component.

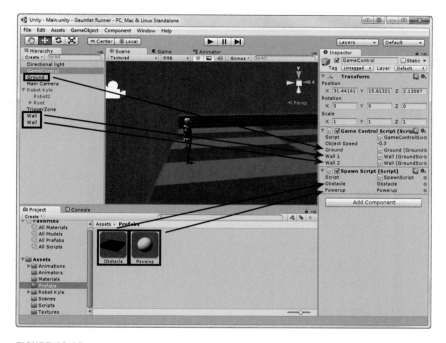

**FIGURE 19.10**
Dragging the objects to their properties.

Next, select the Robot Kyle model in the hierarchy and drag the GameControl object onto the Control property of the Player Script component (see Figure 19.11).

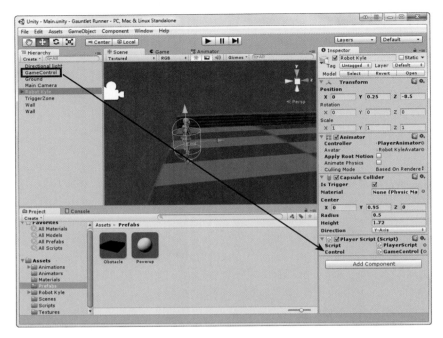

**FIGURE 19.11**
Adding the game control to the player script.

That's it! The game is now complete and playable.

# Room for Improvement

As always, a game is not fully complete until it is tested and adjusted. Now it is time for you to play through the game and see what you like and what you don't like. Remember to keep track of the features that you think really enhance the gameplay experience. Also keep track of the items you feel detract from the experience. Be sure to make notes on any ideas you have for future iterations of the game. Try to have friends play the game as well and record their feedback about the game. All of these things will help you make the game unique and more enjoyable.

# Summary

In this hour, you made the game *Gauntlet Runner*. You started by laying out the design elements of the game. From there, you built the gauntlet and got it to scroll using a texture trick. You then built the various entities for your game. After that, you built the various controls and scripts. Last but not least, you play tested the game and recorded some feedback.

# Q&A

**Q. The movements of the objects and the ground aren't exactly lined up. Is that normal?**

**A.** In this case, yes. A fine level of testing and tweaking is required to get these to sync perfectly. This is one element you can focus on refining.

**Q. The jumping animation looks a little off. Is that normal?**

**A.** Again, this is normal in this circumstance. The animations used in this hour were provided by Unity for their Mecanim demo. Therefore, they are being used in a manner they weren't exactly designed for. (They were meant to control the movement of the player.) So, it looks a little off. Sometimes, game development is a matter of doing what you can with the tools you are provided.

# Workshop

Take some time to work through the questions here to ensure that you have a firm grasp of the material.

## Quiz

**1.** How does the player lose the game?

**2.** How does the scrolling background work?

**3.** What two states did you create in the animator?

**4.** How does the game control the speed of all of the objects in the scene?

## Answers

**1.** The game is lost when time runs out.

**2.** The gauntlet stays stationary. Instead of moving, the texture is scrolled along the object. The result is that the ground appears to move.

**3.** Run and Jump.

**4.** Every object in the scene has a reference to the game control script. The script itself has the speed the objects should travel. Every time an object updates, it gets the speed from the control script to see how fast it should go.

# Exercise

It is time for you to attempt to implement some of the changes you noted when playtesting this game. You should make an attempt to make the game unique to you. Hopefully, you were able to identify some weaknesses of the game or some strengths that you would like to improve. Here are some things to consider changing:

▶ Try adding new/different power ups and obstacles.

▶ Try to refine the object speed to better align with the scrolling ground.

▶ Try to increase or decrease the difficulty by changing how often power ups and obstacles spawn. Also change how much time is added by power ups or how long the world is slowed. You could even try to adjust how much the world is slowed or give different objects different slowed speeds.

▶ Give the power ups and obstacles a new look. Play around with textures and particle effects to make them look awesome.

# Audio

**What You'll Learn in This Hour:**

▶ The basics of audio in Unity
▶ How to use audio sources
▶ How to work with audio via scripts

In this hour, you learn about audio in Unity. You start by learning about the basics of audio. From there, you explore the audio source components and how they work. You also take a look at individual audio clips and their role in the process. Finally, you learn how to manipulate audio in code.

## Audio Basics

A large part of any experience involves the sounds of that experience. Consider taking a scary movie and adding a laugh track to it. All of a sudden, what should be a tense experience becomes a funny one. The same is true for video games. Most of the time players don't realize it, but the sound is a very large part of the overall gameplay. Audio cues like chimes mark when a player unlocks a secret. Roaring battle cannons add a touch of realism to a war simulation game. Using Unity, amazing audio effects are easy to implement.

## Parts of Audio

For sounds to work in a scene, you need three things: the audio listener, the audio source, and the audio clip. The audio listener is the most basic component of an audio system. The listener is a simple component that's sole responsibility is "hearing" the things that are happening in a scene. An easy way to think of them is like an ear in your world. By default, every scene starts with an audio listener attached to the Main Camera (see Figure 20.1). There are no properties available for the audio listener, and there is nothing you need to do to make it work. It is a common practice to put the audio listener on whatever game object represents the player. Note that if you put an audio listener on any other game object, you need to remove it from the Main Camera. Only a single audio listener is allowed per scene.

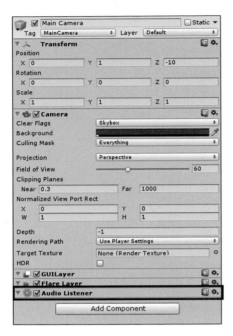

**FIGURE 20.1**
The audio listener.

The audio listener listens for sound, but it is the audio source that actually emits the sound. This source is a component that can be put on any object in a scene (even the object with the audio listener on it). There are many properties and settings involved with the audio source, and these are covered in their own section later this hour.

The last item required for functioning audio is the audio clip. Just as you would assume, the audio clip is the sound file that actually gets played by an audio source. Each clip has some properties that you can set to change the way Unity plays them. Unity supports the following audio formats: .aif, .wav, .mp3, and .ogg. Together, these three items give your scene an audio experience.

## 2D and 3D Audio

One concept to be aware of with audio is the idea of 2D and 3D audio. 2D audio clips are the most basic types of audio. They play at the same (maximum) volume regardless of the audio listener's proximity to the audio source in a scene. 2D sounds are best used for menus, warnings, soundtracks, or any audio that must always be heard the exact same way. The greatest asset of 2D sounds is also their greatest weakness. Consider if every sound in your game played at the exact same volume regardless of where you were. It would quickly spiral out of control.

3D audio solves the problems of 2D audio. These audio clips feature something called *roll off*, which dictates how sounds get quieter or louder depending on how close the audio listener gets to the audio source. In sophisticated audio systems, like Unity's, 3D sounds can even have a simulated Doppler effect (more on that later). If you are looking for realistic audio in a scene full of different audio sources, 3D audio is the way to go.

The dimensionality of different audio clip is managed in the individual settings sound file settings.

# Audio Sources

As mentioned before, the audio sources are the components that actually play audio clips in a scene. It is the distance between these sources and the listeners that determines how 3D audio clips sound. To add an audio source to a game object, select the desired object and click **Component > Audio > Audio Source**.

The audio source component has a series of properties that give you a fine level of control over how sound players in a scene. Table 20.1 describes the various properties of the audio source component.

**TABLE 20.1**  Audio Source Properties

| Property | Description |
| --- | --- |
| Audio Clip | The actual sound file to play. |
| Mute | Determines whether the sound is muted. |
| Bypass Effects | Determines whether audio effects (Pro version only) are applied to this source. Selecting this property turns off effects. |
| Bypass Listener Effects | Determines whether audio listener effects (Pro version only) are applied to this source. Selecting this property turns off effects. |
| Bypass Reverb Zone | Determines whether reverb zone effects (Pro version only) are applied to this source. Selecting this property turns off effects. |
| Play On Wake | Determines if the audio source will begin playing the sound as soon as it is created. |
| Loop | Determines if the audio source will restart the audio clip once it has finished playing. |
| Priority | Importance of the audio source. 0 is the most important, and 255 is the least important. Background music should be set to 0 to avoid being swapped out. |
| Volume | The volume of the audio source where 1 is the equivalent of 100% volume. |
| Pitch | The pitch of the audio source. |

| Property | Description |
| --- | --- |
| 3D Sound Settings | Settings applied to 3D audio clips. Covered in greater detail later. |
| 2D Sound Settings | Settings applied to 2D audio clips. Covered in greater detail later. |

NOTE

### Audio Priorities

Every system has a finite number of audio channels. This number is not consistent and depends on many factors such as the system's hardware and operating system. It is for this reason that most audio systems employ a priority system. In a priority system, sounds are played in the order that they are received until the max number of channels are used. Once all the channels are in use, lower-priority sounds are swapped out for higher-priority sounds. Just be sure to remember that in Unity a lower-priority number means a higher actual priority!

## Importing Audio Clips

Audio sources don't do anything if you don't have any audio to play. In Unity, importing audio is as easy as importing anything else. You just need to click and drag the files you want into the Project view to add them to your assets. These audio files have been graciously given to you to use by Jeremy Handel (http://handelabra.com/).

▼ TRY IT YOURSELF

### Testing Audio

Let's test out our audio in Unity and make sure that everything works. Be sure to save this scene because it will be used in the next section:

1. Create a new project or scene. Locate the **Sounds** folder in the book assets for Hour 20 and drag it into the Assets folder In Project view in Unity.

2. Create a cube in your scene and position it at (0, 0, 0). Add an audio source to the cube (click **Component > Audio > Audio Source**). Locate the file **looper.ogg** in the newly imported Sounds folder and drag it into the Audio Clip property of the audio source on the cube (see Figure 20.2).

3. Ensure that the **Play On Awake** property is checked and run your scene. Notice the sound playing. The audio should stop after about 20 seconds (unless you set it to loop).

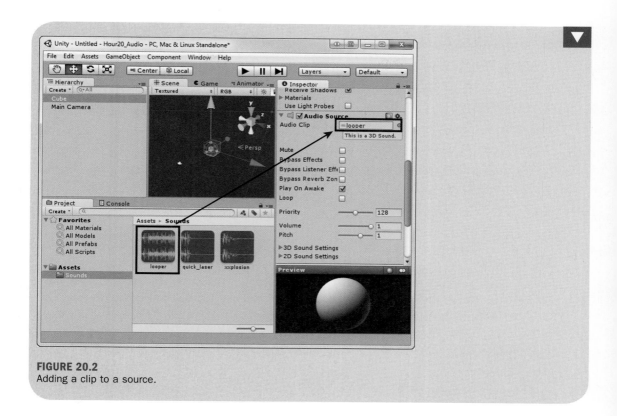

**FIGURE 20.2**
Adding a clip to a source.

## Testing Audio in the Scene View

It would get a bit taxing if you needed to run a scene every time you wanted to test out your audio. Not only would you need to start up the scene, you would also need to navigate to the sound in the world. That is not always easy, or even possible. Instead, you can test your audio in the Scene view.

To test audio in the Scene view, you need to turn scene audio on. Do this by clicking the scene audio toggle (see Figure 20.3). When you do this, an imaginary audio listener is used. This listener is positioned on your frame of reference in the Scene view (not on the position of the actual audio listener component).

**FIGURE 20.3**
The audio toggle.

### Audio in the Scene View

This exercise shows you how to test your audio in the Scene view. It uses the scene created in the previous exercise:

1. Open or create the scene from the previous exercise.

2. Turn on the scene audio toggle (refer to Figure 20.3).

3. Move around the Scene view. Notice how the sound gets louder and quieter based on your distance from the cube emitting the sound. By default, all sound clips are 3D and therefore are subject to the distance between the source and the listener.

## 3D Audio

As mentioned previously, all audio is set to be 3D by default. This means that all audio will be subject to the 3D audio effects that are distance and movement based. These effects are modified by the 3D properties of the audio component (see Figure 20.4).

**FIGURE 20.4**
The 3D audio settings.

Table 20.2 describes the various 3D audio properties.

**TABLE 20.2**   3D Audio Properties

| Property | Description |
|---|---|
| Doppler Level | Determines how much Doppler effect is applied to the audio. A setting of 0 means no effect will be applied. The Doppler effect is how sound is distorted while you are traveling toward or away from it. |
| Volume Rolloff | Determines how the change in sound volume over distance is applied. Logarithmic is set by default. You can also choose Linear or set your own curve with a custom roll off. |
| Min Distance | The distance away from the source you have to be before receiving 100% volume. The higher the number, the farther away you can be and still receive 100% volume. |
| Pan Level | Determines how much effect the 3D engine has on the audio. Setting this to 0 is the same as having a 2D sound. |
| Spread | How spread out the various speakers of a system are. A setting of 0 means that all speakers are at the same position and that the signal is essentially a mono signal. Leave this alone unless you understand more about audio systems. |
| Max Distance | The farthest you can be from the source and still hear some volume. |

# 2D Audio

Sometimes, you want audio to play at full volume regardless of its position in the scene. The most common example of this is background music. To switch an audio clip from 3D to 2D, select the audio file and uncheck the **3D Sound** property in the Inspector view (see Figure 20.5).

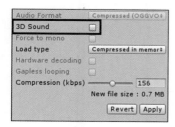

**FIGURE 20.5**
Making a sound clip 2D.

Once an audio clip is set to 2D, only the 2D Sound Settings properties of the audio source will be applied to it. Easily enough, there is only a single 2D property: Pan. The Pan property in this instance controls how the audio is played. With a value of 0, the sound plays equally out of both speakers in a stereo environment (left and right). With a value of –1, the audio will play on only the left side, and a value of 1 makes the audio play only on the right.

**Testing 2D Audio**

Let's try out 2D audio in a scene. This exercise uses the scene created in the previous two exercises:

1. Open or create the scene from the previous exercises.

2. In the Sounds folder, locate the looper.ogg file and select it. In the Inspector, uncheck the 3D Sound property. Click the **Apply** button.

3. With the scene audio toggle turned on, navigate around the scene. Notice how your position to the cube has no effect on the sound being played.

# Audio Scripting

Playing audio from an audio source when it is created is nice, assuming that's the functionality that you want. If you want to wait and play a sound at a certain time, or play different sounds from the same source, however, you need to use scripting. Luckily, there isn't too much difficulty with managing your audio through code. Most of it works just like any audio player you're used to. Just pick a song and press Play. All audio scripting is done using variables and methods that are a part of the object audio.

## Starting and Stopping Audio

The most basic functionality you could want is simply starting and stopping an audio clip. These are controlled by two methods simply named Start() and Stop(). Using these methods looks like this:

```
audio.Start(); //Starts a clip
audio.Stop(); //Stops a clip
```

This code will play the clip specific by the Audio Clip property of the audio source component. You also have the ability to start a clip after a delay. To do that, you use the method PlayDelayed(), which takes in a single parameter that is the time in seconds to wait before playing the clip. This method looks like:

```
audio.PlayDelayed(<some time in seconds>);
```

You can tell whether a clip is currently playing by checking the isPlaying variable, which is a part of the audio object, in code. To access this variable, and thus see if the clip is playing, you could type the following:

```
if (audio.isPlaying)
{
    //The track is playing
}
```

As the name implies, this variable is true if the audio is currently playing and false if it is not.

**Starting and Stopping Audio**

In this exercise, you use scripts to start and stop an audio clip:

1. Create a new project or scene. Import the **Sounds** folder from the book assets if you haven't done so already. Place a cube in your scene at position (0, 0, 0) and put an audio source on it.

2. Drag the looper.ogg file from the Sounds folder onto the Audio Clip property of the audio source on the cube. Also be sure to uncheck **Play On Wake** and to check the **Loop** properties of the audio source.

3. Create a new folder named **Scripts** and create a new script in it called **AudioScript**. Attach the script to the cube. Add the following code to the script:

```
void Update () {

    if (Input.GetButtonDown("Jump"))
    {
        if (audio.isPlaying == true)
        {
            audio.Stop();
        }
        else
        {
            audio.Play();
        }
    }
}
```

4. Play the scene. You can start and stop the audio by pressing the spacebar. Notice how the audio clip starts over every time you play the audio.

TIP
_____

**Unmentioned Properties**

All the properties of the audio source that are listed in the Inspector are also available via script-ing. For instance, the Loop property is accessed in code with the audio.loop variable. As mentioned before, all of these variables are used in conjunction with the audio object. See how many you can find!
_____

## Changing Audio Clips

You can easily control which audio clips to play via scripts. The key is to change the audio clip property in the code before using the Play() method to play the clip. Always be sure to stop the current audio clip before switching to a new one; otherwise, the clip won't switch.

To change the audio clip of an audio source, assign a variable of type AudioClip to the clip variable of the object audio. For example, if you had an audio clip called newClip, you could assign it to an audio source and playing it using the following code:

```
audio.clip = newClip;
audio.Play();
```

You can easily create a collection of audio clips and switch them out in this manner.

## Summary

In this hour, you learned about using audio in Unity. You started by learning about the basics of audio and the components required to make it work. From there, you explored the audio source component. You learned how to test audio in the Scene view, and how to use 2D and 3D audio clips. You finished the hour by learning to manipulate audio through scripts.

## Q&A

**Q. How many audio channels does a system have on average?**

**A.** It truly varies for every system; however it is good baseline knowledge to know that head-phones generally only have two. This doesn't mean that headphones can only play two sounds. It just means that there can only be two sounds played before the system needs to mix the sounds together, slightly degrading the quality.

# Workshop

Take some time to work through the questions here to ensure that you have a firm grasp of the material.

## Quiz

1. What items are needed for working audio?

2. True or False: 3D sounds play at the same volume regardless of the listener's distance from the source?

3. What method allows you to play an audio clip after a delay?

## Answers

1. An audio listener, source, and clip.

2. False. 2D sounds play at the same volume.

3. PlayDelayed().

# Exercise

In this exercise, you create a basic sound board. This sound board will allow you to play one of three sounds. You also have the ability to start and stop the sounds and to turn looping on and off. You can find the completed exercise as Hour20_Exercise in the book assets for Hour 20:

1. Create a new project or scene. Add a cube to the scene at position (0, 0, –10) and add an audio source to the cube. Be sure to uncheck the **Play On Wake** property. Locate the **Sounds** folder in the book assets for Hour 20 and drag it into the Assets folder.

2. Create a new folder called **Scripts** and create a new script named **AudioScript** in it. Attach the script to the cube. Change the script to contain the following:

```
public AudioClip clip1;
public AudioClip clip2;
public AudioClip clip3;

void Start()
{
    audio.clip = clip1;
}

void Update () {
    if(Input.GetButtonDown("Jump"))
    {
        if(audio.isPlaying)
            audio.Stop();
```

```
        else
            audio.Play();
    }

    if(Input.GetKeyDown(KeyCode.L))
        audio.loop = !audio.loop; //toggles lopping

    if(Input.GetKeyDown(KeyCode.Alpha1))
    {
        audio.Stop();
        audio.clip = clip1;
        audio.Play();
    }
    else if(Input.GetKeyDown(KeyCode.Alpha2))
    {
        audio.Stop();
        audio.clip = clip2;
        audio.Play();
    }
    else if(Input.GetKeyDown(KeyCode.Alpha3))
    {
        audio.Stop();
        audio.clip = clip3;
        audio.Play();
    }
}
```

3. In the Unity editor, select the cube in your scene. Drag each of the **looper.ogg, quick_laser.ogg**, and **xxplosion.off** audio files from the Sounds folder onto the Clip1, Clip2, and Clip3 properties of the audio script.

4. Run your scene. Notice how you can change your audio clips with the 1–3 number keys. You can also start and stop the audio with the spacebar. Finally, you can toggle looping with the **L** key.

# HOUR 21
# Mobile Development

**What You'll Learn in This Hour:**

▶ How to prepare for mobile development
▶ How to use a devices accelerometer
▶ How to use a devices touch display

Mobile devices such as phone and tablets are becoming common gaming devices. In this hour, you learn about mobile development with Unity for Android and iOS devices. You begin by looking at the requirements for mobile development. From there, you learn how to accept special inputs from a device's accelerometer. Finally, you learn about touch interface input.

NOTE

## Requirements

This hour covers the development for mobile devices specifically. So, if you do not have a mobile device (iOS or Android), you will not be able to follow along with any of the hands-on exercises. Don't worry, though; the reading should still make sense, and you will still be able to make games on mobile devices. You just won't be able to play them.

# Preparing for Mobile

Unity makes developing games for mobile devices easy. As of Unity version 4.1, the mobile plug-ins are even free! You will also be happy to know that developing for mobile platforms is almost identical to developing for other platforms. This means that you can build a game once and deploy it everywhere. There is no longer any reason why you can't build your games for every major platform. This level of cross-platform capability is unprecedented. Before you can begin working with mobile devices in Unity, however, you need to get your computer set up and configured to do it.

NOTE

## Multitudes of Devices

There are many different types of mobile devices. At the time of this writing, Apple has three devices (iPod, iPad, and iPhone), and Android has an untold number of phones and tablets. Each of these devices has slightly different hardware and steps to configure them correctly. Therefore, this text simply attempts to guide you through the installation process. It would be impossible to write an exact guide that would work for everyone. In fact, several guides by Unity, Apple, and Android (Google) already exist that explain the process better than this text could. You are referred to them when needed.

# Setting Up Your Environment

Before even opening Unity to make a game, you need to set up your development environment. The specifics of this differ depending on your target device and what you are trying to do, but the general steps are as follows:

1. Install the software development kit (SDK) of the device you are targeting.

2. Ensure that your computer recognizes and can work with your device (only important if you want to test on the device).

3. Tell Unity where to find the SDK (required for Android only).

If these steps seem a bit cryptic to you, don't worry. Plenty of resources are available to assist you with these steps. The best place to start is with Unity's own documentation. You can access Unity's documentation at http://docs.unity3d.com.

This site contains the living document of everything that is Unity. By default, it only shows items related to desktop development. You need to enable the documentation for Android and iOS. You should see an Android and iOS icon with a red *X* (see Figure 21.1).

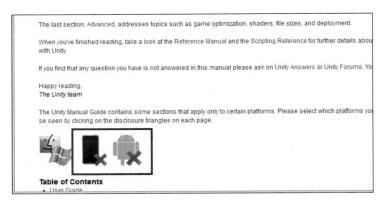

The last section, Advanced, addresses topics such as game optimization, shaders, file sizes, and deployment.

When you've finished reading, take a look at the Reference Manual and the Scripting Reference for further details about with Unity.

If you find that any question you have is not answered in this manual please ask on Unity Answers or Unity Forums. Yo

Happy reading,
*The Unity team*

The Unity Manual Guide contains some sections that apply only to certain platforms. Please select which platforms yo be seen by clicking on the disclosure triangles on each page.

**Table of Contents**
• User Guide

**FIGURE 21.1**
The disabled mobile icons.

Clicking either of these items will put a green check mark on them and enable that documentation (see Figure 21.2). As you can see in Figure 21.2, the Unity documentation has guides to assist you in setting up both the iOS and Android environments. These documents are updated as the steps to set the environment changes. After you have completed the steps to configure your development environment for your target environment, or if you're not planning on following along with a device, continue on to the next section.

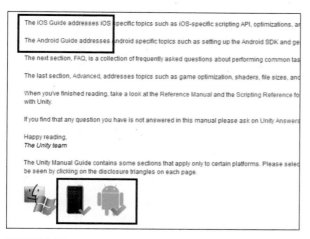

**FIGURE 21.2**
Enabling mobile documentation.

# The Unity Remote

The most basic way to test your games on a device is to build your projects, put the resulting files on the device, and then run it. This can be a cumbersome system and one you're sure to tire of quickly. Another way to test your games is to build the project and then run it through an iOS or Android emulator. Again, this requires quite a few steps and involves configuring and running an emulator. These systems can be useful if you are doing extensive testing on advanced things such as performance and rendering. For basic testing, though, there is a much better way: the Unity Remote.

The Unity Remote is an app you can download from your mobile devices application store that enables you to test your applications out on your mobile device while it is running in the Unity editor. In a nutshell, this means that you can experience your game running on a device in real time alongside development and use the device to send device inputs back to your game. You can find more information about the Unity Remote at http://docs.unity3d.com/Documentation/Manual/unity-remote.html.

To find the Unity Remote application, search for the term *Unity Remote* in your device's application store. From there, you can download and install it just like any other application (see Figure 21.3).

**FIGURE 21.3**
The different application stores.

Once installed, the Unity Remote will act as both a display for your game and a controller. You will be able to send click information, accelerometer information, and multi-touch input back to Unity.

▼ TRY IT YOURSELF

## Testing Device Setup

Let's take a moment to ensure that your mobile development environment is set up correctly. In this exercise, you use the Unity Remote from your device to interact with a scene in Unity. If you don't have a device set up, you won't be able to perform all of these steps, but you can still get the idea of what's happening by reading along. If these steps don't work, it means that something with your environment is not set up correctly:

1. Create a new project or scene. Create a new folder called **Scripts**, and in that folder create a new script called **TestScript**.

2. Attach the test script to the Main Camera and add the following code to it:

```
void OnGUI()
{
    if(GUI.Button(new Rect(Screen.width / 2 - 50, Screen.height / 2 - 50, 100,
➥100), "Click"))
    {
        camera.backgroundColor =
            new Color(Random.Range(0f,1f),Random.Range(0f,1f), Random.
➥Range(0f,1f));
    }
}
```

3. Run the scene and ensure that clicking the button changes the screen's background color. Stop the scene.

4. Attach your mobile device to your computer. Once the computer recognizes your device, open the Unity Remote.

5. Run the scene again. After a second, you should see the scene's blue screen and button appear on your mobile device. You should now be able to tap the button on your device's screen to change the background color of the scene. If you find that tapping the button doesn't do anything, click any of the views other than the Game view. That glitch is due to a slight bug, and clicking a view or one of the tools in Unity will fix it.

# Accelerometers

Most modern mobile devices come with a built-in accelerometer. An accelerometer relays information about the physical orientation of the device. It can tell whether the device is moving, tilted, or flat. It can also detect these things in all three axes. Figure 21.4 shows a mobile device's accelerometer axes and how they are oriented. This is called a *portrait orientation*.

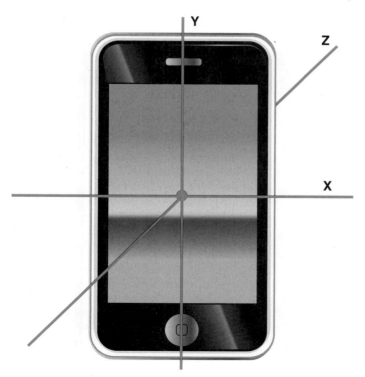

**FIGURE 21.4**
Accelerometer axes.

As you can see in Figure 21.4, the default axes of a device align with the 3D axes in Unity while the device is being held upright directly in front of you. If you turn the device to use it in a different orientation, you need to convert the accelerometer data to the correct axis.

## Designing for the Accelerometer

You need to keep in mind a few things when designing a game to use a mobile device's accelerometer. The first is that you can only ever reliably use two of the accelerometer's axes at any given time. The reason for this is that no matter the orientation of the device, one axis will always be actively engaged by gravity. Consider the orientation of the device in Figure 21.4. You can see that while the x and z axes can be manipulated by tilting the device, the y axis is currently reading negative values. (Gravity is pulling it down.) If you were to turn the phone so that it rested flat on a surface, face up, you would only be able to use the x and y axes. In that case, the z axis would be actively engaged.

Another thing to consider when designing for an accelerometer is that the input is not extremely accurate. Mobile devices do not read from their accelerometers at a set interval, and often have to approximate values. The result is the inputs read from an accelerometer can be jerky and uneven. It is worth noting that the amount of inaccuracy is very small. It exists nonetheless and therefore should be noted.

## Using the Accelerometer

Reading accelerometer input is done via scripts just like any other form of user input. All you need to do is read from the Vector3 variable named `acceleration`, which is a part of the object `Input`. Therefore, you could access the x, y, and z axis data by writing the following:

```
Input.acceleration.x;
Input.acceleration.y;
Input.acceleration.z;
```

Using these values, you can manipulate your game objects accordingly.

---

NOTE

### Axis Mismatch

When using accelerometer information in conjunction with the Unity Remote, you might notice that the axes aren't lining up with the way they were described earlier in the "Accelerometers" section. This is because the Unity Remote bases the game's orientation on the aspect ratio chosen. This means that the Unity Remote will automatically display in landscape orientation (holding your device sideways so that the longer edge is parallel to the ground) and translates the axes for you. Therefore, when you are using the Unity Remote, the x axis runs along the long edge of your device, and the y axis runs along the short edge. It might seem strange, but chances are you were going to use your device like that anyway. This saves you a step.

---

## Moving a Cube with the Power of Your Mind... or Your Phone

In this exercise, you use a mobile device's accelerometer to move a cube around a scene. Obviously, to complete this exercise you need a configured and attached mobile device with an accelerometer:

1. Create a new project or scene. Add a cube to the scene and position it at (0, 0, 0).

2. Create a new script called **AccelerometerScript** and attach it to the cube. Put the following code in the `Update()` method of the script:

```
float x = Input.acceleration.x * Time.deltaTime;
float z = -Input.acceleration.z * Time.deltaTime;
transform.Translate(x, 0f, z);
```

3. Ensure that your mobile device is plugged in to your computer. Hold the device in a landscape orientation and run the Unity Remote. Run the scene. Notice how you can move the cube by tilting your phone. Notice which axes of the phone move the cube along the x and z axes.

# Multi-Touch Input

Mobile devices tend to be controlled largely by touch-capacity screens. These screens can detect when and where you touch them. They usually can track multiple touches at a time. The exact number of touches varies based on the device.

Touching the screen doesn't just give the device a simple touch location. In fact, there is quite a bit of information stored about each individual touch. In Unity, each screen touch is stored in a `Touch` variable. This means that every time you touch a screen, a Touch variable will be generated. That `Touch` variable will exist as long as your finger remains on the screen. If you drag your finger along the screen, the `Touch` variable tracks that. These `Touch` variables are stored together in a collection called `touches`, which is a part of the `Input` object. If there is currently nothing touching the screen, than this collection of touches will be empty. To access this collection, you could enter the following:

```
Input.touches;
```

Using that collection, you could iterate through each touch variable to process its data. Doing so would look something like this:

```
foreach(Touch touch in Input.touches)
{
    //Do something
}
```

As mentioned before, each touch contains more information than the simple screen data where the touch occurred. Table 21.1 contains all the properties of the Touch variable type.

**TABLE 21.1   Touch Properties**

| Property | Description |
| --- | --- |
| deltaPosition | The change in touch position since the last update. This is useful for detecting finger drags. |
| deltaTime | The amount of time that has passed since the last change to the touch. |
| fingerId | The unique index for the touch. For example, these would range from 0 to 4 on devices that allow five touches at a time. |
| phase | The current phase of the touch. The phases can be Began, Moved, Stationary, Ended, and Canceled. |
| position | The 2D position of the touch on the screen. |
| tapCount | The number of taps the touch has performed on the screen. As of the time of this writing, this is implemented only on iOS devices. Taps must be manually managed on Android devices. |

Each of these properties is useful for managing complex interactions between the user and game objects.

▼ TRY IT YOURSELF

**Tracking Touches**

In this exercise, you track finger touches and output their data to the screen. Obviously, to complete this exercise you need a configured and attached mobile device with multi-touch support:

1. Create a new project or scene.

2. Create a new script called **TouchScript** and attach it to the Main Camera. Put the following code in the script:

```
void OnGUI()
{
    foreach(Touch touch in Input.touches)
    {
        string message = "";
        message += "ID: " + touch.fingerId + "\n";
        message += "Phase: " + touch.phase.ToString() + "\n";
        message += "TapCount: " + touch.tapCount + "\n";
```

```
message += "Pos X: " + touch.position.x + "\n";
message += "Pos Y: " + touch.position.y + "\n";

int num = touch.fingerId;
GUI.Label(new Rect(0 + 130 * num, 0, 120, 100), message);
        }
    }
```

3. Ensure that your mobile device is plugged in to your computer. Run the scene. Touch the screen with your finger and notice the information that appears (see Figure 21.5). Move your finger and see how the data changes. Now touch with more fingers simultaneously. Move them about and take them off of the screen randomly. See how it tracks each touch independently. How many touches can you get on your screen at a time?

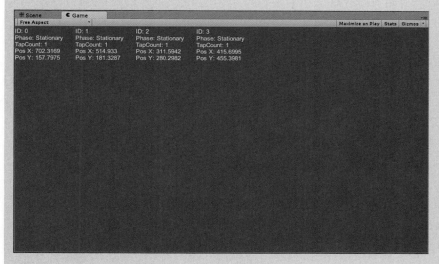

**FIGURE 21.5**
Touch output on the screen.

CAUTION

### Do Because I Say, Not Because I Do!

In the preceding exercise, you created an `OnGUI()` method that collected information about the various touches on the screen. The part of the code where the string `message` is being built with the touch data is a *big* no-no. You should never perform processing in an `OnGUI()` method, because it can greatly reduce efficiencies in your project. This was just the easiest way to build the example without unneeded complexity and for demonstration purposes only. Always keep update code where it belongs: in `Update()`.

# Summary

In this hour, you learned about using Unity to develop games with mobile devices in mind. You started by learning how to configure your development environment to work with Android and iOS. From there, you worked hands on with a device's accelerometer. You finished up the hour by experimenting with Unity's touch-tracking system.

# Q&A

**Q.** Can I really build a game once and deploy it to all major platforms, mobile included?

**A.** Absolutely! The only thing to consider is that mobile devices generally don't have as much processing power as desktops. Therefore, you might experience some performance issues if your game has a lot of heavy processing or effects. You will need to ensure that your game is running efficiently if you plan to also deploy it on mobile platforms.

**Q.** What are the differences between iOS and Android devices?

**A.** From a Unity point of view, there isn't much difference between these two operating systems. They are both treated as mobile devices. Be aware, though, that there are some hardware differences that can affect your games.

# Workshop

Take some time to work through the questions here to ensure that you have a firm grasp of the material.

## Quiz

**1.** What tool allows you to send live device input data to Unity while it is running a scene?

**2.** How many axes on the accelerometer can you realistically use at a time?

**3.** How many touches can a device have at once?

## Answers

**1.** The Unity Remote.

**2.** Two axes. The third will always be engaged by gravity depending on how you are holding the device.

**3.** It depends entirely on the device. If a device doesn't have multi-touch, it can have only a single touch at a time. If it does have multi-touch, it can have many.

# Exercise

In this exercise, you move objects about a scene based on touch input from a mobile device. Obviously, to complete this exercise you need a configured and attached mobile device with multi-touch support. If you do not have that, you can still read along to get the basic ideas. The completed exercise can be found as Hour21_Exercise in the book assets for Hour 21:

1. Create a new project or scene. Add a directional light to the scene.

2. Add three cubes to the scene and name them **Cube1**, **Cube2**, and **Cube3**. Position them at (–3, 1, –5), (0, 1,– 5), and (3, 1, –5) respectively.

3. Create a new folder named **Scripts**. Create a new script called **InputScript** in the Scripts folder and attach it to the three cubes.

4. Add the following code to the `Update()` method of the script:

```
foreach(Touch touch in Input.touches)
{
    if(touch.fingerId == 0 && gameObject.name == "Cube1")
        transform.Translate(touch.deltaPosition.x * .05F, touch.
deltaPosition.y * .05F, 0F);
    if(touch.fingerId == 1 && gameObject.name == "Cube2")
        transform.Translate(touch.deltaPosition.x * .05F, touch.
deltaPosition.y * .05F, 0F);
    if(touch.fingerId == 2 && gameObject.name == "Cube3")
        transform.Translate(touch.deltaPosition.x * .05F, touch.
deltaPosition.y * .05F, 0F);

}
```

5. Run the scene and touch the screen with up to three fingers. Notice how you can move the three cubes independently. Also notice how lifting one finger does not cause the other fingers to lose their cubes or their place.

# HOUR 22
# Game Revisions

## What You'll Learn in This Hour:

▶ How to make *Amazing Racer* mobile capable

▶ How to make *Chaos Ball* mobile capable

▶ How to make *Captain Blaster* mobile capable

▶ How to make *Gauntlet Runner* mobile capable

Let's make a lot of games! More specifically, let's revisit the games you made before and make them mobile capable. You will start by adding movement, looking, and jumping capabilities to *Amazing Racer*. From there, you will add turning and moving controls to *Chaos Ball*. Next, you will change orientations to work in Portrait mode with *Captain Blaster*. Finally, you will add input controls to *Gauntlet Runner*.

NOTE

### Completed Games

Each of the completed *mobile friendly* games is available in the book assets for Hour 22, named after their original game projects.

## Amazing Racer

The first game you made is probably the most difficult one to convert to a mobile device. The reason is that there are three forms of unique input: moving, looking, and jumping. The moving part can easily be read from the accelerometer. The looking and jumping, however, are both derived from touch input. Therefore, you need some way to differentiate between touch inputs.

### Moving and Looking

The first thing you want to do is change the way the player moves. This particular game utilizes a first-person controller. The best way to implement mobile controls is to open the controller and modify the code inside. This is a bit more complex than desired at this point, however, so you will instead be creating new scripts on top of the already existing functionality. You will be making it so that the accelerometer information moves the player forward, backward, and side to side. Any touches that occur on the right half of the screen will allow you to move the view around. Because of the complexity of *looking* mechanics, looking up and looking down will rotate the camera of the controller, while looking left and right will actually rotate the controller itself.

To set up movement and horizontal looking, follow these steps:

1. Open the *Amazing Racer* completed game. Add a new script to the Scripts folder named **MobileInputScript** and attach it to the Player game object.

2. Add the following code to the script:

```
public float speed = 15;
public float jump = 3;

CharacterController control;

void Start () {
    control = GetComponent<CharacterController>();
}

// Update is called once per frame
void Update () {
    float x = Input.acceleration.x * Time.deltaTime * speed;
    float z = -Input.acceleration.z * Time.deltaTime * speed;

    transform.Translate(x, 0f, z);

    foreach(Touch touch in Input.touches)
    {

        //turning
        if(touch.position.x > Screen.width / 2)
        {
            transform.Rotate(0f, touch.deltaPosition.x, 0f);
        }
    }
}
```

3. Attach a mobile device to your computer and run Unity Remote. While holding the device in Landscape mode, run the scene. Notice how you can move around by tilting the phone. Try dragging your finger around the right side of the screen. Notice how you can use a touch on the right side of the screen to look around.

Now that you have added moving and horizontal looking, you want to add vertical looking. You add the vertical looking component directly to the camera of the first-person controller. It will look using the same mechanics as the horizontal looking does. To add this, follow these steps:

**1.** Create a new script in the scripts folder named **MobileLookScript**. Attach the script to the Main Camera, which is nested under the Player game object (see Figure 22.1).

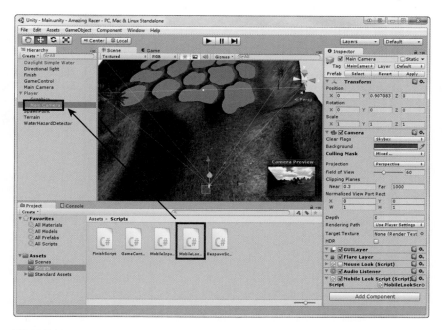

**FIGURE 22.1**
Adding the look script to the controller's camera.

**2.** Add the following code to the Update() method in the look script:

```
foreach(Touch touch in Input.touches)
{
    if(touch.position.x > Screen.width / 2)
    {
        transform.Rotate(-touch.deltaPosition.y, 0f, 0f);
    }
}
```

**3.** Run the scene. Notice how you can now use a finger on the right side of the screen to look up and down. Together with the MobileInputScript, this script will enable you to look all around your scene using a single finger.

# Jumping

The last bit of functionality you want to add to this game is the jumping feature. As mentioned previously, this game was made with a first-person controller. Therefore, the jumping that you will be adding will not function exactly in the same way. The best way to do this is to modify the controller code to allow for the jumping input. Because of the complexity, you will be adding new code instead.

Jumping will work by tapping anywhere on the left side of the screen. In this case, the code is looking for any tap, which will then jump the player up into the air. To do this, follow these steps:

1. You will not be creating a new script. Instead, open the MobileInputScript you created before.

2. Add the following code to the Update() method. You should already have some of the code listed. It is simply there as a reference so that you know where this code should go:

```
foreach(Touch touch in Input.touches) //Here for reference
{
    //jumping
    if(touch.position.x < Screen.width - Screen.width / 2 &&
        touch.phase == TouchPhase.Began)
    {
        control.Move(new Vector3(0f, jump, 0f));
    }

    //turning - Here for reference
    if(touch.position.x > Screen.width / 2)
//...
```

3. Run the scene. Notice how you can now jump as well as move and look with a mobile device.

At this point, all the mobile conversion should be complete for *Amazing Racer*.

---

NOTE

## Game Quality

When running this game on a mobile device, you might notice a lack of control quality. The jump mechanic is jerky, and the move and turn mechanics are a bit twitchy. This is correct and in no way indicates a problem with your mobile device. The fact of the matter is, you are adding new functionality on top of an already functioning game. Not all mechanics integrate easily. These mechanics could be smoothed out, but doing so would take too much time. Remember, you still have three games to go. Instead, use these games as an indicator of what is possible with mobile controls and as a guideline to the basics of how they can be implemented.

---

# Chaos Ball

The second game you creating, *Chaos Ball*, is a bit simpler of an implementation. The idea again is that the accelerometer will control the paddle's movement. You can then use a touch to control the looking. Because no other input is required, you don't need to split the screen or use touching for anything else. The scripts here will look similar to the previous game because they use similar controls. To convert this game, follow these steps:

1. Open the *Chaos Ball* project in Unity. Disable the **Mouse Look (Script)** component on the Main Camera of the first-person controller game object (see Figure 22.2).

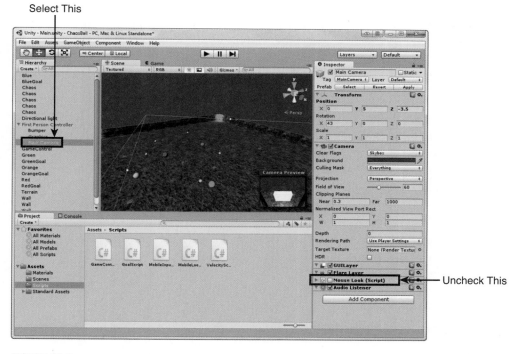

**FIGURE 22.2**
Removing the Mouse Look component.

2. Add a new script to the Scripts folder named **MouseInputScript**. Attach the script to the first-person controller game object. Add the following code to the script:

```
public float speed = 15;

void Update () {
    float x = Input.acceleration.x * Time.deltaTime * speed;
    float z = -Input.acceleration.z * Time.deltaTime * speed;
```

```
transform.Translate(x, 0f, z);

foreach(Touch touch in Input.touches)
{
    //turning
    if(touch.position.x > Screen.width / 2)
    {
        transform.Rotate(0f, touch.deltaPosition.x * 10, 0f);
    }
}
}
```

3. Add another script named **MouseLookScript** and attach it to the Main Camera of the first-person controller game object (see Figure 22.1). Add the following code to the Update() method of the script:

```
foreach(Touch touch in Input.touches)
{
    transform.Rotate(-touch.deltaPosition.y, 0f, 0f);
}
```

4. Run the game. Notice how you can now move around and look about with the accelerometer and touch input.

That is all you need to do to convert this game to mobile inputs (and make it very difficult). One thing to be aware of is that now the player can move through the walls and fall off of the level. This is because you are now using a Translate() and not the controller to move the player about. You could fix this in a couple of ways: by using the already existing character controller or by raycasting from the player to see if the player is too close to a wall.

# Captain Blaster

The game *Captain Blaster* is unique among the games you have made so far, in that it is treated as a 2D game and it is a vertical-oriented game. That means that you do not have to worry about the z axis. It also means that you need to configure your game to work in Portrait mode. If you recall, a *portrait orientation* is what you get when you hold a mobile device upright so that its short edge is parallel to the ground while its long edge is perpendicular to the ground.

To get the Unity http to work in Portrait mode, you will need to make some changes to the Unity editor. You must tell it that you want to operate in Portrait mode. To do this, follow these steps:

1. Open the *Captain Blaster* Unity project.

2. Choose **File > Build Settings** to bring up the Build Settings dialog. Do not worry too much about what is in here; it is covered more extensively in the next hour. In the left menu, select either **Android** or **iOS** depending on which type of device you are using, and then click **Switch Platform**. When you have finished, click the **X** in the upper-right corner to exit this dialog (see Figure 22.3). If you are on a Mac machine, you have a similar button in the upper-left corner.

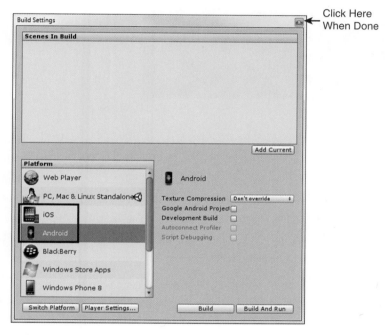

Click Here
When Done

**FIGURE 22.3**
Switching platforms.

3. In the Game view, choose the resolution for your game. It is best if you choose the dimensions of the mobile device you are using. If you don't know what the dimensions are, choose the generic **3:2 Portrait** (see Figure 22.4).

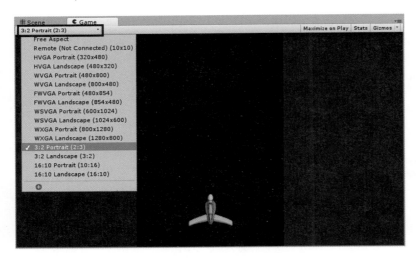

**FIGURE 22.4**
Changing the scene resolution.

NOTE

**Console Errors**

During this process, you might see a bunch of red errors in the console. You can safely ignore those at this point. They are generated when the textures and models in a scene get converted. As soon as you play the scene, they will go away, and everything will correct itself.

Now your scene is ready to go. When run in the Unity Remote, it should display in the proper portrait orientation. Now all you need to do is map the accelerometer and taps to game input. This is easy this time because you didn't use one of the built-in controllers when you made this game originally. Now you can just modify the code you wrote to work with a mobile device:

1. In the Scripts folder, locate the PlayerScript and open it.

2. To make movement work, place the line

```
transform.Translate(Input.acceleration.x * speed * Time.deltaTime, 0f, 0f);
```
underneath the line
```
transform.Translate(Input.GetAxis("Horizontal") * speed * Time.deltaTime, 0f,
0f);
```

3. To make shooting work, modify the line

```
if(Input.GetButtonDown("Jump"))
```
to be
```
if(Input.GetButtonDown("Jump") || Input.touches.Length > 0)
```

Now your mobile inputs are set up. You might have noticed that you left the original controls in. This is nice because it allows the game to run on both a mobile device and a computer. One thing to mention is that because the resolution has changed to be narrower, many meteors are spawning offscreen. To improve this, you would need to change the dimensions of the area the meteors can spawn.

# Gauntlet Runner

The last game that you made, *Gauntlet Runner*, is also the easiest to convert to a mobile device. All you need to do to make this game work is apply the code changes that you also applied to *Captain Blaster*. Because that is boring, you are going to implement a different system for the player to move around.

This time, players will move left and right by dragging their finger left and right. To jump, players must "flick" their finger upward. Both of these actions rely on the deltaPosition variable inside the Touch variable. To implement this, follow these steps:

1. Open the *Gauntlet Runner* project in Unity.

2. Locate and open the PlayerScript script inside the Scripts folder. Modify the Update() method to contain the following:

```
transform.Translate(Input.GetAxis("Horizontal") * Time.deltaTime *
strafeSpeed, 0f, 0f);

//if there is a touch
if(Input.touches.Length > 0)
{
    //use the position of the first one
    transform.Translate(Input.touches[0].deltaPosition.x * Time.deltaTime *
➥strafeSpeed,
        0f, 0f);
}

if(transform.position.x > 3)
    transform.position = new Vector3(3, transform.position.y, transform.
➥position.z);
else if(transform.position.x < -3)
    transform.position = new Vector3(-3, transform.position.y, transform.
➥position.z);

if (anim.GetCurrentAnimatorStateInfo(0).IsName("Base Layer.Jump"))
{
    anim.SetBool("Jumping", false);
    jumping = true;
}
else
```

```
{
    jumping = false;
    if(Input.GetButtonDown("Jump"))
    {
        anim.SetBool("Jumping", true);
    }
    //check for "flick" if there are touches
    else if(Input.touches.Length > 0)
    {
    if(Input.touches[0].deltaPosition.y > 2)
        anim.SetBool("Jumping", true);
    }
}
```

**3.** Run the game. Notice how sliding a finger back and forth moves the player side to side. Also notice how you are able to jump by flicking your finger upward.

As you work through the code for this game, you may notice the following line:

```
if(Input.touches[0].deltaPosition.y > 2)
```

You might be wondering why a value of 2 was used here. The basic idea is that although you might be flicking your finger upward very fast, the game is cycling 60 times a second. This means that compared to the game, you are actually going quite slow. Therefore, the value to determine whether you are flicking your finger is very low. By setting this value any higher, your game may not recognize slower flicks. By setting it lower, the game may think you are flicking your finger when you aren't.

# Summary

In this hour, you rebuilt your four previous games to include mobile device controls. You started with *Amazing Racer*, to which you added movement, jumping, and looking controls. From there, you modified *Chaos Ball* to allow mobile accelerometer and touch inputs. You changed gears in the next game, *Captain Blaster*, where you modified the game to be in a mobile portrait orientation. You also added accelerometer movement and tap shooting. In your final game, *Gauntlet Runner*, you tried a new style of control. You added swiping and flicking motions to control the player.

# Q&A

**Q.** Some of the games didn't seem to translate well to mobile. Is that normal?

**A.** Yes, it is. Often, when a game is not made with mobile platforms in mind, it is difficult to transition it. Computers and gaming consoles have many more control options available to them than the simple mobile device. Always ask yourself when designing a game if a mobile version is possible in the future.

# Workshop

Take some time to work through the questions here to ensure that you have a firm grasp of the material.

## Quiz

1. How did you handle needing to use the screen to both jump and look in *Amazing Racer*?
2. What is the major problem with using translations to move the player in *Chaos Ball*?
3. True or False: *Captain Blaster* was modified to be in landscape orientation.
4. What constitutes a "flick" in *Gauntlet Runner*?

## Answers

1. Half the screen was used for jumping input and the other half was for looking.
2. The player is able to move through the walls and fall off of the world.
3. False. It was modified to be in portrait orientation.
4. A flick is when the player moves their finger upward really quickly.

# Exercise

In this hour, you worked through a lot of control mechanics on four different games. When developing games, major mechanics overhauls can sometimes take place. It is not uncommon to change how inputs or controls work to try to build a better user experience. As with any major change, always retest afterward to see what impact the changes had. For this exercise, go back through and replay these games again. This time, play them with mobile controls. Like always, take notes on what you like and what you don't like. When you finish playing, compare these notes to the notes you took when you originally made the games. (You kept those, right?) See what changes you can make to the controls, or the game, to make the *mobile experience* better. Try to implement some or all of those changes.

# Polish and Deploy

---

**What You'll Learn in This Hour:**

▶ How to manage scenes in a game

▶ How to save data and objects between scenes

▶ The different player settings

▶ How to deploy a game

In this hour, you learn all about polishing a game and deploying it. You start by learning how to move about different scenes. Then, you explore ways to persist data and game objects between scenes. From there, you take a look at the Unity player and its settings. You then learn how to build and deploy a game.

## Managing Scenes

So far, everything you have done in Unity has been in the same scene. Although it is certainly possible to build large and complex games in this way, it is generally much easier to use multiple scenes. The idea behind a scene is that it is a self-contained collection of game objects. Therefore, when transitioning between scenes, all existing game objects are destroyed, and all new game objects are created. However, you can prevent this, as discussed in the next section.

---

NOTE

### What Is a Scene? Revisited

What a scene is was discussed early on in this book. It is time, however, to revisit that concept with the knowledge you now possess. Ideally, a scene is like a level in a game. With games that get consistently harder or games that have dynamically generated levels, though, this is not necessarily true. Therefore, it can be good to think of scenes as a common list of assets. A game consisting of many levels that use the same objects can actually consist of one scene. It is only when you need to get rid of a bunch of objects, and load a bunch of new objects, that the idea of a new scene really becomes necessary. Basically stated, don't split levels into different scenes just because you can. Only create new scenes if required by the gameplay and asset management.

---

# Establishing Scene Order

Transitioning between scenes is relatively easy. It just requires a little setup to function. The first thing you do is add the very scenes of your project to the project's build settings, as follows:

1. Open the build settings by clicking **File** > **Build Settings**.

2. With the Build Settings dialog open, click and drag any scenes you want in your final project into the Scenes in Build window (see Figure 23.1).

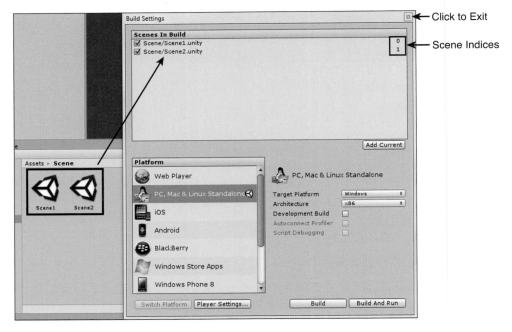

**FIGURE 23.1**
Adding scenes to the build settings.

3. Pay attention to the number that appears next to the scenes in the Scenes in Build window. These are used later. When done, click the X in the upper-right corner to exit the window. If you are on a Mac, you have a similar button in the upper-left corner.

Now the scenes can be referenced and changed.

## Adding Scenes to Build Settings

In this exercise, you add scenes to the build settings of a project. Keep the project you make here; you will be using it in the next section:

1. Create a new project. Add a new folder under Assets named **Scenes.**

2. Click **File > New Scene** to create a new scene and then **File > Save Scene** to save it. Save the scene in the Scenes folder as **Scene1**. Repeat this step to save a **Scene2**.

3. Open the build settings (click **File > Build Settings**). Drag Scene1 into the Scenes in Build window first, and then drag Scene2 in. Scene1 should have an index of 0, and Scene2 should have an index of 1. Save the project for later.

# Switching Scenes

Now that the scene order is established, switching between them is easy. To change scenes, use the method LoadLevel(), which is a part of the Application object. This method takes a single parameter that is either an integer representing the scene's index or a string representing the scene's name. Therefore, to load a scene that has a name of GameOverScene and has an index of 4, you could write either of these two lines:

```
Application.LoadLevel(4) ;              //Load by index
Application.LoadLevel(GameOverScene); //Load by name
```

This method call immediately destroys all existing game objects and loads the next scene. Note that this command is immediate and irreversible, so make sure that it is what you want to do before calling it.

## Changing Scenes via a Button

In this exercise, you switch between two scenes by using a graphical user interface (GUI) button. This exercise requires the project created previously this hour. If you have not completed it yet, do so before continuing. Be sure to save this project; you will be using it again in the next section:

1. Load the project created previously. Load Scene1 by finding the Scene1 file in the Scenes folder and double-clicking it. Add a cube to your scene and place it at (0, 0, 0).

2. Create a folder called **Scripts** and add a script to it named **LoadSceneTwo**. Attach the script to the Main Camera and add the following code to it:

```
void OnGUI()
{
    if(GUI.Button(new Rect(5, 5, 100, 100), "Load Scene2"))
    {
        Application.LoadLevel(1);
    }
}
```

3. Save the scene (click **File > Save Scene**), and then open Scene2. (See step 1 if you don't remember how.) Create a new script in the Scripts folder named **LoadSceneOne**. Attach it to the Main Camera and add the following code to it:

```
void OnGUI()
{
    if(GUI.Button(new Rect(5, 5, 100, 100), "Load Scene1"))
    {
        Application.LoadLevel(0);
    }
}
```

4. Save the scene and load Scene1 again. Run the scene. Notice how you can now transition between the two scenes by clicking the button that appears on each. Also notice how the cube only exists in Scene1. It is destroyed in Scene2.

# Persisting Data and Objects

Now that you have learned how to switch between scenes, you have undoubtedly noticed that data doesn't transfer during the switch. In fact, so far all of your scenes have been completely self-contained, with no need to save anything. In more complex games, however, saving data (often called *persisting*) becomes a real necessity. In this section, you learn how to keep objects from scene to scene and how to save data to a file to access later.

## Keeping Objects

An easy way to save data in between scenes is just to keep the objects with the data alive. For example, if you have a player object that has scripts on it containing lives, inventory, score, and so on, the easiest way to ensure that this large amount of data makes it into the next scene is just to make sure that it doesn't get destroyed. There is an easy way to accomplish this, and it involves a method called DontDestroyOnLoad(). The method DontDestroyOnLoad() takes a single parameter that is the game object that you want to save. Therefore, if you want to save a game object that was stored in a variable named Brick, you could write the following:

```
DontDestroyOnLoad(Brick);
```

Because the method takes a game object as a parameter, another great way for objects to use it is to call it on themselves using the this keyword. For an object to save itself, you put the following code in the Start() method of a script attached to it:

```
DontDestroyOnLoad(this);
```

Now when you switch scenes, your saved objects will be there waiting.

---

**TRY IT YOURSELF ▼**

### Persisting Objects

In this exercise, you save a cube from one scene to the next. This exercise requires the project created previously this hour. If you have not completed it yet, do so before continuing. Be sure to save this project; you will be using it again in the next section:

1. Load the project created previously. Ensure that Scene1 is the currently loaded scene. Notice that the cube that exists in the scene that you created earlier.

2. Create a new script in the Scripts folder named **DontDestroyScript**. Attach the script to the cube and replace the Start() method with the following:

```
void Start ()
{
    DontDestroyOnLoad(this);
}
```

3. Save and run the scene. Notice now that when you switch scenes, the cube stays. The cube is now persisted between scenes. Be sure to save this project for future use.

---

## Saving Data

Sometimes, you need to save data to a file to access later. Some things you might need to save are the player's score, configuration preferences, or inventory. There are certainly many complex and feature-rich ways to save data, but a simple solution is something called the PlayerPrefs. PlayerPrefs is an object that exists to save basic data to a file locally on your system. You then use PlayerPrefs to pull the data back out.

Saving data to the PlayerPrefs is as simple as supplying some name for the data and the data itself. The methods you use to save the data depend on the type of data. For instance, to save an integer, you call the SetInt() method. To get the integer, you call the GetInt() method. Therefore, the code to save a value of 10 to the PlayerPrefs as the score and get the value back out would look like this:

```
PlayerPrefs.SetInt("score", 10);
PlayerPrefs.GetInt("score");
```

Likewise, there are methods to save strings, SetString(), and floats, SetFloat(). Using these methods, you can easily persist any data you want to a file.

### Using PlayerPrefs

In this exercise, you save data to the PlayerPrefs file. This exercise requires the project created previously this hour. If you have not completed it yet, do so before continuing:

1. Open the project you created previously and ensure that Scene1 is loaded. Add a new script to the scripts folder named **SaveData** and attach it to the Main Camera. Add the following code to the script:

```
string playerName = "";

void OnGUI()
{
    playerName = GUI.TextField(new Rect(5, 120, 100, 30), playerName);
    if(GUI.Button(new Rect(5, 180, 50, 50), "Save"))
    {
        PlayerPrefs.SetString("name", playerName);
    }
}
```

2. Save Scene1 and load Scene2. Create a new script called **LoadData** and attach it to the Main Camera. Add the following code to the script:

```
string playerName = "";

void Start()
{
    playerName = PlayerPrefs.GetString("name");
}

void OnGUI()
{
    GUI.Label(new Rect(5, 120, 50, 30), playerName);
}
```

3. Save Scene2 and reload Scene1. Run the scene. Type your name into the text field and click the **Save** button. Now click the Load Scene2 button to load Scene2. Notice how the name you entered is written on the screen. The data was saved to PlayerPrefs and then reloaded from PlayerPrefs in a different scene.

CAUTION

**Data Safety**

Although using PlayerPrefs to save game data is very easy, it is also not very secure. The data is stored in an unencrypted file on the player's hard drive. Therefore, players could easily open the file and manipulate the data inside. This could give them an unfair advantage or break the game. Be aware that the PlayerPrefs, just as the name indicates, is intended for saving player preferences. It just so happens that it is useful for other things. True data security is a difficult thing to achieve and is definitely beyond the scope of this book. Just be aware that PlayerPrefs will work for what you need to it for now, but in the future you want to look into more-complex and secure means of saving player data.

# Unity Player Settings

Unity provides several settings that affect how the game works once it is built. These settings are called the *player settings*, and they manage things like the game's icon and supported aspect ratios. There are many settings, and many of them are self-explanatory, but take your time looking through them and learning what they do. You can open the Player Settings window by clicking **Edit > Project Settings > Player**. The Player Settings window will open in the Inspector view.

## Cross-Platform Settings

The first settings you see are the cross-platform settings (see Figure 23.2). These are the settings applied to the built game regardless of the platform (Windows, iOS, Android, Mac, and so on) you built it for. Most of the settings found in this section are self-explanatory. The product name is the name that will appear as the title of your game. The icon should be any valid texture image file. Note that the dimensions of the icon have to be a square power of 2, such as: 8 x 8, 16 x 16, 32 x 32, 64 x 64, and so on. If the icon doesn't match these dimensions, the scaling may not work properly, and the icon quality might be very low. You can also specify a custom curser in the Cursor setting and define where the cursor hotspot is.

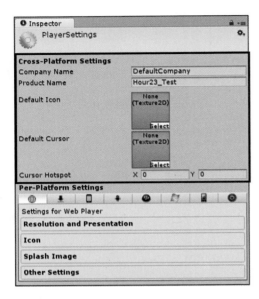

**FIGURE 23.2**
The cross-platform settings.

# Per-Platform Settings

The per-platform settings are the settings specific to each platform. Even though there are several repeat settings in this section, you still have to set up each one of them for every platform you want to build your game for. You can select a specific platform by choosing its icon from the selection bar (see Figure 23.3).

Many of these settings require a more specific understanding of the platform you are building on. These should not be modified until you better understand how that particular platform works. Other settings are rather straightforward and need to be modified only if you are trying to achieve a specific goal. For instance, the Resolution and Presentation settings deal with the dimensions of the game window. For desktop builds, these can be windowed or full screen, with a large array of different supported aspect ratios. By enabling or disabling the different aspect ratios, you allow or disallow different resolutions that the player can choose when playing the game.

The icon settings are autopopulated for you if you specify an icon image for the Default Icon property in the Cross-Platform Settings section. You can see that various sizes of the icon image will be generated based on a single provided image. This is why it is important for the provided image to have the correct dimensions. You can also provide a splash image for your game in the splash image settings. A splash image is an image that is added to the Player Settings dialog when the actual player first starts up the game.

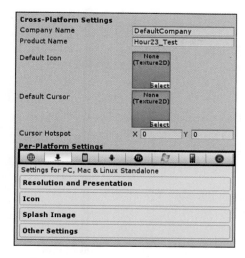

**FIGURE 23.3**
The platform selection bar.

NOTE

## Too Many Settings

You probably noticed the large number of settings in the Player Settings that weren't covered in this section. The truth is that most of the properties are already set to default values so that you can just quickly build a game. The other settings all exist to achieve advanced functionality or polish. You shouldn't toy with most of the settings if you don't understand what they do, because they can lead to strange behaviors or prevent your game from working at all. In short, only use the more basic settings for now until you get more comfortable game-building concepts and the different features you have use.

NOTE

## Too Many Players

The term *player* is used a lot this hour because there are two ways in which the term can be applied. The first is, obviously, is the player who actually plays your game. This is a person. The second way the term can be used is to describe the Unity Player. The Unity Player is the window that the game is played in (like a movie player or a TV). This exists on the computer (or device). Therefore, when you hear *player*, it probably means a person, but when you hear *Player Settings*, it probably means the software that actually displays the game.

# Building Your Game

Let's say that you've finished building your first game. You've completed all the work and tested everything in the editor. You have even gone through the Player Settings and set everything up the way you wanted. It is now time to build your game. You need to be aware of two settings windows during this process. The first is the Build Settings window, which is where you determine the final results of the build process. The second is the Game Settings window. These settings are seen by the actual player and are how players pick resolution and control configurations.

## Build Settings

The Build Settings window contains the terms under which the game is built. It is here that you specify the platform the game will be built under as well as the various scenes in the game. You have seen this dialog once before, but now you should take a closer look at it.

To open the Build Settings dialog, click **File** > **Build Settings**. Once the Build Settings dialog opens, you can change and configure your game as you want. Figure 23.4 shows the Build Settings dialog and the various items on it.

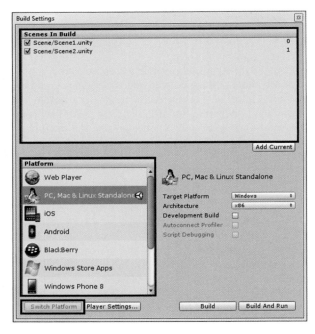

**FIGURE 23.4**
The Build Settings dialog.

As you can see, in the Platform section you can specify a new platform to build for. If you choose a new platform, you need to click **Switch Platform** to make the switch. Clicking the **Player Settings** button opens the Player Settings dialog in the Inspector view. You have seen the Scenes in Build section before. This is where you determine which scenes will make it into the game and their order. You also have the various build settings for the specific platform that you chose. The PC, MAC, & Linux Standalone settings are simple and should be self-explanatory. The only thing to note is the Development Build option, which will allow the game to run with a debugger and profiler (pro features).

When you are ready to build your game, you can either click **Build** to just build the game or **Build and Run** to run the game after it has finished building. The file that Unity creates will depend on the platform chosen.

## Game Settings

When the built game is run from its actual file (not from within Unity), the player will be presented with a Game Settings dialog (see Figure 23.5). From this dialog, players choose options for their game experience.

Name of Game

**FIGURE 23.5**
The Game Settings dialog.

The first things you may notice is that the name of the game appears in the title bar of the window. Also, any splash image you provided in the Player Settings dialog will appear at the top of this window. This first tab, Graphics, is where players specify the resolution at which they want to play the game. The list of available resolutions is determined by the aspect ratios you allowed or disallowed in the Player Settings dialog. Players can also choose to run the game in a window or full screen and can pick their quality settings.

Players can then switch over to the Input tab (see Figure 23.6). On this tab, players can remap any of the input axes to the buttons that they want.

NOTE
_____

**Told You So!**

You might recall earlier in this book where you were informed that you should always try to ensure that the input you are reading from a player is based on one of the input axes and not the specific keys. This is why. If you had looked for specific keys instead of axes, the player would have no choice but to use the control scheme you intended. If you think that this isn't a big deal, just remember that a lot of people out there (people with disabilities, for instance) use nonstandard input devices. If you deny them the ability to remap controls, they might not be able to play your games. Using axes instead of specific keys is a negligible amount of work on your part and can be the difference between players loving or hating your game.
_____

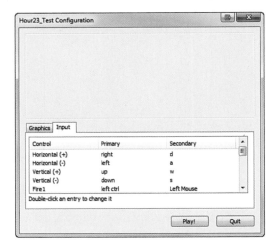

**FIGURE 23.6**
The input settings.

After players choose the settings they want, they just click **Play!**. They can finally begin enjoying your game.

# Summary

In this hour, you learned all about polishing and building games in Unity. You started by learning how to change scenes in Unity using the LoadLevel() method. From there, you learned how to persist game objects and data. After that, you learned about the various player settings. Finally, you wrapped up the hour by learning to build your games.

# Q&A

**Q.** **A lot of these settings looked important. Why didn't we cover them?**

**A.** Truth be told, most of those settings are unnecessary for you. The fact is that they aren't important... until they are important. Most of the settings are platform specific and are beyond the scope of this book. Instead of spending many pages going over settings you might never use, it is left up to you to learn about them if you ever need them.

# Workshop

Take some time to work through the questions here to ensure that you have a firm grasp of the material.

## Quiz

1. How do you determine the indices of each scene in your game?

2. True or False: Data can be saved using the PlayerPrefs object.

3. What dimensions should an icon for your game have?

4. True or False: The input settings in the game settings allows the player to remap all inputs in your game.

## Answers

1. After you add the scenes to the list of Scenes in Build, they will have an index assigned to them.

2. True.

3. Game icons should be a square with sides that are powers of 2: 8 x 8, 16 x 16, 32 x 32, and so on.

4. False. The player can only remap inputs that were established based on input axes, not specific key presses.

# Exercise

In this exercise, you build a game for your desktop operating system and experiment with the various features. There isn't much to this exercise, and you should spend most your time trying out various settings and watching their impact. Because this is just an example to get you building your games, there isn't a completed project to look at in the book assets:

1. Pick any project you have created previously, or create a new project.

2. Go into the Player Settings dialog and configure your player however you want.

3. Go into the Build Settings dialog and ensure that you have added your scenes to the Scenes in Build list. Ensure that the **PC, MAC, & Linux Standalone** platform is chosen. Build the game.

4. Locate the game file that you built and run it. Experiment with the different game settings and see how they affect the gameplay.

# HOUR 24
# Wrap Up

---

**What You'll Learn in This Hour:**

▶ What you've accomplished so far

▶ Where to go from here

▶ What resources are available to you

In this hour, you wrap up your journey with Unity. You start by looking at exactly what you've done so far. From there, you will see where you can go to continue improving your skills. Then you are introduced to the various resources available to help you continue learning.

# Accomplishments

When you have been working on something for a significant amount of time, you may sometimes forget everything that you have accomplished along the way. It is helpful to reflect on the skills you had when you began learning something and compare them to the skills you have now. There is a lot of motivation and satisfaction to be found in discovering your progress. Let's look at some numbers.

## 19 Hours of Learning

First and foremost, you spent 19 hours (possibly more) intensely learning the various elements of game development with Unity 4. Here are some of the things you have learned:

▶ How to use the Unity editor and many of its windows and dialogs.

▶ About game objects, transforms, and transformations. You learned about 2D versus 3D coordinate systems and about local versus world coordinate systems. You became a pro at using Unity's built-in geometric shapes.

▶ About models. Specifically, you learned how models consist of textures and shaders applied to materials, which in turn are applied to meshes. You learned that meshes are made up of triangles that consist of many points in 3D space.

▶ How to build terrain in Unity. You sculpted unique landscapes and gave yourself the tools needed to build any kind of world you could ever dream of. (How many people can say that?) You improved those worlds with ambient effects and environmental detail.

▶ All about cameras and lights.

▶ To program in Unity. If you had never programmed before this book, that's a big deal. Good job!

▶ About collisions, physical materials, and raycasting. In other words, you took your first steps in object interactions through physics.

▶ About prefabs and instantiation.

▶ How to build GUIs using Unity's built-in GUI controls. You even learned what GUI stands for.

▶ How to control players through Unity's character controllers. On top of that, you built a custom 2D character controller to use in your own projects.

▶ How to make awesome particle effects using various particle systems. You learned to use the new Shuriken system, but you also got to try out some legacy system effects.

▶ The legacy animation system. This includes learning about the anatomy of animations and a little bit about how they are made.

▶ How to use Unity's new Mecanim animation system. While learning that, you learned how to remap the rigging on a model to use animations that weren't made specifically for it. You also learned how to edit animations to make your own animation clips.

▶ How to manipulate audio in your projects. You learned how to work with both 2D and 3D audio, in addition to how to loop and swap audio clips.

▶ How to work with games made for mobile devices. You learned how to test games with the Unity Remote and to utilize a devices accelerometer and multi-touch screen.

▶ How to polish a game by using multiple scenes and data persistence. You learned how to build and play your games.

That's quite a list, and it's not even complete. As you read through this list, I hope you remembered experiencing and learning each of these items. You've learned a lot!

# 4 Complete Games

Over the course of this book, you created four games: *Amazing Racer*, *Chaos Ball*, *Captain Blaster*, and *Gauntlet Runner*. You designed each of these games. You worked through the concept, determined the rules, and came up with the requirements. Once done, you built all the entities of the games. Every object, player, world, ball, meteor, and more was put in the games specifically by you. You wrote all the scripts and built all the interactivity into the game. Then, most importantly, you tested all the games. You determined their strengths and their weaknesses. You played them, and you had peers play them. You considered how they could be improved, and you even tried to improve them yourself. Take a look at some of the mechanics and game concepts you used:

▶ *Amazing Racer*: A 3D foot-racing game against the clock. This game utilized the built-in first-person character controller as well as fully sculpted and textured terrain. The game used water hazards, triggers, and lights.

▶ *Chaos Ball*: Another 3D game that truly earns its namesake of *Chaos*. This game featured a large amount of collision and physical dynamics. You utilized physics materials to build a bouncy arena. You even implemented corner goals that turned specific objects into kinematics.

▶ *Captain Blaster*: A retro-style 2D space shooter. This is the first game to use a scrolling background and 2D effects. It is also the first game you made where the player can lose. Third-party models and textures ensured that this game had a high level of graphical style.

▶ *Gauntlet Runner*: A 3D-ish running game where you had to collect power ups and avoid obstacles. This game utilized Mecanim animations and third-party models, as well as clever manipulations of texture coordinates to achieve a 3D scrolling effect.

Don't forget that you also went back and modified each of these games to work on a mobile device. You have gained experience in designing games, building them, testing them, and updating them for new hardware. Not bad. Not bad at all.

# 58 Scenes

Over the course of this book, you created 58 scenes while following along. Let that number sink in for a moment. That means that while reading through this book, you specifically got hands-on with at least 58 different concepts. That is quite a lot of experience for you to draw upon.

By now, you probably get the point of this section. You've done a lot, and you should be proud of that. You have personally used a huge part of the Unity game engine. That knowledge will serve you well as you go forward.

# Where to Go from Here

Even though you have completed this book, you are far from done with your education in making games. In fact, it is fairly accurate to say that no one is ever truly done learning in an industry that moves as quickly as this one. That said, here is some advice on what you can do to keep going.

## Make Games

No, seriously, make games. This cannot be overstated. If you are someone who is trying to learn more about the Unity game engine, someone who is trying to find a game job, or someone who has a game job and is looking to get better, make games. A common misconception with people newer to the game (or any software) industry is that knowledge alone will get you a job or improve your skills. This couldn't be further from the truth. Experience is king. Make games. They don't even have to be big games. Start by making several smaller games like the ones you've done in this book. In fact, trying a large game right away can lead to frustration and disappointment. No matter what you decide to do, though, make games (was that mentioned yet?).

## Work with People

There are many local and online collaborative groups looking to make games for both business and pleasure. Join them. In fact, they would be lucky to have someone with as much Unity experience as you. Remember, you have four games under your belt already. Working with others teaches you a lot about group dynamic. Furthermore, working with others allows you to achieve higher levels of complexity in the games you can make. Try to find artists and sound engineers to make your games full of rich media goodness. You will find that working in teams is the best way to learn more about your strengths and weaknesses. It can be a great reality check as well as a confidence boost.

## Write About It

Writing about your games and your game development endeavors can be a great boon to your personal progress. Whether you start a blog or just keep a personal notebook, your observations will serve you well in the present and in retrospect. Writing can also be a great way to hone your skills and collaborate with others. By putting your ideas out there, you can receive feedback and learn through the input of others.

# Resources Available to You

Many resources are available to you to continue your education on both the Unity game engine and in game development in general. First and foremost is the Unity documentation. This manual is the official resource for all things Unity. It is important to know that this site (http://docs.unity3d.com) covers Unity from a technical approach. Don't think of the site as much of a learning tool as it is a manual.

Unity also provides a great assortment of online training on their Learn site. You can access this site accessed from http://unity3d.com. There, you will find many videos, projects, and other resources to help you improve your skills.

If you find that you have a question that you cannot answer with these two resources, the Unity community is very helpful. You can find the forums at http://forums.unity3d.com. This is where you can take part in general conversations and broad questions. There is also the Unity Answers site, at http://answers.unity3d.com. This is where you ask specific questions and get direct answers from Unity pros.

Aside from the official Unity resources, several game development sites are available to you. Two of the more popular ones are http://www.gamasutra.com and http://www.gamedev.net. Both of these sites have large communities and regularly publish articles. Their subject matter is not limited to Unity, so they can provide a large and unbiased source of information.

# Summary

In this hour, you reviewed everything you have done so far. You also looked forward. You started by examining all the things you have accomplished over the course of this book. Then, you looked at some of the things you can from here to continue improving your skills. Finally, you looked at some of the free resources available to you on the Internet.

# Q&A

**Q. After reading this hour's materials, I can't help but feel that you think we should make games. Is that true?**

**A.** Yes. I believe I mentioned it a few times. I cannot stress enough how important it is to continue to hone your skills through practice and creativity.

# Workshop

Take some time to work through the questions here to ensure that you have a firm grasp of the material.

## Quiz

1. Which game involved 3D item collection?

2. Should you be proud of the things you have accomplished so far?

3. What is the single best thing you can do to continue increasing your skills in game development?

4. How many Unity community sites are available to you?

## Answers

1. *Gauntlet Runner.*

2. Absolutely.

3. You can make games!

4. Two: the Unity forums and Unity Answers.

# Exercise

The theme behind this final hour is that of retrospect and solidifying the things that you have learned. The final exercise for this book follows that same theme. It is common in the game industry to write something called a *post-mortem*. The idea behind a post-mortem is that you write an article about a game you have made, with the intention of other people reading it. In a post-mortem, you analyze the things that worked in your process and the things that didn't. You aim to inform others of the pitfalls that you discovered so that they won't fall into the same.

In this exercise, you write a post-mortem about one of the games you made. You don't necessarily have to have anyone read it. It is the writing of it that is important. Be sure to spend some time on this, because you might want to read it again further down the road. You will be amazed at the things you found difficult and at the things you found enjoyable.

After writing the post-mortem, print it out (unless you wrote it by hand) and put it in this book. Later, when you come across this book again, be sure to open the post-mortem and read it.

# Index

# FREE
# Online Edition

## Safari
### Books Online

Your purchase of *Sams Teach Yourself Unity Game Development in 24 Hours* includes access to a free online edition for 45 days through the **Safari Books Online** subscription service. Nearly every Sams book is available online through **Safari Books Online**, along with thousands of books and videos from publishers such as Addison-Wesley Professional, Cisco Press, Exam Cram, IBM Press, O'Reilly Media, Prentice Hall, Que, and VMware Press.

**Safari Books Online** is a digital library providing searchable, on-demand access to thousands of technology, digital media, and professional development books and videos from leading publishers. With one monthly or yearly subscription price, you get unlimited access to learning tools and information on topics including mobile app and software development, tips and tricks on using your favorite gadgets, networking, project management, graphic design, and much more.

## Activate your FREE Online Edition at
## informit.com/safarifree

**STEP 1:**   Enter the coupon code: KKRKGWH.

**STEP 2:**   New Safari users, complete the brief registration form.
Safari subscribers, just log in.

If you have difficulty registering on Safari or accessing the online edition,
please e-mail customer-service@safaribooksonline.com